Whose Improv Is It Anyway?

whose

improv is it

anyway?

beyond

second city

Amy E. Seham

University Press of Mississippi / Jackson

www.upress.state.ms.us

09 08 07 06 05 04 03 02 01   4 3 2 1
∞

Library of Congress Cataloging-in-Publication Data

Seham, Amy E.
    Whose improv is it anyway? : beyond Second City / Amy E. Seham.
        p.   cm.
    Includes bibliographical references and index.
    ISBN 1-57806-340-X (alk. paper)—ISBN 1-57806-341-8 (pbk. : alk. paper)
    1. Improvisation (Acting).   2. Comedy.   3. Stand-up comedy.   I. Title.
PN2071.I5 S45   2001
792'.028—dc21   00-068659

British Library Cataloging-in-Publication Data available

To the memory of Paul B. Williams—a man of the theatre

Contents

Acknowledgments

First, I want to thank my three mentors for this project: my advisor, Sally Banes, for her invaluable insight and guidance through the research, original composition, and beyond; Anne Stascavage, for championing it at the University Press of Mississippi; and John Rezmerski, for his wisdom, expertise, and support through every word of the revisions.

I am also grateful to Gustavus Adolphus College for funding additional research, to my colleagues and students there, and especially to the Department of Theatre and Dance at Gustavus for improvising with me every semester.

Thanks also go to Philip Auslander, Natalya Baldyga, Karen Bovard, Carolyn Bronstein, Phil Bryant, Eric Carlson, Noël Carroll, Nicole Chrissotimos, Laurie Beth Clark, Julie D'Acci, Jill Dolan, Jeanie Forte, Patty Gallagher, Rob Gardner, Anita Gonzalez, Tim Good, Steve Griffith, Nancy Hanway, Dorinda Hartmann, Melissa Hillman, Cassandra Holst, Jan Jensen, Marna King, Pat Kewitsch, Derek Kompare, Mariangela Maguire (feminist on call), Betsy Morgan, Terence Morrow, Lisa Myrhe (for always listening), Elizabeth Nafpaktitis, Peg O'Connor, Tasha Oren, Lisa Parks, Michele Rusinko, Carrie Sandahl, Terry Smith, Patrick Sutton, Tamara Underiner, Michael Vanden Heuvel, Phil Voight, and my friends, professors, and colleagues at the University of California, Berkeley, and the University of Wisconsin, Madison, for suggestions and encouragement along the way.

From Performance Studio in New Haven, Connecticut, I am thankful to Andrew Rubenoff, Margaret Kurland, Deanna Dunmyer, the cast of *Oops, I Forgot to Get Married!* and the many idealistic improvisers, actors, artists, and musicians who collaborated with me through the years.

Much appreciation is also due to the photographers, publicists, theatre companies, and private collectors who have provided photographs for the book. Thank you all.

This book would not have been possible without the generous way that many improvisers (performers, producers, directors, and teachers) shared their lives, thoughts, and experiences with me. My profuse thanks go to Sean Abley, Andrew Alexander, Jody Amerling, Gwyn Ashley, Baby Wants Candy, Zoe Beckerman, Joe Bill, Jennifer Bills, Bo Blackburn, Molly Cavanaugh,

Kecia Cooper, Dick Chudnow, Joan Cloonan, Del Close, Liz Cloud, Steve Cowdrey, Martin de Maat, Stephanie DeWaegeneer, Doug Diefenbach, Rachel Dratch, Andrew Eninger, Mary Fahey, Tom Farnan, Jo Forsberg, Lillian Francis, Aaron Freeman, Robert Galinsky, Susan Gaspar, Dave Gaudet, Sara Gee, Michael Gellman, Scott Goldstein, Noah Gregoropoulos, Charna Halpern, Melanie Hutsell, Brandon Johnson, Aaron Krebs, Kelly Leonard, Khristian Leslie, Lisa Lewis, Anne Libera, Jennifer Liu, Ken Manthey, Rachael Mason, Sue Maxman-Gillan, Jerry Minor, Kevin Mullaney, Mary Olivieri-Mullins, Cordell Pace, Jay Patrick, Jonathan Pitts, Kathleen Puls, Stewart Ranson, Ronald Ray, Dante Richardson, Rob Reese, Dee Ryan, Tami Sagher, Abby Schachner, Keli Semelsberger, Lynda Shadrake, Angela Shelton, Abby Sher, Randy Smock, Faith Soloway, Jill Soloway, Gail Stern, Jackie Stone, Ellen Stoneking, David Summers, Hans Summers, Jeffrey Sweet, Nicole Tinnin, Lisa Trask, Bill Underwood, and Stephnie Weir, among many others, and *most especially* to Frances Callier, Mark Gagné, Shaun Landry, Susan Messing, Mick Napier, Keith Privett, and Mark Sutton for in-depth and ongoing conversations.

Finally, my love and appreciation goes out to my extended family in California, New York, and New Jersey—and to Lucy, Lee, Jenny, and, most of all, Mom and Dad for their unwavering support of all my academic and artistic ventures.

Preface

This study of gender, race, and power in improv-comedy has its origin in my own experience and practice of improvisation and my desire to understand this complex genre. In the 1980s, as the artistic director of Performance Studio, an independent theatre company in New Haven, Connecticut, I saw improvisation as an ideal mode of group creation. For our young troupe, improvisation provided a means by which actors and directors could move beyond the confines of scripted drama to forge our own brand of theatre and to take control of the roles we would play in it. At our best, improvisation allowed us to be inclusive, to break down boundaries, to tell our own stories, and to imagine new realities. We experimented with new ways to involve the audience in our interactive performances. As our company grew, we were able to escape the casting limitations of scripted plays by improvising new works designed to fit our members' talents regardless of race, gender, or "type." Later, I worked with groups of actors to develop original feminist shows through improvisations based on our personal experiences.

Though the process was not without friction, our use of improvisation gave many of the performers a sense of connection to the group, but a sense also of individual power and self-expression. This combination of community with self-expression was crucial in my work as a feminist artistic director and for my own life in the theatre. New Haven audiences responded enthusiastically to the new shows we created through improv and to our improvisational style of acting in scripted productions.

In 1986, a group of actors proposed we present weekly improvised comedy as a supplement to our regular season. Improv-comedy performance was growing in popularity at colleges and universities across the country, and many of the young members of our company were very eager to turn our experimental workshops into paying gigs. I agreed to sponsor a trial run at our theatre, and one of the actors stepped in to direct the new improv troupe, which was dubbed Snazz 'n' Guffaw.

In very short order, our improv-comedy shows became extremely popular with local young club-goers. Our skilled improvisers were willing to take exciting theatrical risks and could be very funny. And yet, something in the improv troupe's performances began to make me uncomfortable. The Chicago-style improv technique we studied in our workshops taught actors to create scenes spontaneously, using a number of game structures to invent characters, relationships, and situations based on audience suggestions. The only unbreakable rule for this improv play was *agreement*, a cooperative method of scene building. In theory, *agreement* requires each improviser to accept, support, and enhance the ideas expressed by the other performers on stage without *denying* a fellow player's reality. In practice, however, Snazz 'n' Guffaw's comedy performances were often extremely aggressive and competitive. Moreover, the troupe's tone both on and off stage seemed increasingly misogynist, and rehearsals began to take on the tone of a "boy's club."

Although I personally encouraged some of our best female actors to join Snazz, very few felt comfortable enough to stay with it. The women who remained with the troupe were rarely powerful in performance, most often appearing in the stereotypical support roles of wife, mother, girlfriend, or sex object. The male actors sometimes even made jokes—and got laughs—on such subjects as wife beating and date rape.

As artistic director, I attempted to steer the troupe away from the most negative humor. But members of the group closed ranks and fiercely resisted what they saw as censorship. After all, they argued, improvisations are spontaneous; they just happen. They can not and should not be controlled. I found myself confused—not wanting to be a censor or a prude—but also wondering how and why this "free" form now seemed so oppressive.

One anecdote may help to illustrate the way improvised comedy scenes often reinscribe conventionally gendered relationships despite (or because of) the politics of the players. In one early performance, I was to play a scene with Patrick, one of the leaders in the troupe. When the MC of the show asked the audience to suggest a location for the improvised scene, someone shouted, "Sultan's harem!" I entered the stage miming a notebook and pen, intending to be a reporter who had come to interview the sultan. But before I had time to speak, Patrick shouted, "Wife! On your knees!"

In the few seconds before I had to reply, I became painfully aware of many things. Patrick had ignored my initiation; perhaps my opening had been tentative and hard to read. Patrick had clearly set a relationship and an action, as improvisers were taught to do. At the same time, I felt that Patrick's offstage attitude toward me as the artistic director of the theatre had entered into his improvised choice. Not only was a sultan ordering his concubine to her knees, but Patrick was demonstrating his power over a female authority figure. Nevertheless, in front of a paying audience, I felt I had no choice within "good" improv technique but to *agree* and go along with Patrick's initiation. I dropped my imaginary pad and pen and sank to my knees. The audience guffawed, and from that point on, Patrick controlled the action of the sketch. In hindsight, I now imagine that I could have resisted Patrick's power play without denying the premise of the scene. If I had it to do again, I would say, "Yes, I am your wife, but I have come to tell you that I am no longer willing to bow and grovel. You see, there's this American named Gloria Steinem . . ."—or something like that. But the moment passed too quickly, and my instincts reverted to the rules of the game and to the same conventional narrative that Patrick and I both knew.

Despite my strong belief in improvisation's potential to invent alternative realities, and my commitment to comedy as a liberating force, I played my part like a "good girl." The alternative scenario I had imagined did not prevail. Instead, the woman was once again the butt of the joke and not the jokester. I had participated, however unwillingly, in recreating and representing that dynamic. But it was not a question of this one sketch, nor of the occasional classic comic situation. For most of the troupe's female performers, the pattern of marginalization continued, in scene after scene, through two years of weekly shows. Something between improv's theory and its practice was just not working. Still, there were times when I found the improv performances exhilarating, felt true connection to another player onstage, or witnessed leaps of faith and imagination that thrilled the audience. The idea of it was hard to let go.

We eventually disbanded Snazz 'n' Guffaw in 1988, despite its continued popularity. That difficult decision left me with many unanswered questions. Why couldn't women (including myself) seem to hold their own on the improv-comedy stage? Was the problem confined to our particular group—or did this happen elsewhere? Was it the form itself? The principles of comedy or of improvisation? The pressures of a paying audience? Our upbringing and socialization? And could improv-comedy be done another way—or would any rule designed to make things more equitable only succeed in destroying improv's vitality? I was too close to see clearly.

Years later, my study of the history of improvisation in theatre, and of feminist theories of gender and comedy, prompted me to take another look at my own history with improv-comedy. I became interested in the gap between improv-comedy's utopian philosophies and the highs and lows of my own experience. To study the question from its very roots, I traveled to improv's Mecca, its birthplace—Chicago. I attended a wide variety of improv-comedy performances, conversed with scores of players, and gathered oral histories. I discovered that not only were issues of race, gender, and power visible in the performances, they had been a continual source of struggle throughout the Chicago improv community. Before I had spent a week there, players were seeking me out: "Have I got a story for you!"

Improvisers debate and theorize about their art form in classes, bars, and over the internet. On a web site called *Impravda,* for example, a 1997 discussion labeled "Improv = Boys Club?" drew comments from well-known directors, veteran players, and beginners. A male player blamed improv's gender imbalance on the way "society teaches women to be scared of making fools of themselves." A female player responded, "The REAL truth is that the majority of improv spaces and performers are pumping with so much testosterone that no one else (women) can get a word in edgewise" *(Impravda).* Opinions poured in from every side—women need to be more aggressive, men should learn to listen, power plays only happen when improv is played badly, it's the director's/teacher's/group's fault for not correcting it, or it's your own fault—do something about it.

Two years later, in 1999, a heated debate over the YES*and* bulletin board retraced many of the same points, including questions of race, sexual preference, and age. List members from Chicago, New York, Indiana, and points west were willing to concede that a problem remained, but offered a wide variety of solutions: get angry, get over it, demand respect, form your own group, turn that dick joke into something better. One post asked, "Why can't we talk about funny *people* instead of funny men or women?" to which another replied, "That would be great in an ideal world—but we're not there yet" (YES*and*).

Similar challenges face improvisers everywhere. In Australian Theatresports, for example, director Lyn Pierse was troubled by the stereotypical roles her female actors consistently played: "Offstage, women had held positions such as artistic director, national coach, lighting and production manager. . . . Yet they found they were being railroaded by the men on stage. Women would go on to establish a scene and be removed by a funnier offer made by a male player. The original offer given by the female was destroyed" (303). At a workshop in 1990, Pierse also noticed that some women seemed to demote themselves, initiating low-status roles they would not accept in the "real world," but which, nevertheless, emerged in the spontaneous responses of improvised play. Pierse believes this reflects women's cumulative life experience, demonstrating how embedded our social training is, despite any advances we have made.

Improv-comedy's complex power relations exist on many levels—as obvious as a bulldozer or as unconscious as an archetype. The opportunity extensively to observe and analyze Chicago performances and to interview many players in depth provided me with the means to explore the extraordinary idealism and the equally bitter disappointment improv can evoke in its participants. My hope for this study is not to debunk improv's claims of community and freedom, but to discover its potential for genuine transformation.

Introduction

The term "improvisation" has many meanings and uses in the world of art and philosophy. Chicago-style improv-comedy, or *improv*, however, refers to the specific form of improvised comedy that originated with the Compass Players and the Second City comedy theatre in the 1950s and continues to be performed by troupes throughout the world.[1] Chicago-style improv-comedy is a form of unscripted performance that uses audience suggestions to initiate or shape scenes or plays created spontaneously and cooperatively according to agreed-upon rules or game structures, in the presence of an audience—frequently resulting in comedy. It is usually performed by small groups of players who often develop strong bonds and relationships as a result of their work together.

At its inception, Chicago improv came together as an amalgam of elements drawn from *commedia dell'arte*, cabaret, and children's games, along with a variety of other potent but often incompatible influences, including everything from Brecht, baseball, and beatnik jazz to stand-up comedy and psychotherapy. From the beginning, the disparate strands of improv-comedy sometimes meshed, sometimes clashed productively to create exciting performances, and sometimes strained and pulled apart. The uneasy alliance of improvisation and comedy, process and product, shamanism and showbiz, personal growth and sociopolitical satire is intrinsic to improv's nature. These built-in conflicts are the cause both of improv's appeal and of the constant quest to reform and perfect the art form.

Chicago is a mecca for young improvisers who travel from as far away as Texas, New York, and California to study improv-comedy at its source. At the same time, Chicago techniques have infiltrated classrooms, workshops, rehearsals, and comedy clubs across North and South America, Europe, Australia, and Japan. The Second City, which creates comedy revues through improvisation, has earned recognition as the center of improv training and the incubator of such comic talents as John Belushi, Gilda Radner, and Mike Myers. The theatre is widely seen as a stepping-stone to *Saturday Night Live* and other opportunities in television and film. But there is far more to the theory and practice of improv than the sketches of *Saturday Night Live* or the games on *Whose Line Is It Anyway?* might suggest.

Since the mid-eighties, the *Chicago Reader* theatre listings have included more than two dozen separate offerings by improv-comedy troupes in any given week, as well as several additional shows billed as developed through improvisation. A sizeable subculture of improv devotees—audiences and practitioners—circulates and fluctuates throughout the city. Improv's birthplace has become a laboratory where players experiment with rules and structures in a never-ending search for the freedom and connection this genre seems to promise. For a number of its idealistic proponents, improv is a serious art form, a mission, even a way of life.

African American improviser Frances Callier thinks of herself as *practicing* improvisation, as one might practice a religion: "This is a lifelong art form that I will forever be doing no matter what I do. . . . You HAVE to live it. I believe in what I do. It has purpose and voice and it gives meaning to my life in a deeper spiritual sense" (personal interview).

Despite Callier's commitment to the improv ideal, she is equally clear that the reality of improv practice puts women and people of color at a distinct disadvantage. Chicago improv-comedy is dominated—both in numbers and in the control of content and style—by young, white, heterosexual men. Women and minorities are often marginalized by the mode of play on stage, through the manipulation of rules and structures, and by the rigid control of what improvisers acknowledge as *funny*.

Why should that be remarkable? Why not assume that improv would reflect the power dynamics of society as a whole? In part, because the powerful rhetoric of improv insists on process, mutual support, and individual liberation. In part, because so many intelligent, passionate, and sincere players believe in that rhetoric. In part, because women and people of color have historically found a voice through improvisational modes of cultural expression—including feminist theatre and jazz—but to the notable exclusion of improv.

This book is a historical and theoretical study of the important innovations in Chicago improv-comedy that both encompass and move beyond Second City's famous tradition. I examine the exponential growth and influence of this art form in the 1980s, 1990s, and into the millennium. Tracing the evolution of improv-comedy in Chicago, I investigate improv's ideals of community, spontaneity, and liberation, contrasting its rhetoric with the real experience of much of its actual practice. In particular, I address the issues of race, gender, and power as they shape the outcome of each spontaneous comic performance, asking the question, Whose improv is it anyway?

Growing divergence between the teachings of improv's early visionaries and the pragmatics of popular entertainment has created great tensions throughout the Chicago improv community. At two key moments described in the book, conflicting values and goals caused a significant break with prevailing modes of improv play. New troupes with alternative approaches emerged to coexist and compete with older companies. I use the metaphor of *waves* to mark these major redefinitions, which were created as a response to the perception that the earlier wave had failed to keep faith with the true spirit of improv.

As I have defined it, the first wave of Chicago-style improv-comedy consists of the Second City and its progenitor, the Compass Players, where the specific genre of Chicago-style improv-comedy was created and developed beginning in the mid-1950s. Part of my examination of Second City focuses on its influential training center, established in 1984, which has operated to define and teach classic improv-comedy to new generations of improvisers.

The second wave includes ImprovOlympic and ComedySportz, theatres that significantly diverged from Second City in the early 1980s. Now well-established, both companies run training programs of their own. Their distinct variations on classic improv, both inspired by the work of British teacher-director Keith Johnstone, have influenced emerging third-wave troupes and have circled back to affect the later playing style of Second City as well.

By the late 1980s to 1990s, a significant third wave of improv-comedy began to evolve. While the second wave focused on hierarchies of process and product and the revival of community and spontaneity, the third wave directly addressed political issues of power, difference, and identity. I examine three companies that define themselves specifically as alternatives to the more established improv theatres in terms of approach, casting, and structure: the Annoyance Theatre, the Free Associates, and Oui Be Negroes.

In each of the following chapters, I focus on the distinctive structures and practices of a specific improv-comedy troupe and the historical context of that company's role in the development of the genre. Because the overarching issues are so complex, I employ a variety of theoretical and analytical approaches throughout the book. In response to limitations of space and time, I have confined this discussion to Chicago-based troupes and innovations. I wish to acknowledge, however, that improvisers throughout the United States, Canada, and the rest of the world have made and continue to make important contributions to the art form. These developments will, I hope, soon be the subject of another book. The next few pages briefly outline key elements of improv theory and practice relevant to every wave.

* * *

Improvisation can have a number of meanings, from a pragmatic inventiveness within limitations ("I didn't have all the right ingredients for the cake, so I just had to improvise") to a shamanic channeling of extraordinary art, truth, and beauty ("When I improvise, I lose myself—it feels as if a greater power is speaking *through* me"). Improvisation means *making do,* a conscious creativity within restraints, through the rearrangement of available elements (de Certeau xxii). Improvisation also means *letting go,* the surrender of conscious control that allows the performer to serve as a channel or instrument for artistic or divine inspiration. Most improvisational performance combines or fluctuates between making do and letting go.

Improv's magic lies in its spontaneity and virtuosity—the illusion of a comic scene created from thin air, with actors anticipating each other's every move, spouting punch lines "too good" to be improvised. Audiences delight in its sense of danger and potential failure as they enjoy the escape act or the high-wire routine. Improvisation's unpredictable immediacy may also allow the artist to evade censorship—both internal and external—subverting "official" representations of life.

Cultural studies theory discusses improvisation as a tactic of the disenfranchised, one which, "because it does not have a place . . . depends on time—it is always on the watch for opportunities that must be seized 'on the wing' " (de Certeau xix). It can also be a link to something spiritual and outside of politics. According to a number of African American cultural theorists, many African Americans see improvisation both as a tactic for survival and as part of an oral culture that expresses the spiritual notion of "flow" or ecstatic possession through music, dance, preaching, and testifying (e.g., Jones; Ventura). African American jazz musician Cecil Taylor asserts that "improvisation is . . . the magical lifting of one's spirits to a state of trance" (qtd. in Ventura 138).

Throughout the twentieth century, improvisation was used by avant-garde artists—from Dada, Futurism, and Surrealism, to the countercultural and feminist theatres of the '60s and '70s—in their rebellious rejection of "establishment" art and society. Social activists, such as Brazilian director Augusto Boal, use improvisational theatre as a means of involving and empowering spectators to take action against oppression. Theatre educators and practitioners have explored spontaneous improvisation as a means of freeing the creative spirit.

In *Improvisation for the Theatre,* Viola Spolin writes, "Through spontaneity we are re-formed into ourselves. It creates an explosion that for the moment frees us from handed-down frames of reference, memory choked with old facts and information and undigested theories and techniques of other people's findings. Spontaneity is the moment of personal freedom when we are faced with a reality and see it, explore it and act accordingly. In this reality the bits and pieces of ourselves function as an organic whole. It is the time of discovery, of experiencing, of creative expression" (4).

Post-structuralist theorists, too, have been attracted to the idea of improvisation as a means of embodying the free play of meaning. In her discussion of Spolin and other improvisational theatre artists, Natalie Crohn Schmitt writes, "The emphasis on the moment suggests that human existence is potentially redefinable at any moment: it consists in the shifting currents of our most immediate consciousness. In improvisation, actors do not reveal characters or move through predetermined actions, rather, they make choices to get from moment to moment. . . . We are to view the world as something that we make at each moment, as we make ourselves" (118–19).

The combined effect of these theories implies a promise of direct access to organic wholeness, authentic truths, agency, and free expression. It inspires, in some, a passionate commitment to improvisation as not only an art form, but also a belief system. However, most improv-comedy practice demonstrates that spontaneous group creation usually taps into reserves of shared references, received truth, and common knowledge rather than, as Spolin claims, challenging "old facts and information." Because the spontaneous performer seems not to have time to construct images consciously, the social construction of those images seems invisible. Through improvisation, these representations come together, as if by magic, in narratives that appear natural, inevitable, and true, but that are more likely to be drawn from archetype, stereotype, and myth.[2] In addition, in the pressure cooker of performance, players may be driven to reach for the most familiar, most popular references and are often rewarded with the laughter of recognition.

Like improvisation, comedy is often seen as an instrument of the disempowered. Anthropologist Mary Douglas says that jokes challenge dominant social structure in "a victorious tilting of uncontrol against control" (297). Historian and performer Ron Jenkins asserts that laughter provides a "liberating release" from oppressive authority (1–2).

However, a number of theorists, from Aristotle to Henri Bergson to Susan Purdie, describe comedy as a conservative force—disparaging the lowly, ridiculing the outsider, and enforcing societal norms, hierarchies, and conventions. Women and other oppressed people are often effectively barred from wielding the weapon of humor by two obstacles: mainstream society's refusal to acknowledge their ability to create comedy, and its punishment of those who try. Cultural critic Philip Auslander writes, "Our society . . . stigmatizes the funny woman. Joke telling is a male preserve because humor is linked with power; women are supposed to be the objects of jokes, not joking subjects" (*Presence and Resistance* 205).

Similarly, as Mel Watkins' definitive history of African American humor documents, comedy has historically posed great risks for blacks because their joking and laughter often seemed threatening to white society. As a result, much of the humor of African Americans, women, and other marginalized people has been stealth humor, "based on a knowledge of shared oppression," unrecognized by those in power (Weisstein 90).

The collaborative and spontaneous nature of subordinated humor is, in theory, the very essence of improv-comedy. Site-specific, improvisational humor is the comedy version of *making do*—using tactics of irony and observations of incongruity to challenge the status quo, if only temporarily. Watkins points out that black humorists avoid "set" jokes—preferring to find comedy in the here and now—and writes that "one reason traditional jokes do not assume greater importance among blacks is that improvisation is as much esteemed in black humor as it is in music. . . . The highest regard is reserved for spontaneous wit and inventiveness" (476–77).

Sociological studies show that most women are culturally conditioned to base their humor in complex characters and relationships and to use humor in conversation to achieve intimacy. Men usually concentrate on comic narratives and are more likely to tell jokes that subordinate others—tendencies that seem more in tune with stand-up comedy than with improvisation (Crawford passim). Linguist Deborah Tannen calls joking an "asymmetrical" activity, in which men seek status by making others laugh, while women "habitually take the role of appreciative audience" (90). In improv, everything from the tempo of play and the aggressiveness of the jokes to the content of the scenes can be affected by these contrasting values.

Many sincere improvisers insist that improv-comedy must be based on the humor of emerging truths—incongruities, character, and situation—rather than jokes. Although this approach (pioneered by Spolin) is theoretically a feminine mode of comedy, Chicago improv tends to privilege a heterosexual white male joking subject.[3] According to some women in improv-comedy, not a few male improvisers have justified their control of scenes by asserting that women have no sense of humor and are simply *not funny*. A number of women, determined to play hardball with male improvisers, emulate the quick, aggressive, macho qualities associated with stand-up—even within the context of group improvisation. Others may recede into support positions or seek structured, theatrical forms of improv.

Yet improvisation also provides a valuable means of creating original material—particularly for women and marginalized people whose lives and histories are underrepresented in mainstream performance. Improv attracts many artists seeking to express and share the unique humor of their backgrounds and experience—to show that they, too, can be funny.

Improvisers are known as players; most structures are referred to as games. These terms originate with Spolin and Johnstone, yet equating improv with play also implies freedom, connection, and a creativity that "undermines, transforms, and re-creates" the rigidity of law and tradition (Schechner, "Drama Performance" 279). However, play is only distinguishable as play by its framing in terms of time and place, rules and structures, us and not-us. Descriptions of the ideal improv situation resonate with Johan Huizinga's claim that "the first main characteristic of play" is "that it is free, is in fact freedom" (8).

Long-time Chicago improviser Susan Messing explains her passionate dedication to this art form in similar terms: "Why am I an improviser? Because it's an opportunity to be a fifth grader playing in your backyard, doing whatever the hell you want to do. . . . You can be whoever you want. You can explore whatever you want. There's no limitation of script. There are *no* limits. There are no limits. . . . And if that isn't freedom, man, . . . I keep thinking what else is left?" (personal interview).

Limits do, in fact, exist—in the parental "real world" outside improv's childlike exploration of fantasy. Messing's description of improv play is linked to the second of Huizinga's characteristics of play, "namely, that play is not 'ordinary' or 'real' life. It is rather a stepping out of 'real' life into a temporary sphere of activity with a disposition all of its own" (8).

On the other hand, Huizinga points out that play, to be distinguished from real life, must be limited in time and place, must have rules and create order. Moreover, he explains that play is marked by pleasure in being in on the game, deriving a sense of belonging and community through exclusiveness. Huizinga relates that players often tell one another, "[T]his is for us, not for the *others*" (12). In the tight-knit Chicago improv community, many troupes work to maintain the homogeneity of goals, backgrounds, and values required in a utopian society. This intensity of group feeling often creates insider-outsider categories that can manifest themselves in terms of gender and race.

Quite a few male improvisers also believe that women interfere with the unfettered fun of improv play. If a female player appears overly timid or concerned with "the rules," or desires to protect herself psychologically, she may indeed seem to be a "spoil sport [who] threatens the fragile play-world" (11). Huizinga describes the spoilsport in terms often applied to women in Chicago improv: "He [sic] robs play of its *illusion*—a pregnant word that means literally 'in-play' . . . he must be cast out, for he threatens the existence of the play-community. The figure of the spoil-sport is most apparent in boys' games. The little community does not enquire whether the spoil-sport is guilty of defection because he dared not enter into the game or because he is not allowed to. Rather, it does not recognize 'not being allowed' and calls it 'not daring.' . . . The spoil-sport breaks the magic world, therefore he is a coward and must be ejected" (11).

For many male improvisers, women are the spoilsports—whether because they are "good girls" who don't feel entitled to play hard or trouble-making feminists who want to make new rules for the game. Women often feel trapped by the limited number of images improv seems to create for them. Nevertheless, in Chicago, many women, people of color, and other marginalized people want to play. Here, we can look at a third sense of the word "play"—in its meaning as a little bit of "give," and the possibility for movement or maneuver. This book focuses on the play in improv, the play that might allow improv to work for everyone.

There are tensions in improv-comedy between the rhetoric of freedom and self-expression and the rather rigid rules that govern performance. The structures of classic improv-comedy, beginning with Spolin's teachings, have evolved through trial and error over the decades into a handful of primary principles. Leading improv troupes teach their own versions of improv basics in classes for adults and high school students. Second City urges students to build improvised scenes through give-and-take, avoiding *questions* and *story* in order to concentrate on the "now" moment (Second City manual). But the key principle shared by virtually every improv troupe is *agreement*. The founders of ImprovOlympic say, "*Agreement is the one rule that can never be broken*: The players must be in agreement to forward the action of the scene. When improvisers meet on stage, they agree to accept each other's initiations; they must completely commit to the reality they create for each other without a moment's hesitation" (Halpern, Close, and Johnson 47).

Dick Chudnow, creator of ComedySportz, gives his disciples the following commandment: "If you believe in the art, the science, the religion of improvisation, you know nothing moves until someone says 'YES . . . and . . .' " (10).

Students are taught to respond to a fellow player's initiation by saying, "YES*and*—" to accept the other player's offer (or *gift*), then add to it by exploring or heightening the given idea.[4] Players who *deny* are told that they are thinking too much, setting up *blocks* that obstruct their spontaneous response to each moment of play. No idea is to be rejected—all offers must be accepted and supported. In this way, junior improvisers learn, they may achieve *groupthink* or *groupmind*—the entire troupe working intuitively together toward the same goals.

The perfect working of groupmind is often called *the zone* or *flow*, a magical kind of high, akin to perfect teamwork in sports or even great sex. Players and teachers often equate groupmind with the Jungian "collective unconscious" and believe that through it they are able to tap into something universal, genuine, and true. The Second City Training Center manual includes a long poem written by the school's artistic director, Martin de Maat, in which a flock of birds metaphorically evokes groupmind. An excerpt follows:

> The birds seem to have a *common mind, a common goal*. They each surrender to the *power of the group*. No bird questions the flow. They simply flap and fly to support it whichever way it turns.
>
> This is the way of natural order and the emergence of creativity. It is the flow that we seek when improvising.
>
> . . . .
> No bird is questioning the flock's movement.
>
> . . . .
> No bird thinks he has a better idea.
> No bird doubts his ability to fly.
>
> . . . .
> Nothing is important but the flight itself. (11)

For some, this bird's-eye view is a utopian picture of belonging, but for those who feel marginalized by the group, it can seem more like a frightening loss of identity. While the pleasure of groupthink consists in its seeming connection to a natural order of things, social scientist I. L. Janis argues that it does not achieve genuine consensus. In his work on group processes, Janis contends that groupthink forces conformity and narrows the range of options that groups are able to consider (qtd. in Brown 158).

Despite improv training's insistence on teamwork and give-and-take, the first person who speaks, or who speaks most forcefully, usually controls the premise of a given scene. Women are often less comfortable taking initiative and focus on stage than the male players. They frequently find themselves *agreeing* to play the supportive, backseat position in scenes that express the male perspective, allowing men to define them with a word ("Honey!"), or, in improv terms, to *endow* them exclusively as convenient wives, girlfriends, and mothers.[5] When they do initiate a relationship, women often default to familiar low-status reactive characters, while men take active roles. Australian Theatresports director Lynn Pierse confesses that she and other female players too often choose clichéd gender activities on stage such as "washing dishes . . . ironing and filing" instead of high status action (303).

African American and other minority improvisers often find that their references, allusions, and perceptions of incongruity are not immediately grasped by white players, and thus their distinctive humor falls by the wayside. While some minority performers have little or no problem assimilating, and indeed enjoy being seen as "just another member" of the troupe, others are troubled by the feeling that they must "whitewash their humor" in order to have the opportunity to perform (Callier interview).

In the striving for agreement, any form of difference—whether it is based on gender, race, or sexuality—is subsumed into the larger groupmind. Anyone whose views diverge too far may be accused of trying to impose an inappropriate personal or political agenda. Feminist, ethnic, and gay perspectives are often viewed warily and allowed only in the most homogenized constructions. Thus, it seems that the universal groupmind for which classic improv strives is too often simply the heterosexual white male mind.

Practitioners divide improv-comedy into two basic formats: *short form* and *long form*. Short-form improv usually consists of brief scenes developed from audience suggestions and built on various game structures—including many of Spolin's original exercises and status games developed by Keith Johnstone. Long-form improvisation, on the other hand, requires players to sustain original improvisation for extended periods of time—based on a pre-written scenario or a more complex game structure. In some versions, such as ImprovOlympic's *Harold*, long-form improvisers begin with a single audience suggestion and create impromptu performances that last up to thirty minutes and more.

For some improvisers, short-form games seem like shallow, vaudevillian comedy, while long form presents the opportunity for a more artistic and spiritual exploration of the truth. Others claim that long-form improv lends itself to self-indulgent meandering, while short form provides genuine, accessible entertainment. Some women say they feel pressured by the short form's quicker tempo and competitive focus on comedy. Long form tends to allow for more evolved character development and subtler scene work and is therefore sometimes considered a more woman-friendly mode. But not every female improviser prefers this style of play.

The automatic or "no-minded" response is privileged in most forms of improv as the best expression of the "innermost self" and closest to the truth

(Johnstone 111). Spolin's teaching instructs group leaders not to rush their students, but also not to give them time to preplan: "Pre-planning 'How' constitutes the use of old material even if that material is but five minutes old . . . it makes process impossible . . . and no 'explosion' or spontaneity can take place" (37). But the value placed on fast-paced, unthinking creations often results in a devaluation of the more nuanced, character-based humor preferred by many women and a reversion to unexamined stereotypes of gender, sexuality, and race.

In its post-show improv sets, Second City habitually provides a period of time after the audience suggestions for players to make a few decisions backstage. When performers take a few moments to agree on a political point of view, or common context, says Second City administrator and director Anne Libera, the company is able to create smarter, more pointed scenes than pure improvisation permits (personal interview). Indeed, strictures against being too much *in your head* work against the creation of anything but personal or perhaps social observations through improv. Political commentary and satire usually do require a conscious scripting process. Some improvisers view Second City's planning sessions as cheating on the whole notion of improv, while others acknowledge the liabilities of the no-minded approach.

Improvised comedy is made up of those fragments of the performers' personal memories, beliefs, and individual libraries of cultural reference that are most easily and immediately accessed under the pressure of the moment and simultaneously most likely to be accepted by fellow players and approved of by audiences. Much of the excitement and pleasure—as well as the danger and misuse—of improv stems from its exploitation of each player's "self." Unlike legitimate theatre, where actors' roles are (more or less) clearly delineated by the text, improvisers must negotiate across the far more permeable boundaries of real (offstage, social, personal) interaction and performance—learning to play the game on many levels.

Some schools of improv give considerable attention to techniques of character construction. Others ask performers to share their own personal memories and feelings. Most performance emerges as a mix of these approaches, leaving little room to distinguish between actor and role. What, then, if a player improvises a bullying racist or sexist character? What if another consistently portrays prostitutes or bimbos? Theories of spontaneity and groupmind often protect players, giving them permission to explore and express socially unacceptable behavior. But improvisers without the skill both to inhabit and to contextualize or comment on a character's actions are vulnerable to being conflated with the roles they play.

Improv-comedy also leaks off the stage, mingling with the offstage lives of its participants. Despite many teachers' insistence that humor will emerge naturally out of the "truth" in a scene, players know that witty routines, characters, or *bits* are often rewarded with coveted stage time. Bits are developed not only in workshops or rehearsals, but backstage, in the bar after a show, or in the van on the way to a gig. In this context, white male improv culture can further alienate and exclude women and minorities. In a typical rehearsal process, women almost always have to ally themselves with powerful male performers to be included in sketches being workshopped.

The practice of Chicago-style improv-comedy extends beyond the interactions of improvisers on stage (or off stage) to include the entire improv subculture and its complex relationship with the audience. The more successful an improv troupe becomes, the more players feel they have to provide dependably funny performances at any cost. One improviser posted his opinion: "Men think they need to be loud, violent, and just a tad abusive to get laughs. This is positively reinforced by the men in the audience who are laughing, so it is continued, but then again, who's in the audience?" (*Impravda*).

Despite the dissonance between improv's powerful rhetoric and its actual practice, most players from every wave of Chicago improv-comedy believe that, regardless of its pitfalls, improv-comedy can be freeing, connecting, egalitarian, spiritual, truthful, and funny all at the same time. Faced with the dualities and contradictions of its hybrid nature, each player must sort out and piece together a workable definition of improv for him- or herself. What element in this complex and multifaceted art form beckons me with a promise of fulfillment? What do I hope to find within it? What do I want to express through it? Where do I want it to take me? These choices are inexorably linked to questions of identity—gender, race, class, sexual orientation, and education—along with artistic, career, and personal goals. Eloquent, articulate, and passionate about their art, improvisers continue to theorize, practice, and theorize again in hopes of finding solutions to improv's inequalities without destroying its energy or sense of play.

Whose Improv Is It Anyway?

CHAPTER 1

the first-wave paradigm

In 1995, one of the *Chicago Reader's* recommended theatre selections was a bitterly funny show at the tiny Factory Theatre entitled *Second City Didn't Want Us or Is There a Part in the Touring Company for My Girlfriend?* Developed through improvisation and modeled on a Second City comedy revue with sketches and songs, the show spoofed Second City's "improv doctrine," teaching styles, and institutional practices and parodied the sexism, racism, and homophobia encountered there. Amidst the jokes, this independent company accused Chicago's biggest and best-known comedy factory of manipulating idealistic young improv students through favoritism, hypocrisy, and both economic and sexual exploitation. Each player announced the amount, in thousands of dollars, that he or she had spent on Second City classes. In one sketch, a little girl asked her father why there were no funny roles for women in the Second City performance they attended. She then naively resolved to be a *real* improviser when she grew up, despite all attempts to persuade her that women "just aren't funny." A later parody contrasted the New Age, feel-good spirituality of a well-known instructor's teaching style with the cutthroat competition among his students. At one December performance of *Second City Didn't Want Us,* a small band of spectators (mostly other Chicago improvisers) laughed and nodded in recognition at every reference.

Chicago Tribune reviewer Lawrence Bommer (whose style was also mimicked in the revue) suggested in his critique that "the fearless Factory folks pay Second City too great a compliment, by assuming Chicago has no other path to comedy success" ("Bitter Second City"). Yet, Second City does have a powerful influence—both real and symbolic—on improvisers and comedy hopefuls in Chicago and throughout the United States. For more than forty years, the company has been largely unchallenged as the origin, the model, the norm, and the watchdog of classic American improv-comedy. By the year 2000, the Second City Training Center was serving over three thousand students a year, offering introductory workshops and a more advanced conservatory program that prepares players to create "Second City–style" shows (Second City Training Center manual). First level classes emphasize Viola Spolin's fundamental games and techniques while later sessions gear that work toward satirical comedy material. The company has generated (directly or indirectly) a number of similar theatres throughout the United States (including the Premise, the Committee, the Proposition, the Groundlings, Ace Trucking Company, and others) as well as its own branch theatres in the Chicago suburbs (now closed), Toronto, Los Angeles, and Detroit. In addition, three touring companies perform "Best of Second City" revues throughout the country.

On a practical level, this entertainment institution has launched quite a number of successful comedy careers. More importantly, as the "first wave" of Chicago improv, Second City, and its precursor, the Compass Players, defined a technique and a philosophy that many believe embodies cherished notions of truth, freedom, and community. Young improvisers often mythologize early first-wave improv as a utopia of pure improvisation, progressive politics, self-discovery, brilliant comedy, and communal cooperation. This interpretation of the past has been encouraged and even taught at the Second City Training Center, where players also study Spolin's principles of agreement, acceptance, trust, and support.

However, the Compass Players/Second City's struggle to create and sustain their new art form was far more complicated than the utopian myth makes it appear. The direction of the Compass (and then the Second City) shifted over the decades as idealistic dreams were shaped not only by conflicting artistic visions, but also by financial concerns, the desires and power relations of the performers, the pressure and participation of audiences, and the changing cultural context. But, while the requirements for success on stage morphed to fit fluctuating needs, the credo of first-wave training workshops remained comparatively constant. Performers and other students learned a far purer form of Chicago-style improv—its techniques, values, and philosophy—than they would have the chance to use on the Second City stage. Thus, in every generation of management and each successive cast of performers, new pressures strained the relationship between Second City's philosophical legacy and its practice. As the Factory's performance illustrates, many second- and third-wave players have felt disillusioned, even betrayed by these inconsistencies. These feelings and expectations (realistic or not) have sometimes been the impetus for a show (Second City Didn't Want Us) or a whole new movement (wave) in improv theory and practice.

Because there are already several books that detail the history of the Compass Players and Second City, I will not attempt to provide a complete chronicle of the first wave. Instead, this chapter focuses on the development of Chicago improv's early rhetoric—its promise and philosophy. I concentrate on several key struggles among first-wave practitioners—particularly the important debates over the relative merits of art and activism, spirituality and entertainment, individuality and community, personal growth and political satire, and, especially, of process and product. I work to identify the tensions within the developing improv-comedy form as well as the critical gaps between first-wave rhetoric and practice, problems that would become catalysts for the emergence of the second and third waves of Chicago improv in the 1980s and 1990s. I show how these and other questions of power are embodied in performance, often played out in terms of race, gender, and other forms of difference. First-wave improvisers rarely acknowledged race and gender issues, often simply excluding those who did not "fit" the group, until the mid-nineties, when a number of affirmative-action initiatives were implemented.[1] It remains the case, however, that successful improv-comedy often depends on some improvisers being literally freer than others.

Nevertheless, improv's promise of truth, freedom, and community has been a powerful part of its appeal for many young intellectuals and performers from the 1950s through the millennium. In order to understand the meaning of these utopian concepts for the original first-wave improvisers—and thus to understand the first-wave paradigm—it is important to begin with the historical context in which the Compass Players emerged.

The year was 1955. Allen Ginsberg read "Howl" to beatnik audiences; Rosa Parks refused to give up her seat on the bus to a white man; Elvis Presley hit big as the white singer who could rock like a black man; and in Chicago the Compass Players presented its first improv performance. It was the decade of McCarthyism, suburban affluence, "the Bomb," and *Father Knows Best*. After the shocks of the Great Depression and the Second World War, many Americans were eager to assert an aura of prosperous normalcy at all costs.

For many, maintaining the good life seemed to depend on obedience to authority and willful ignorance of the gaps between the utopian view of American capitalism, democracy, family, and nation—and their realities. Others sought enclaves of "avant garde culture and political dissonance" that combined an alternative sense of community with countercultural expression (Gitlin, *Sixties* 28). The main channel of resistance, according to cultural historian Todd Gitlin, rested with the Beat writers and poets, who—though apolitical in any active sense—rejected the postwar "bargain of workaday routine in exchange for material acquisition" and embraced poverty, sexual libertinism, and eastern philosophies (28). Gitlin also notes the emergence of other "tiny bohemias" including the Living Theatre, jazz clubs, and other "subcultures where exotic practices attracted a hard core of rebels, a fringe of hangers-on, and a larger penumbra of the part-time, the tempted, and the vicarious participants" (28).

Jazz represented "hipness"—an insider's knowledge of what really counts and a rejection of "square" establishment values. Cultural theorist Andrew Ross suggests that "black culture, and especially jazz, was cast as a vital and natural source of spontaneous, precivilized, anti-technological values—the 'music of the unconscious,' of uncontaminated and untutored feeling and emotion" (*No Respect* 74). White Beats like Jack Kerouac often envied what they perceived as the intensity, immediacy, and free form of African American expression, without fully appreciating the oppression and marginalization that shaped blacks' artistic and life choices.

The mid-fifties marked the first stirrings of what comedy producer and historian Tony Hendra calls "Boomer Humor," a cynical, "sick" sense of comedy and satire ranging from *Mad Magazine* to Mort Sahl and designed to cope with the ambiguity, absurdity, and hypocrisy of postwar society. For Hendra, the most important quality of boomer-humor performance was its *liveness:* "Rejecting both the terrifying impersonality of the Bomb and the hallucinatory self-absorption of the Box [television], it quite literally went out, collared the nearest human by the lapel, and started talking. . . . Secondly, it rejected the patter and sketches of the previous generation of comedians, material which for some performers had lasted them, unchanged, for a lifetime, and instead started *improvising,* alone or in groups, a new kind of material that was never the same two nights in a row . . . the danger [of failure] gave the whole affair an added thrill when it worked" (17).

In these performances, *liveness* meant the possibility of connection and community. Improvisation offered "freedom" through its open form and produced "truth" in its spontaneous observations of life's inconsistencies. Other postwar art forms were taking a similar tack. From action painting to jazz, American improvisation "emphasized the *process* of the subjective artist as well as the content of his objectified art—through improvising, the creator becomes a performer" (Brustein 28).

Chicago-style improv was born in 1955 at the University of Chicago when the idealistic and eccentric David Shepherd joined forces with theatre student Paul Sills to invent a new art form. Shepherd wanted to create a populist theatre based on *commedia dell'arte* but set in a Brechtian-style smokers' cabaret. He envisioned a troupe of performers who would improvise original works, from politically progressive scenarios, that would comment comically on the issues of the day. At the same time, Shepherd realized, "[A]s we develop a new kind of play and audience, we may have to develop an entirely new style of acting" (qtd. in Sweet xxii).

Sills, an accomplished young director also interested in Brecht and avant-garde theatre, had the components for a new approach to acting, one that could respond to Shepherd's vision. In the 1930s, Sills's mother, Viola Spolin, had created a series of games and exercises designed to encourage children to play cooperatively and creatively together. In 1955, her techniques seemed to provide the perfect way to train young performers in the lost art of *commedia*-style improvisation. Shepherd and Sills formed the Compass Players and began the work of creating their new style of acting—the hybrid genre that became Chicago-style improv.

Histories of the Compass and Second City tell us that each of these three principal architects of Chicago-style improv made a distinctive contribution to the genre's ideology.[2] At the outset, powerful contradictions were built into the very foundations of first-wave improv through the often-conflicting goals and methods of its creators. It was in fact the negotiation of these conflicts that *created* the amalgam that is Chicago-style improv and that continues to provoke discussion and invention today.

Spolin was devoted to improvisation's spiritual and psychological release of human potential. Shepherd wanted a political community theatre that would fight class oppression through dialogic interaction between actors and "real people." Sills was interested in both the spiritual and the political, as long as improv also produced authentic "art." Each artist subscribed to the notion that improvisation (and by extension improv-comedy), when properly practiced, could allow participants to bypass limiting and disciplinary structures—whether internal or external—and to have the freedom to express a greater truth. Their combined work and writings, along with the larger history and mythos of improvisation and comedy, have blended to form a belief system fervently held by many if not all Chicago improvisers. The underlying assumptions, beliefs, and philosophies of improv are rooted in the specific artistic and cultural movements that inspired its three midwives.

As the "High Priestess of Improvisation" (according to Compass historian Janet Coleman), Spolin linked spontaneity and group connection to feelings of spirituality and belonging. Spolin taught that improvisation, which she also called "transformation," is an embrace of the unknown and a trust that all things are ultimately connected and meaningful—notions influenced by theosophy and borrowings from several Eastern religions. She believed that intuitive and spontaneous group improvisation had the power to link improvisers with one another and with the larger universal truths of the cosmos. She claimed to have developed "a learning system which can reach the intuitive power of the individual and release genius" and called group improvisation a "communion" among players (Coleman 23; Spolin 45).

Spolin's methodology is based on structured play, or the *game*, which she defines as "a natural group form providing the involvement and personal *freedom* necessary for experiencing" (4). In her influential book of exercises, *Improvisation for the Theatre*, Spolin writes that the feeling of personal freedom is too often stifled by society's mechanisms of approval, disapproval, and authoritarianism. Accordingly, she instructs workshop leaders to forego judgments and tells performers to avoid "showing off"(7). Instead, participants must work together in their group to "solve the problem" of the game by focusing on a "Point of Concentration." Spolin explains, "It is understood during playing that a player is free to reach the game's objective in any style he chooses. As long as he abides by the rules of the game" (5).

Spolin taught that "Individual freedom (expressing self) while respecting community responsibility (group agreement) is our goal" and that the "right of individual choice is part of group *agreement*" (44). True improv, according to Spolin, must have no stars, nor may anyone impose any intentional message or political agenda on the organic truth that must emerge through group agreement. The difficulty of maintaining this balance between self and group, freedom and agreement, has been a source of significant friction in Chicago improv. Nevertheless, the goal of achieving *groupthink* and the supremacy of *agreement* are still central to improv-comedy's credo.

Like Spolin, Shepherd was committed to involving the larger community, both by taking spectators' suggestions for scenes and by encouraging local amateurs to join the company on stage. Unlike Spolin, Shepherd wanted the audience to be aroused into political action. A fervent admirer of Brecht, Shepherd was intrigued by "the notion of letting people eat and smoke [in] a popular theatre where [they can] be comfortable and not think of the theatre as something holy and untouchable" (qtd. in Sweet 5). He dreamed of neighborhood cabarets where working-class audiences could watch and participate in improvised scenarios relevant to their lives.

Brecht described a "smoker's theatre," where the thoughtful spectator, puffing on a cigar, was an active participant in the performance event—a "theatre full of experts, just as one has sporting arena full of experts"(Brecht 44). For Brecht, the expertise of the sports fan represented the ideal blend of distance and passion. Every sports fan understands the techniques and choices in play in the contest being staged. Fans can see how things could have gone, even should have gone, because the sporting event is open ended and (like improvisation) capable of different outcomes. Thus, the spectator is inspired to think instead of feel, to work for social change and take action against injustice rather than to weep over inevitable miseries. Summing up his ambitions for the Compass, Shepherd wrote, "I saw that the goal of our theater should be a riot in the audience" (Sweet xxi).

Shepherd believed *commedia*-style scenarios were the best way to harness improvisation in service of a political statement. In *commedia dell'arte*, actors playing stock character types improvised dialogue around preset plot outlines. Players mastered large repertoires of *lazzi*—or comic bits—and memorized poetic speeches appropriate to various dramatic situations. Thus, while the elements of each performance were not necessarily invented in the moment, there was an infinite number of ways in which known fragments could be recombined. As in Chicago improv, the success of each performance depended heavily on the range of each actor's knowledge and the ability of fellow players to recognize every reference and play along.

Such preplanning was antithetical to Spolin's notion of improvisation as exploration of the unknown, but Shepherd saw the predetermined narrative as an essential means of focusing on political issues. He also preferred *commedia*'s bold, comic acting style over the realistic, psychological approach of Stanislavsky's Method, saying, "[W]hat we are after is a more vigorous idea . . . the kind of mask or prototype that you come across in Brecht or Jonson or Molière: didactic theatre" (qtd. in Coleman 56). *Commedia*'s legacy lingers in modern improv through rigidly gendered character archetypes, shared cultural references and bits, and in long-form improv.

Like Shepherd, Sills held that not only the satiric, antiestablishment content of the early scenarios but the very form of improvisational performance could be liberating. Sills told *Chicago Magazine* in 1955, "Compass, if carried to its logical conclusion, is a sort of 'do it yourself' movement. I'd like to see neighborhoods all over the city form groups like this. It's a search for community" (Sweet xxvi). Sills, like many avant-garde artists of the late forties and fifties, believed that the dialogic nature of improvisation made it "a model of democratic interaction" and a "technique for bringing ideologically inadmissible possibilities into awareness" (Belgrade 9).[3]

Sills was more in tune with his mother than he was with Shepherd in his views on *how* theatre should effect social change: "[The purpose of theater is] the liberation of the people. The possibility of this country liberating itself. I'm not talking about tearing down buildings and things like that. I'm talking about personal liberation. . . . To me it's very important the people get a little heart and spirit back" (Sweet 17).

Intrigued by primitivist ideas of myth, magic, and ritual, Sills spoke of channeling the subconscious, or tapping an even deeper collective unconscious, to find a cosmic truth that would link his artistic expression to both the personal and political uses of improvisation, saying: "It's Orpheus. They send a poet into the nether regions and he comes back with the message. He is supposed to come out with the truth. He is supposed to be the oracle" (qtd. in Mee 63).

Sills's interest in the shamanic aspects of improv was often at odds with his commitment to the more intellectual and political Brechtian theatre. One of his friends commented, "Brecht influenced Paul more than any other playwright. But there are two lines in him. He's never fused them. There's the Brecht thing. And there's the Viola thing: the fairy-tale thing" (Coleman 38). This unresolved contradiction later grew to be the source of deeper rifts in the entire genre. It was Sills's finesse and his directorial skills that made viable theatre out of Shepherd's dreams and Spolin's games.

In the early days of the Compass, this fusion seemed to be working. Many players and spectators remember the exhilaration of hearing their own secret thoughts, dreams, and desires spoken aloud on stage. Original Compass player Andrew Duncan recalls, "To suddenly find something that was . . . an applied form in which to get up and start expressing the things we were thinking about and feeling at that time, with all those repressed political, social, psychological feelings . . . I mean the *freedom!*" (Sweet 47).

The first days at the Compass have been described as a time of rough innocence and creative anarchy.[4] Shepherd and Sills recruited players drawn largely from their earlier repertory group at the Playwrights Theatre Club and the University of Chicago.[5] They set out to create new plays through the scenario format, to attract new audiences through a cabaret atmosphere, and to develop a new acting method through improvisation.

There was some question whether Spolin's techniques were appropriate for the new theatre's purpose. Spolin was reportedly displeased at first to find that her process-oriented exercises were being used by the Compass Players to create a commercial performance product. Yet, she gave the project her support. Sills led the players in several months of workshops based on her games in the spring of 1955. Spolin herself instructed the group for one month that spring before going home to California (ironically, she never saw the Compass Players in performance). Barbara Harris remembers the liberating sensation of Spolin's workshops, where improvisation "swept us into another realm, another consciousness . . . a new language which asked for spontaneity and freedom on stage that followed nothing I had ever heard of before" (Sweet 66).

Shepherd's main project was the longer scenarios, with often quite serious themes, written by various members of the company. These were always followed by a set of improvised scenes based on audience suggestions, frequently using one of Spolin's games as a base structure. Known as "spot improvs," they soon became the acknowledged highlight of each show.

The fledgling company struck a chord with its young audiences and appeared to capture the Brechtian smoker's theatre atmosphere that Shepherd and Sills wanted. A journalist for *Chicago Magazine* reported, "The audience is informal, spontaneous, heckling, comes from all over. . . . People hate to leave, clamor for more, and the actors . . . often keep it up for a couple of extra hours" (qtd. in Sweet xxv). Barbara Harris recalls, "If there is such a thing as altruism, then it was altruistic, with a kind of generosity of energy and spirit. . . . It wasn't very practical. It wasn't realistic. But it filled a need that made sense" (Coleman 113).

At first, the Compass was open to participation on stage by performers from a wide variety of backgrounds and occupations. Membership in the first ad hoc company fluctuated greatly, as Sills tended to cast "whoever show[ed] up" (Sweet interview). Spolin had always held that "anyone can improvise" and Shepherd wanted to keep workshops and performances open to real workers and members of the community, preferring what he considered to be the authenticity of amateurism to the skill of professional performers. For all three, the purpose of the theatre was to awaken new consciousness—in both the performer and the spectator—not merely to entertain.

But Shepherd failed to interest the southern Illinois proletariat in his idea of a worker's theatre. Instead, the company appealed to people like themselves—highly educated middle- and upper-class misfits, restless in the conformist atmosphere of the 1950s. In fact, with the exception of Harris, Sills, and Elaine May, none of the original players had professional theatre experience or ambition. Rather, the theatre was a means of expression, a refuge, a surrogate family. Duncan remembers, "The idea of Compass, and later Second City, was a theater of us . . . we'd be in a theater that was concerned with the community. The issues of the community, the politics, the social issues" (McCrohan 26).

While they tried to be inclusive, the Compass was in fact a minority theatre with an outsider's sensibility based partly on ethnicity and religion. A majority of the Compass and early Second City companies were Jews, while many others were Catholics from immigrant families (Sweet interview). According to historian and playwright Jeff Sweet, Second City's comedy "came very much out of Jewish rhythms. The irony, the satire, the love for the intellectual and finding the contradiction and dialectic in things" (interview). In 1955, the Compass was a theater of "us" formed from outsiders, misfits, and pioneers determined to discover a new community to which they could belong.

Perhaps because of their outsider status, Compass management moved by stages to shut down the all-inclusive, "anyone can play" nature of the founders' original concepts. The theatre of us began to define a "them," who were not eligible to play. For example, Duncan points out, "[Shepherd] really expected people in the troupe to have other jobs. But [that] meant passing up workshops. Or, if you had a night job, you couldn't perform at night. There was an elitist thing behind his premise, no matter how based it was in Brechtian-Marxist whatever. You had to have money to support it . . . [and] to assume that you had a leisured group of people" (Sweet 45).

Participation in the Compass was increasingly dependent on specific training, shared cultural references, and significant amounts of unpaid workshop and rehearsal time. Pointing to their policies of openness, most improvisers have blamed self-selection for the shortage of women and the almost complete absence of nonwhite players in first-wave improv. It is more likely that people of color who were aware of the troupe did not feel welcome or financially able to participate.

The Compass rarely addressed the issue of racism directly in the content of their scenarios and sketches, or in the makeup of the troupe. They believed, perhaps, that ignoring race was the best way to show a lack of prejudice, a typical approach by liberals at the time. The only player of color to appear with the Chicago Compass was Bob Patton, one of the amateur actors who performed, unpaid, in the earliest days of the company. Patton had no particular political agenda; he just wanted to act. "I was aware that I was the only black member of the group. That was pretty obvious. But it really played no part. I took whatever roles came along" (Coleman 108). When Patton played a dope dealer in one early sketch, some of the very few blacks in the Compass audience objected to his stereotypically immoral character. But Patton rejected their disapproval: "I was just playing a part. [They're stupid to] complain about my great role" (108).

However, Patton did encounter overt racism in his short stint with the Compass. Duncan remembers, "[I]t bothered one of the bartenders there was a black guy onstage. I mean this was 1955 . . . this bartender would crawl under [the stage] and pound, interrupting rehearsals. . . . Finally, he leaped onstage one night during a performance where Bobby kissed one of the white girls" (Sweet 52). If many in the Compass Players' university-based audiences were willing to see Patton's kiss as a hip understatement about racial equality, the theatre's bartender was unwilling to pretend that nothing shocking had taken place.

White players often portrayed ethnicity with stereotypical gestures or mannerisms that were instantly recognized by the audience. They did not hesitate to play Asian, black, Jewish, and other ethnic types, which they could take on or discard in the spirit of improvisational transformations. White players were able to represent blackness, but the reverse was not the case. No matter what role Patton might choose to play, the white spectator could not recognize him as a "white character."

After Patton left to concentrate on his career in city management, players Mark and Bobbi Gordon remember "blacks being in the audience," but "rarely." Mark feels that racial issues were handled badly: "What I remember was people not afraid to play black. . . . I was very sensitive to it. I felt that we should have had a black actor if we were going to do it. Anything that came out of improvisational theater would have to be a recognizable cliché. . . . So if someone did black, they would do black in stereotype" (qtd. in Sweet 107). The racial issues Patton's presence had raised, however, would not be addressed again for decades.

As with many avant-garde or radical movements, the Compass Players often used women as metaphors, decorations, or enabling support characters rather than fully equal subjects. Few women attracted to the Compass found the artistic home available to the men. At first only Harris and May stuck it out. An extremely shy woman, Harris began very quietly. Her talent, and, arguably, the protection of Sills, who became her husband, allowed Harris to blossom into a significant force in the Compass troupe. May, on the other hand, fought fearlessly for her share of artistic control, using the sheer force of her personality to broaden the scope of the troupe's satire.

Spolin's insistence on mutual cooperation, a nonjudgmental atmosphere, and the valuing of process over product had a significant impact on gender relations in the early improvisation sessions at the Compass. Harris describes the games as "very equalizing. . . . The exercises gave you a point of concentration outside yourself. You didn't have to be brilliant. It wasn't competitive" (Coleman 94–95).

Many of the long, slow-paced character scenes that made Harris and May famous were originally improvised in an environment of tolerance for exploration. When the improvisation became fast-paced, competitive, and more focused on comedy, however, many of the women who came through the Compass (with the notable exception of May) faded into support and background roles. As psychologist Rose Laub Coser asserts, "In this culture . . . a woman who has a good sense of humor is one who laughs (but not too loudly!) when a man makes a witticism or tells a good joke. . . . The man provides; the woman receives" (qtd. in Barreca 7).

The notion of open-ended process is not innately feminine, nor is a results-oriented focus on product innately masculine. Yet, many gendered behavior patterns, however socially constructed, served to reinforce the association of female players with pure improvisation and male players with performance-ready entertainment. For most women improvisers, particularly in the pre-feminist '50s and '60s, exploring and supporting relationships, giving up control of unfolding events, or subjugating self-interest for the benefit of the group simply reinforced their gender training. Men, on the other hand, often felt uncomfortable until they had imposed a through line or, at the very least, produced a punch line for a scene—reinforcing the more goal-oriented, heroic role that males were expected to play in society. This comedy dichotomy was a productive one for the famous Nichols and May partnership at the Compass. Mike Nichols remembers working with May on their scenes: "By and large, I would shape them and Elaine would fill them. . . . What she's interested in is character and the moment. What I'm interested in is moving on and giving it a shape. I was always very concerned with beginning, middle, and end, and when it's time for the next point to be made and when it's time to move because after all, we're telling a story. . . . She could go on and on in character" (qtd. in Sweet 82–83).

For other players, it often seemed natural for male improvisers to dominate in the shared group or pair improvs. Men's creative freedom was frequently built on women's agreement. Spolin's (and Sills's) theory that improvisation revealed universal truths often helped to reinforce the gender stereotypes that no-mindedly emerged in scenes. By the time second- and third-wave women began to challenge sexism in improv-comedy, the notion that Spolin's rules and process were uniformly beneficial for female players was also seriously questioned.

The Compass Players' success was immediate—and overwhelming. Meeting audience demand required a grueling rehearsal, workshop, and performance schedule, but the actors' low pay could not support this exhausting commitment. Many core players left. Shepherd and Sills were forced to find ways both to preserve the actors' energy and to increase their income. They hired several professional actors in New York as replacements and eased the strain of constant production by presenting each show for a longer run. To Shepherd's dismay, the scenario format gave way to collections of audience-pleasing shorter scenes, which the players often polished and repeated instead of newly improvising every night (though some scenario work hung on throughout the Compass's life). The Compass Players became an enormously popular satirical comedy troupe.

But the target of their barbs was not the capitalist system, as Shepherd would have liked, but their own families and upbringing, social mores and pretensions. Societal ills were presented in terms of individual dis-ease and anxiety. With psychoanalysis a newly fashionable pastime, scenes were often set in a psychiatrist's office and characters defined through their neuroses. In keeping with the therapeutic style of Spolin-inspired improv, players used a psychological style of confessional free-association for other situations as well.

Without a scenario to focus it, improvisation was unlikely to create a pointed political message. Challenged also was the experimental spirit of the improvisation, as the players began to "freeze" lines and repeat jokes. None-theless, according to Duncan, "The artistic work, the acting, was worlds apart from the early stuff. It was more entertaining. The audience reaction was much better. I know. I was there. I never heard such laughter in my life" (Coleman 138). It seemed that the Compass had deliberately traded process for a more sure-fire product.

As the Compass grew in reputation, standards for a successful performance rose, and the pressure to produce quick-thinking comedy intensified. Most of the remaining amateurs dropped away. Performers felt they had less and less of a right to fail at the risky onstage improvisations. This shift away from process had a particular effect on the women in the troupe—most of whom had been cast for their ability to act a role (or for their looks or type) rather than for aggressiveness or broad comic abilities. Bobbi Gordon recalls, "And then it was funny time and who could be funnier than whom. I never felt as much competition onstage as around this time" (Sweet 68). Annette Hankin remembers that when she felt the loss of group support, "[T]hat was the end of it for me" (Coleman 137). As feminist journalist Julia Klein has commented, "Comedy itself is an aggressive act; making someone laugh means exerting control, even power. But a woman cannot come off as over-aggressive or she will lose" (116). May was the only woman performer who insisted on an equal voice in the writing and directing of scenes and longer scenarios. Severn Dar-den remembers, "She was always good. But she had this fierce competitive-ness. We argued. She terrified me" (McCrohan 29).

Even as the Compass grew in popularity, tensions, rivalries, exhaustion, and disillusionment increased. Players were forced to acknowledge that, de-spite Spolin's original insistence on mutual support and shared focus, impro-visation could be manipulated to give some performers star status at the expense of others, male and female. After many defections, firings, and re-criminations, the group finally disbanded in the winter of 1957.

In the meantime, performer-director Ted Flicker had won Shepherd's per-mission to start a branch of the Compass in St. Louis. The new partners both hoped this venture would expand to include a New York City branch of the theatre, and they agreed that Flicker would begin work in St. Louis while they both sought backers for the New York company.

The next phase of first-wave improv-comedy was a further structuring of the "proper" use of improvisation for comedy performance. Flicker polished and disciplined performances to make them more entertaining. Instead of street clothes, Flicker's performers wore costumes in black and white, giving the actors a uniform look. The men wore shirts and slacks; the women, long shirts and revealing tights—a look that increased the entertainment value of the women's appearance as well. Flicker also established time limits on the improvisations and openly acknowledged the idea of including jokes and playing for laughs—a notion deeply disdained by improv purists.

When Elaine May joined the St. Louis Compass, she and Flicker worked together to develop a coherent theory of improvisation in performance. They codified techniques for adapting the freedom of the workshop to the pressures of the stage, concentrating on how to minimize the failure rate of improv. Flicker recalls that he and May made a distinction between *private* and *public* improvisation. Private improvisation, according to Flicker, belongs in the classroom or the workshop. Its purpose is "to sensitize yourself to your inner creative force" (Sweet 161). But Flicker and May believed that this kind of work was boring for an audience to watch. In their definition, public improvisation "first of all had to entertain" (161).

The rules Flicker and May defined in St. Louis had a significant impact on the way improv would be taught in the decades that followed—particularly at the Second City Training Center. Their rules for public improv—including the prohibition against denial or negation of another player's established reality—extend Spolin's general notion of group agreement. Other rules instruct actors to take the active, even the unlikely, choice in each improvised situation; to base characterizations on exaggerations of key aspects of the actor's "self"; and to train extensively in the techniques of establishing place, character, and circumstance. Flicker and May systematized and superseded the various ad hoc adaptations of Spolin, *commedia*, and other techniques with the express goal of creating nightclub entertainment. For Flicker, the bottom line was training and technique. Despite the ethos of improv as a free-for-all, Flicker insisted, "The freer the form, the greater must be the underpinnings of discipline" (qtd. in Sweet 161).

But after seeing one "circus-like" performance of the St. Louis Compass, Shepherd told Flicker, "You've turned it into entertainment. You've ruined my dream" (Coleman 220). The two men dissolved their partnership, and the St. Louis Compass disbanded after less than a year in operation. Flicker went on to found his own improv-comedy troupe, the Premise, which flourished in New York from 1960 to 1963.

Both Flicker and Shepherd made a stab at racial integration in improv-comedy in 1963. Shepherd cast actress Diana Sands for his Compass venture in Hyannisport, Massachusetts. She was the first black performer to play with any of the Compass or Second City troupes since Bob Patton's brief stint eight years earlier. But Shepherd then turned down the highly talented actor Godfrey Cambridge. He explains, "I went to Hyannisport with only one black— Diana Sands—because I thought there was room for only one black person in a company that was going to play in such a lily-white area. I would have loved to have worked with Godfrey Cambridge" (Sweet 8).

Later that year, Flicker cast Cambridge, along with Sands and Al Freeman Jr., to perform improv-comedy in a Premise offshoot called the Living Premise. This integrated troupe filled the seats of a Bleecker Street cabaret for a brief run, but the actors soon dispersed into individual projects. First-wave improv-comedy's virtual exclusion of African American performers is ironic, particularly in the 1960s, when the improvisational quality of black art, performance, and music (especially jazz) was imitated and "seized on by [white] avant-garde artists as a potent emblem of freedom" (Banes 156).

In 1959, Sills teamed with commercial theatre producer Bernie Sahlins and actor-manager Howard Alk to create the Second City. No longer willing to be burdened with Shepherd's Marxist notions and personal eccentricities, Sills was interested in creating marketable social and political satire. The new company would generate scripted comedy revues by using the techniques developed at the Compass. Yet Sills was still quite committed to improv as a means of personal discovery and social change, and he grounded every rehearsal in Spolin's exercises.

The formative years at Second City are seen by many as another utopian moment of real improvisation. Spolin returned to teach the new cast her games and her philosophy of improvisation, both of which became required and integral elements of the Second City system. But Sahlins had little faith in improvisation as a performance mode, saying, "Essentially, improvisation for me is a tool, like mime, used to arrive at material in the absence of a writer. And in the absence of a writer you can only arrive at certain kinds of material: short things, things without subtext, and so forth" (Adler, "The 'How' of Funny" 16). He (and others) believed that sophisticated satire required more conscious craft. This familiar process-product debate still resonates in Chicago improv, where some purists believe that Sahlins' attitude seriously damaged Second City's improvisational spirit.

Duncan recalls, "Rather than the anarchy which reigned at the Compass, Sills planned every second from the minute the lights dimmed to the applause and bows" (Sweet 55). The troupe focused on short blackout sketches, created either through improvisations or outright scripting, which were then strung together to make revues. Post-revue improvs based on audience input tended to be topical and drawn from audience concerns of the moment, including Chicago politics and contemporary social trends. The best impromptus were refined and developed for later revues. Alan Arkin remembers these early days as a time when, after performing the set revue, the actors were allowed to experiment with risky improvised material and were "virtually encouraged to fail" (Sweet 225). The audiences, says Arkin, were hip to the nature of improvised work, they "understood the process and were very excited. It was like verbal-physical jazz [with] the same kind of audience [that] appreciates good jazz musicians" (Sweet 225).

Second City performers were mostly white, male, middle class, and more than half Jewish. They were highly educated, well read, and well informed on current events. An important rule for each Second City performance was to improvise from the "top of your intelligence." This meant avoiding cheap jokes; and, in the early days, it also assumed a literate, well-informed audience. Allusions to Freud, Kafka, or Hemingway were common. References to television were usually laced with contempt. The company prided themselves on presenting smart social satire, and their general tone was rebellious and antiestablishment, "bringing to bear an ironic point of view on the difference between what people profess and what they do, what ought to be and what is" (Sahlins qtd. in McCrohan 41). But the troupe's critiques were aimed mostly at the family, or the cultural scene, with far less attention paid to the social and political issues Shepherd once promoted.

Sahlins admits, "We were never as political as people remember us" (Sweet 180). Second City created a sensation partly because even the mildest political humor was a novelty in 1959 and the early 1960s—"you just said Eisenhower on stage and it was orgasmic" (180). But Sahlins insists that Second City's best work consisted of more than the simple violation of taboos. Rather, it created a space where young audiences saw and recognized their own concerns being played out and where they could "form a community with the people on stage" (McCrohan 41).

Yet, while hip young audiences saw the troupe speaking out against corporate greed and social hypocrisy, the internal politics of Second City reflected conventional hierarchies based on gender, race, and the power of money and knowledge. Second City performers were even less attuned to racial, ethnic, and gender issues than the Compass had been. For many members of the troupe, it became part of the game to pretend ignorance of all these disparities. For the women in the company, this game was part of their survival as players.

In conscious recreation of *commedia dell'arte*, the performers were strongly typecast—particularly in the early scenes of each show. According to Alk, "The audience should have a sense of what the people in troupe are. Thus, Gene Troobnick is the schlemiel, Andy Duncan is the All-American boy, and Severn Darden is the Madman" (McCrohan 54). Actors were often pigeon-holed in essentializing roles—where Jewish players were schlemiels and blond Christians were all-American. Alan Arkin became well known for his portrayal of a Puerto Rican drifter who teaches a social worker the pleasures of unemployment, and "samurai" characters were popular long before they would be seen on television in *Saturday Night Live*. In the pressure to create quick characterizations, it was fairly simple to adopt stereotypical ethnic attributes. Yet, in the first twenty-nine years of Second City performances, only two African Americans appeared on that company's mainstage. And, while several Asian American women were cast in touring companies in the 1990s, the millennium turned without an Asian American on the Chicago mainstage in forty-one years.[6]

True to its roots in *commedia*, Second City offered many comic masks for men, but only one or two for women. Anne Libera, one of a handful of women to direct for Second City, observes, "If you look at photos of Second City casts over the years you can see the pattern.[7] In every company you see four or five men and two women—the pretty one and the funny one" (personal interview).

Barbara Harris and Mina Kolb used very different tactics to maintain their positions as artists in the original cast. Obviously "the pretty one," Harris brought depth, intelligence, and poignancy to her portrayal of girlfriends, wives, and objects of desire in many Second City sketches. Known for her "people scenes"—pieces that were often longer, slower, and more subtly comic than the other blackout sketches—Harris thought of herself as an actress rather than a comedian, and she rarely challenged conventional gender roles either on or off the stage.

Mina Kolb, "the funny one," was often described as the "clubwoman" type. She played a vacuous, upper-class suburban matron but was, in fact, a savvy survivor. In a typical Second City rehearsal process, women were forced to ally themselves with powerful male performers to be included in the sketches being developed. Kolb recalls, "It was almost always that a man insti-gated a scene. . . . Sure, I had a lot of ideas, but they weren't always acceptable to who was in power at the time. . . . You had to make it somebody else's idea. . . . I've been playing that game all my life" (Sweet 206).

Kolb was often able to deflect male control with non-sequiturs—to great comic effect. For example, in one improv, when she was quizzed on her opinion of a famous sculptor's work, Kolb replied, "Well, I really haven't seen it.

I've been out of town" (Coleman 257). She was able to make her *character* misunderstand—and thus was able to passively resist being dominated in the scene.

"Mostly," Kolb says, "I think I would make comments in scenes. Barbara . . . and some of the others could really develop scenes dramatically, but I don't think I was very good at that. Perhaps I should have worked more on Viola's games" (Sweet 204). Yet, Kolb's more distanced style may have been the key to her relative independence. Cultural theorist Elin Diamond recommends that a feminist actor use Brechtian alienation techniques to stand aside from and comment on the difference between her *self* and the (often male-created) character she represents (83–84).

Comic performance often permits a similar kind of distancing. Second City audiences were able to witness the essential machinery of their presentation of each stock character—from the "dizzy blonde" to the "mad professor." In this way, says Tony Hendra, "those figures themselves were, subtly, targets of the humor. The performer conveyed to the audience that he or she was now *acting*. The audience could enjoy both the character that was being played, and the fact that they knew a character was being played. And not the smallest part of the audience's enjoyment was that it was flattered to be let in on the process" (63).

This Brechtian-comic approach is usually at odds with female improvisers' traditional refuge and ally—Spolin's process—which requires the surrender of self-consciousness. At both the Compass Players and Second City, women were encouraged to play in a dramatic, character-based mode, partly to avoid threatening male comic power. Because women at Second City were given such limited and gendered roles, spectators were more likely to conflate a female actor with her "type." Thus, in order to comment on stereotypically gendered characters, the woman player may risk a more extreme representation of distance—resulting in accusations that she is improvising badly, or without the appropriate commitment. For the women players who try to maneuver between them, the uneasy marriage between Brechtian and Violan techniques in improv-comedy has created both pitfalls and opportunities.

In the 1960s, the original Second City cast courted the critics in London, Los Angeles, and New York, requiring producers to train replacement players who could hold the fort in Chicago. The company created systems of financing, touring, and training, systems that would have long-term implications for all Chicago improv. In 1960, Spolin taught a series of classes as she honed the text of *Improvisation for the Theatre*, recruiting a new group of converts to her techniques and philosophies. Contested, modified, and expanded over the years, Spolin-based workshops and structures have been used in every decade not only for inspiration but also for authority, discipline, and control over Chicago-style improvisers.

At first, although the new actors learned Second City's improv methods and ideology, they were not asked to create fresh material but to step into roles left behind by the original troupe. This process in itself, however, was fairly improvisational. Richard Libertini, who joined the company a bit later, recalls, "When we inherited material, it was like the old vaudeville days. Someone says, 'You're going to do Floogle Street. Here's how it goes.' They'd kind of show you. So you're watching it, then you jump in . . . then you're on your own. Things continue to transform . . . it depends on who inherits what from whom" (McCrohan 79).

While it became a point of honor for most players to add their own personal touch to inherited scenes, women found themselves more circumscribed in their roles than the men were. Women were almost always the object of the joke, their clichéd behavior a critical, and therefore immutable, part of the humor's mechanism. They were often portrayed as sexually repressed or withholding, the cause of comic frustration for male characters.

In one famous scene developed with Mina Kolb, a woman begs her husband not to leave her, pleading, "No, George, don't." But the moment he relents and comes to embrace her, the wife turns a cold shoulder, again saying, "No, George, don't."

Joan Rivers replaced Kolb in 1961. She recalls, "[I] realized instinctively that the men would be perfectly content to let me fill in the secondary slots that needed a prop female, let me go on saying, 'No, George, don't,' while I slowly withered and eventually died. I could see that they regarded Second City as a male art form, that they did not want a girl pushing in and saying, 'I can do that scene' " (McCrohan 156). Rivers challenged both the training and the typecasting she was offered. But resistance was translated as *denial* (or non-agreement)—a particularly incendiary crime in the world of Second City improv.

Improv veterans retell one particular story of Rivers' willingness to sacrifice agreement, reality, and team spirit for the sake of a laugh. Rivers was on stage in an improv set one night when a male player entered the scene with a clear initiation. He was a tired businessman home from work, talking to his wife about the house, the kids, the dog, and the neighbors. Rivers patiently waited out her partner's opening, then, in a matter-of-fact voice, replied, "What are you talking about? I've never seen you before in my life." The audience's shocked laughter brought down the house; but Rivers' tactics infuriated the rest of the troupe.

While a number of men—from David Steinberg to John Belushi—have gotten away with breaking improv's rules, Rivers was ostracized for similar behavior. The comedian acknowledges that she owes much of her later success to lessons learned at Second City, but Rivers feels she was never supported or encouraged there. Undercutting and undermining the men was the only way she saw to get a laugh of her own.

Workshops continued in the mid-sixties, advocating the values of collectivity in an increasingly individualistic performance context and stressing cooperation in a genre that was becoming ever more competitive. According to Anthony Holland, improvisers began to divide themselves into separate interest groups. "There was the wit group, the kind of object-reality group, and there was the surreal group [which was] much more into the emerging drug culture . . . we were all members of the same church, but there were sects" (Sweet 264).[8] Del Close, one of those in the surrealist group, experimented so often with mind-altering drugs that he was forced to take extended vacations from his acting and directing responsibilities. Nonetheless, his pioneering work with new structures would greatly influence second-wave improv.

Most players reveled in the interactive creativity of those years and remember the competition as a natural byproduct of its intensity. Comedian Jack Burns recalls, "In only two places in my life have I felt that camaraderie. One was in the Marine Corps and the other was Second City, and they both had a sense of discipline. They both had a leader like Paul Sills. It was like a commune. It was the sixties" (McCrohan 166). Sandy Holt was far more troubled by the divergence between ideology and reality. She remembers, "The whole idea of Second City is not to be competitive. In the workshops, it's not. But in our contracts was a two-week clause. You could be canned at any time. I had to fight for everything. Once I knew that I could fight for it, then I became part of the company" (McCrohan 166).

Sahlins asserted primacy of the company over the importance of any single player. He resisted any demand for pay increases or artistic control on the grounds that Second City was a family, where everyone pitched in equally and everyone benefited. If Sahlins was the patriarch, associate producer Joyce Sloane was the den mother. Sloane nurtured individual players while raising funds for the company through theatre parties and donations. But even as Second City began to be a huge success, Sahlins kept salaries low, partly out of genuine financial concerns, but also to maintain control over the company. He viewed escalating actor demands, along with fickle commitment to the troupe, as personal betrayals. In the early '60s, when Second City performers joined Actors' Equity and AFTRA, the unions for stage and screen actors, Sahlins protested, "But we're a family!" He closed the theatre temporarily rather than accede to their demands (McCrohan 162).

Second City's increasing celebrity in the early '60s brought in "the mink-coat crowd," raising the troupe's income even as it lowered the hipness factor of its audiences; many believe it lowered the quality of the comedy as well. According to Avery Schreiber, the shift to a more mainstream, middle-class audience was reflected in their suggestions for the improvs: "Before, we'd ask for characters and we'd get 'Dido and Aeneas.' Then it shifted and we would get 'Jackie Kennedy at the hairdresser' "(Sweet 299). It seemed to many of the old guard that commercial success and artistic purity were incompatible and that Second City was selling out.

In the mid-sixties a new style of stand-up comedy, inspired by Lenny Bruce and Mort Sahl, used personal observances, characters, and an improvisational style instead of set routines made of up of jokes and one-liners. Important early proponents of this approach included Richard Pryor, Lily Tomlin, and Bill Cosby, along with David Steinberg and Robert Klein—who both did stints with Second City. From his first appearance on the Second City stage, Steinberg saw that the rules around group cooperation masked the real operations of power in the troupe. As a new player, he felt completely shut out of the improvisations, until he finally stole focus by *breaking the reality* of his teammates' scene. He got a laugh. Steinberg says, "For me, the lesson of that night persisted. Break any rule you can get away with" (McCrohan 130).

In 1964, Spolin returned to California to create the more process-oriented Games Theatre. Meanwhile, Sills's frustration mounted as he felt Second City was becoming increasingly commercial, its revues contrary to Violan values. He declared, "The sooner the improvisational theatre breaks away from the idea of repeating itself, the closer it will be to real improvisational theatre. What I'm after is a *total* reversal of values" (Mee 180). Sills took long leaves of absence, forcing the company to cultivate a stable of alternative directors, including Del Close, Larry Arrick, and Alan Myerson.[9]

In 1965, Sills sold his interest in the company to Sheldon Patinkin, who stepped in as supervising artistic director. According to Coleman, Sills's abdication left Sahlins "free to begin the transformation of The Second City into what a William Morris Agent called the 'Superbowl of Comedy' " (290). Nonetheless, the workshops forged ahead under the direction of Spolin's assistant, Jo Forsberg.

Second City was softening its satiric edge, presenting less and less challenge to the "establishment" that had become a large part of its audience. Patinkin said, "The place had to become more commercial or die. . . . As a result, the workshops for the most part are and always have been about how to be funny, which is part of what drove Paul and Viola out. The point became how to do

Viola and Paul's work and make sure you were trying to be funny at the same time" (McCrohan 128).

Despite nostalgia for an improv utopia, Second City's history does not represent any direct progression from purity to corruption. While some moves emphasized commercialism and mainstream ideology, there were also periodic resurgences of commitment to the ideals of iconoclastic improvisation. And although the troupe's underlying sexism remained fairly constant, the need to achieve broader audience appeal forced the company to reevaluate its entrenched class- and education-based elitism.

Years later, producer Sahlins would say that, in hindsight, the early Second City "played for the elite and were the elite. Looking back, all of our democratic impulses were arrogant in many ways. We were educated, interested in high-level reference. While our hearts were in the right place politically and socially, we were nevertheless snobs, cultural snobs" (Sweet 177).

But in 1967 Second City brought in several stand-up comics from the Improvisation comedy club in New York. J. J. Barry recalls, "I think that's when Second City changed from a satirical, intellectual group to a sort of broader based Saturday night humor . . . we introduced what you could call a blue-collar approach to satire, down-home, nitty-gritty, on the street" (McCrohan 145). While Second City producers needed the energy and mainstream appeal of a new breed of comic, they were also very clear that these actors had to be trained and disciplined to create the Second City way. Barry had worked at New York's Improvisation as a stand-up for several years. He began doing free-form comedy improvisations with fellow comic Richard Pryor. It was improv without rules, without technique. Barry says, "I just know Richie used to say, 'Come on, let's get up and fool around.'. . . The thing I loved about it was the freedom of it. In not knowing what we were doing we were being brilliant . . . it was the freedom of ignorance" (Sweet 355).

Although it was Pryor who instigated these improvisations, he was not one of the actors recruited by Second City. This choice could reflect Pryor's determination to make a solo career. On the other hand, it was likely that producers saw Pryor as less trainable and, as a black man, less castable in Second City sketches. For all their liberal protestations, first-wave producers could be quite conservative on race issues, often preemptively sparing their audiences the challenge of accepting African American performers. Second City's proprietary attitude about the art of improvisation may have made them undervalue alternative modes of play. For example, while Pryor was performing a style of spontaneous comedy well entrenched in African American tradition, Second City's producers believed that, without the proper training and technique, neither he nor anyone else could do genuine Second City improv. Despite the affinity that early Compass Players and Second City improvisers felt for the beatnik, hipster aesthetic associated with blackness, African Americans themselves were notably absent from the Second City stage—with the single (brief) exception of comedian Bob Curry in 1966.[10] More than ten years would pass before a second black actor appeared with the company in any capacity.

In 1967, Second City also moved to a larger theatre at 1616 North Wells Street and created permanent touring companies that played a "Best of Second City" show around the country. This arrangement, which expanded further in the '90s, established "farm teams" to cultivate players for the major league of Second City's mainstage. Spolin returned to Chicago to help train the new cast. The workshops she established eventually expanded to become a major element of Second City's empire. Before long, Second City management would stop seeking replacement performers in New York and elsewhere but would produce their own improvisers through a progression of Second City workshops, touring companies, Children's Theatre Company, and regional troupes.

In 1968, the Second City troupe was drawn into political issues—both on- and offstage. Their Wells Street address was only a few short blocks from the Cabrini-Green housing projects, and the neighborhood was in a constant ferment of racial tensions. At the Democratic National Convention in Chicago, Mayor Daley's "Gestapo tactics" and police brutality against originally peaceful antiwar protesters galvanized Second City's political sensibilities.[11]

On the heels of the convention, and just before Chicago's Southside race riots, Second City mounted a show called *A Plague on Both Your Houses*. The first scene showed a Chicago policeman beating a young man he thinks is a demonstrator. When the victim pleads, "Wait, I'm a reporter!" the officer stops the beating, takes out a gun—and shoots the reporter. *A Plague on Both Your Houses* brought gasps of dismay and cheers of solidarity from audiences for months. Barry remembers the effect of the show's stirring title song: "[T]he entire audience got up, tears in their eyes, and the arms went up in peace symbols. It was like a revival, man! Everybody . . . started singing with us" (Sweet 359). Second City's reputation as an antiestablishment theatre was briefly revived.

The 1970s brought additions to the Second City family. Sahlins and Sloane launched a second Second City in Toronto, but it floundered until Canadian producer Andrew Alexander invested in the venture in 1973. In Chicago, the new mainstage troupe was known on Wells Street as "the Next Generation." They were the first group to be entirely cast out of Second City's touring company system. Weaned on countercultural values, the idealistic young company seemed genuinely to embrace Spolin's philosophies of collectivity and spontaneity. When surrealist improviser Del Close returned to direct for Second City, the troupe was eager to create both true, unplanned improvisation and hard-hitting political satire. Some of their most daring work, however, proved unsuccessful at the box office. Audiences wanted lighter, less abrasive subject matter—they wanted the old cast back.

In 1971, Sahlins "discovered" John Belushi, who rose rapidly to become a Second City star, breaking every improv rule in the process. He was an audience favorite—a visceral, earthy scene-stealer who also defied the company's restrictions on obscenity and low humor. Although teammates resented his upstaging, many followed this pied piper, even as he moved deeper into a drug culture that had become an accepted part of Second City's beatnik-hippie lifestyle.

The advent of feminism in the '70s made small difference to backstage politics, and women still had to maneuver for stage time by attaching themselves to influential male players. Although women rarely appeared in partner scenes with one other, the changing times produced the phenomenon of "the chick scene." Women would go through most of the rehearsals for a Second City revue playing support roles and walk-ons in sketches that centered on the male players. At the last minute, when a director realized he might be criticized for giving the women too little stage time, he would throw the two female players together in a room and tell them to write a chick scene.

In the mid-seventies, Betty Thomas saw this "ghettoization" as a form of disempowerment. She quickly realized that a woman player had to hang out with the guys if she wanted to get in on the next show. "Maybe you'd play a whore or a wife," says Thomas, "but at least you'd be in it. At the beginning, I wasn't even doing that" (McCrohan 156). Thomas was so determined to make it in a man's world of comedy that she deliberately avoided the other woman in her troupe. She remembers, "[W]hen Deborah Harmon came into the company . . . I told her, 'Harmon, don't even talk to me. Don't ask me to do a scene or anything else because I am busy forming a power base' " (McCrohan 156). Once she had established herself, however, Thomas did collaborate with Harmon on a number of woman-oriented sketches. Thomas notes that she could tell her male colleagues thought her scenes were funny when they began trying to *enter* them.

Working conditions were complicated by what Ann Elder remembers as a "sexually charged atmosphere." A high number of romances blossomed among the actors because "the whole art of improv and whole idea of working together creates a certain bonding, and out of that bonding and that atmosphere, you're going to have a sexual situation occur" (qtd. in McCrohan

160). Personal relationships were often played out in performance. When things fizzled off stage, life could get ugly on stage. Elder recalls one night when an unrequited lover "annihilated" a woman on stage, "in character of course, and I remember she came off stage sobbing. . . . But she couldn't fault him, because it was legitimate within the terms of an improv. It was a perfect crime" (160).

Robin Duke, who followed Thomas to Second City, realized early that she had to start writing: "All the guys are going to write for guys, and then a woman comes in, but not a really developed character. If you want to be fulfilled in your performing, then you have to create something for yourself" (McCrohan 227). But writing or improvising good material was not in itself enough. Players had to fight for stage time.

Many of the women at Second City hesitated to be competitive—both because they were uncomfortable being aggressive and because they believed confrontation was counter to the values of ensemble improvisation. By the late '70s, however, performers like Thomas and Duke were willing to battle for their own opportunities. In improv, says Duke, "[T]hey can talk you down backstage but they don't have the control *on* stage"(158).

Some women were able to earn the grudging respect of their male colleagues by going to one extreme or another—either by showing a macho aggressiveness or (like Gilda Radner) by demonstrating willingness to do anything for a laugh, even to being the obliging butts of physical or abusive humor. Sills himself would sometimes provoke women to assert themselves. Valerie Harper remembers a workshop where "Paul really lit into [the women] for being so docile. 'Don't you know about women's liberation? Don't you know what's going on? Show some power!' and he was right" (McCrohan 159). Yet, despite his awareness of this problem, the entire improv-comedy culture that Sills had co-created continued to discourage women's power. [12]

In 1976, Roger Bowen was asked to explain the absence of black performers at the Compass or Second City. In a now infamous statement, Bowen opined,

I think that satiric improvisational theater is definitely a cosmopolitan phenomenon and the people who do it and its audience are cosmopolitan people who are sufficiently liberated from their ethnic backgrounds to identify with whatever is going on throughout the world. They know what a Chinese poem is like and what Italian food tastes like. But I don't think most black people are cosmopolitan. I think they're more ethnic in their orientation, so when they're black actors, they want to do black theater. . . . Now a cosmopolitan has to fight every single battle there is, because he can't say, "Me and my tribe say, 'Fuck you,' " because he has no tribe anymore. The cosmopolitan . . . is in a position of having to improvise a whole way of life, whereas in the ethnic society, much of it is handed to you, it's a received tradition (qtd. in Sweet 40–41).

Bowen is not alone in many of the assumptions and ignorant generalizations that characterize his comments. The fact is, however, that improvisational comedy in America is largely derived from African American cultural influences. White improvisers consistently and explicitly compare their performances to those of African American athletes, musicians, and religious figures.

Bowen's discussion of "cosmopolitan man" not only reveals an egocentric assumption that white male intellectuals are able to discover and reveal universal truths through satire or improv-comedy, but also shows the kind of lonely disconnectedness he felt, having detached himself from his own "tribe." This isolation of the cosmopolitan man may help to explain the attraction many white men feel toward an art form that seems to offer them an opportunity to create new traditions and new rules—or a tribe of their own.

In 1976, producer Sloane encouraged Aaron Freeman, a young black actor, to try out for one of the theatre's touring companies. After touring for more than a year, Freeman graduated to Second City's satellite resident company at Chateau Louise in Dundee, Illinois. Freeman enjoyed his work there but recalls that both the director of his touring company and the director at Chateau Louise nervously forbade him to play any character who would be the blood relative of someone played by a white actor, saying that "the audience would never accept it" (personal interview). To Sahlins' credit, when he finally heard about this practice, he angrily ordered the "no relative" policy changed. Nevertheless, Freeman was fired from Chateau Louise because, he says, he was not a good improviser.

According to Freeman, Sahlins liked the young actor personally (the two maintain an ongoing friendship) and later gave him another opportunity to work with Second City. By 1986, Freeman was drawing sellout crowds to his own comedy project, *Council Wars*. He was rehired for the mainstage company in 1987, the second African American ever to perform in that resident troupe.

Freeman stayed with Second City for two years before he was "laid off" once again. He insists that he was not a victim of racism but of his own individual fears and baggage, saying, "I certainly was never good on stage, because I was just always so frightened at Second City. So intimidated, because everybody was better than me" (personal interview). However, he does allow that race was a factor in his discomfort: "But I will tell you one skin color thing that was a *huge* deal at Second City, and one of the big huge

Steve Assad and Aaron Freeman perform a scene from the 1987 Second City revue *Kuwait until Dark*. Freeman was the second African American ever to be cast for Chicago's mainstage troupe. Photo: Jennifer Girard

reasons I sucked—which is that I always, always was representing the race. . . . It wasn't just me—I was representing brown people everywhere. . . . I couldn't live up to it. I couldn't carry the 40 million people on my back on stage at the Second City . . . and I was so worried about it . . . that I could never relax—I couldn't be as good as I actually am" (personal interview).

When Andrew Alexander bought Sahlins' interest in the Chicago operation in 1990, the new producer and his associate, Kelly Leonard, began to be concerned that the lily-white Second City companies were out of touch with modern times and were therefore unable to reflect and satirize their own society (Libera interview). In the next several years, Alexander would hire more people of color to perform in Second City's two Wells Street theatres (and three touring companies) than had appeared in the previous three decades. [13] But it would take a more comprehensive effort truly to engage with the complex issues of integrated improv that confronted Freeman.

In the early years, Chicago improv defined itself in opposition to the "mindless" entertainment of television, assuming an audience attuned to the literary, cultural, and social references of the intelligentsia. With the next generation of the '70s, the backgrounds and experience of both players and audiences had shifted significantly. Now, television *was* the common denominator, providing a different set of references that performers could assume most people shared. By the middle of the decade, television also began to transform Second City from a local comedy club to a nationally recognized spawning ground for screen talent. Millions became aware of Second City through a single television program—*Saturday Night Live*.[14]

Saturday Night Live's first company included John Belushi, from the Chicago troupe, with Dan Aykroyd and Gilda Radner, from Second City in Toronto. Television exposure made Second City famous as a source of comedians and comic technique. It also disseminated a highly commercial approach to improv still somewhat at odds with the company's underlying philosophy. Hopeful young comedians flocked to Chicago—less to learn the art of improvisation than to use Second City as a stepping-stone to television or film.

The popularity of *Saturday Night Live* heightened the aura of anarchy and machismo associated with improvised comedy and often equated with the genre's commitment to freedom. Historians Hill and Weingrad write, "John Belushi, Dan Aykroyd, and then Bill Murray embraced, consciously and proudly, the romance of the outlaw, the flat-out, no-holds-barred ethic that writer Hunter S. Thompson called 'Gonzo'"(232). This macho lifestyle included hard drinking, extensive drug use, and voluble disrespect for authority, "wimps," and women. Some of the young men who arrived in Chicago to pursue the allure of improv-comedy brought with them a desire to imitate the Gonzo aesthetic—intensifying the sexism already in place in the genre.

In the mid- to late seventies, Second City's workshops had already begun producing more improvisers than the company was able to cast. Groups of unemployed trainees often formed to produce independent improv shows around the city. Some, such as the Reification Company, were briefly successful. But not until the 1980s did a significantly new movement in Chicago improv emerge and establish itself as an alternative to the first-wave paradigm.

As the number of would-be players grew, several questions became increasingly urgent: What were improv's rules, and who could break them? Who was qualified to participate and why? In other words, whose improv was it anyway?

the second wave

Even as their numbers increased, many improvisers involved in the first wave began to believe that Second City had lost sight of the most important ideals of improv: spontaneity and community. By the late '70s that comedy institution appeared to be minimizing the improv sets, creating pat revue sketches, and catering more and more to tourist audiences. Group feeling continued to erode as Second City actors moved through the company on their way to jobs in television, and scores of hopefuls on the fringes of the first wave jockeyed for each open position in the troupe. Second-wave founders, by contrast, were determined to make spontaneity and community synonymous with success by selling the *process itself* as product. ImprovOlympic and ComedySportz deliberately parted ways with Second City's practice of classic improv, in part by insisting on the primacy of improvisation as a performance medium rather than as merely a method for developing comedy material to be scripted later.

Four things contributed to the exponential expansion of the numbers of players, students, and spectators involved in Chicago improv-comedy in the 1980s: the growing popularity of comedy performance throughout the United States; the appeal of belonging to the growing local improv subculture; the increased activity of first- and second-wave training centers; and the second wave's inclusive performance policies.

For many players, the second wave represented a reaction against Second City's commercialism and perceived hypocrisies. For others, who had been shut out or marginalized by first-wave practices, the second wave provided a new opportunity to get in the game.

Both ImprovOlympic and ComedySportz have flourished since the early '80s. Each used a sports-based structure to generate multiple *teams* that provided student players with early and frequent access to stage time. Improv-Olympic focused on the improvisational process as a means of self-discovery and cosmic connection, while ComedySportz declared a guiltless devotion to comedy and competition. Changes in structure and approach by second-wave companies, however, did little to change the underlying power dynamics regarding race, gender, and difference.

The conservatism of the Reagan era differed from Eisenhower's postwar return to normalcy. Baby boomers had lived through the discrediting of many cherished myths that shaped American history, and many former activists were exhausted and discouraged. At the same time, a number of baby boomers who had been students, and even members of the counterculture during the '60s and '70s, were beginning to have families, homes, and obligations of their own. The forcibly upbeat and cheerful Reagan era became a time to set aside the disturbing images and issues of the recent past and to call once again on the older ideals of self-reliance and individualism that had forged the American dream.

For those boomers born in the late '50s and early '60s, the '80s produced a feeling of having somehow missed all the excitement. Most young adults of this era were unwilling to give up the economic privileges that Reaganism offered, but they were nonetheless nostalgic for the '60s. This decade represented a time in their youth, or even childhood, when it seemed possible to find real substance—a time when authentic passion, belief, and even transcendence could be achieved through individual activism and community cooperation.

For women and people of color, the '80s were a time of retrenchment and backlash against the gains of the previous decades. Cultural theorist Michael Omi writes that there was a "new twist" in the question of representation for racial minorities: "Increasingly, the problem . . . is not that of misportrayal but of 'invisibility' . . . racial minorities are no longer the focus of sustained media attention; when they do appear they are cast as colored versions of essentially 'white' characters" (121). As Susan Faludi has documented, the Reagan-Bush decade also saw a "powerful counter-assault on women's rights" (xi).

Within this general context of conservatism and nostalgia, second-wave improv's promise of spontaneity and community had great appeal. Dualities of conservatism and resistance, surface and authenticity, self-spirituality and success in second-wave improv-comedy are a response to the ambivalent feelings of many baby boomers (and post-boomers) living through the '80s.

Ironically, television, the medium blamed for the demise of live comedy performance in the '50s, was now responsible for its major resurgence. The new cable television industry, suddenly faced with countless hours of airtime to fill, found stand-up comedy both popular and inexpensive to produce. Numerous "Nights at the Improv" were taped, edited, and shown throughout the country.[1] Spectators in the '80s were willing to listen to favorite comedy routines over and over again, leading to an upsurge in live performance in a new type of venue—"comedy clubs" (Auslander, *Presence and Resistance* 131).

Comedy performance, says performance theorist Philip Auslander, had changed from the burlesque or Borscht Belt ghettos of urban, immigrant stand-ups who spoke as outsiders in a hostile environment to a brand of comedy by and for "the socially and culturally enfranchised: white, middle-class professionals of the baby-boom generation" (*Presence and Resistance* 129). These new audiences associated comedy, no matter how bland, with nonconformity, authenticity, and idealism (134). Yet, according to Auslander, while spectators often gave these performers the status of dissident for poking fun at the establishment, most comedians' jokes about growing up in '60s suburbia completely ignored the larger issues of that decade and their link to contemporary politics.[2]

While stand-up comedy enjoyed a renaissance, *Saturday Night Live* and its many improv-trained stars helped to popularize sketch comedy nationally, bringing new attention to Second City. In his analysis of *Saturday Night Live* as a postmodern phenomenon, Fred Pfeil writes that the empty parodies in this once-hip television show reflect the structure of feeling, the "social experience and constitution" of the baby-boom professional-managerial class (PMC) in the '80s (109). Raised on television and working in a meaningless netherworld between labor and capital, the baby-boom PMC, according to Pfeil, is disconnected from any sense of community. They construct selves from fragments of commodity culture. Improv-comedy, at Second City and in the second-wave companies, has always dealt in the reassembling of disconnected images and appropriated memories to create comedy and community. Improv-comedy techniques could be easily adapted to newer, postmodern methods of expression.

New Age religions, televangelism and fundamentalist religious sects, and "self-religionist" or self-actualization movements such as est (Erhard Seminars Training) and Scientology emerged to fill the empty place of any unifying or collective belief system for many Americans in the '80s. Improv was strongly linked to New Age notions of human potential and theosophical pan-religious beliefs through Spolin's teaching and writing. Spolin's belief in spontaneity's ability to create personal freedom and to break through old frames of reference resonates with New Agers' focus on "magical power and liberation from social conditioning" (Heelas 25). Cultural historian Todd Gitlin writes that, as the radical counterculture movement burned out, many veteran activists looked for meaning in the human potential movement. Gitlin's litany of New Age benefits echoes first- and second-wave claims for the pleasures of improv: "This melange of encounter groups, therapies, and mystical disciplines promised to uncover authentic selves, help people 'live in the present,' 'go with the flow,' 'give themselves permission,' 'free themselves of shoulds,' 'get in touch with their feelings,' 'get in touch with their bodies'—promises of relief for besieged individuals burdened by obligations; promises of intimate personal relations for those who had lost the hope of God or full community; promises of self-expression for the inhibited and cramped, the bored and spoiled" (424).

But, by the '80s, the New Age movement's primary focus on self-spirituality had begun to move in two, sometimes opposing, directions. One end of the spectrum emphasized "the best of the inner world," a detached focus on personal transcendence. The other end dealt with achieving "the best of the outer world," using self-actualizing techniques as a means to achieve "empowerment and prosperity" through capitalism (Heelas 30). These two approaches, which historian Paul Heelas calls the "purist" and the "empowerer," parallel the ways that ImprovOlympic and ComedySportz work with the rhetoric of spirituality. While ImprovOlympic offers "universal truths" and transcendence through groupmind, ComedySportz empowers players to "sell" themselves and their comedy.

Improv techniques were becoming increasingly popular with university students, aspiring actors, and comedians across the country—many of whom yearned for a shot on *Saturday Night Live*.[3] Student troupes were formed at many universities in the Chicago area and elsewhere, notably the *Mee-Oww Show* at Northwestern University. In 1981, a number of *Mee-Oww Show* alumni formed the Practical Theatre Company, whose key players (including Julia Louis-Dreyfus and Brad Hall) were swiftly hired by *Saturday Night Live* talent agents. Although their departure destroyed the Practical Theatre troupe, their success again demonstrated that Chicago improv was a gateway to national television. By the mid-eighties, Second City spin-offs were an important part of the golden age of Chicago improv, a period of growth that peaked when as many as a hundred groups offered performances in a given week. Second City was at the height of its popularity with popular performers such as Mike Myers and Bonnie Hunt drawing capacity crowds.

Bernie Sahlins, longtime controlling visionary at Second City, had always held that improvisation was "just a game"—no more than a tool for creating comedy "in the absence of a writer" (Adler, "Love" 22). In fact, Sahlins believed that the presentation of raw improvisation as performance was "a cheat" (Adler, "Love" 22). When Sahlins took over the artistic directorship of Second City in 1980, improvisation workshops continued, but without their former prestige in the overall process.

For several years, Sahlins' improv-minimizing approach at Second City prevailed and, indeed, sold tickets quite successfully. The company established a second, smaller theatre in Piper's Alley, next door to the mainstage, in 1982.

Dubbed the "e.t.c." stage, the abbreviation has sometimes been interpreted as "experimental theatre company," but producer emeritus Sloane says that when she named it, she "didn't really have anything in mind" (Patinkin 141). The new theatre was first designated as a home performance space for Second City touring companies (or TourCo's) doing recycled material and catering to the overflow crowd from the mainstage. Within a short time, however, the e.t.c. troupe became a full-fledged, if second-tier, resident company—with somewhat edgier original material and its own, often younger, following.[4]

In 1985, however, Sahlins sold his interest in the company (though he continued as a part-time director). The buyer was Andrew Alexander, owner and producer of Second City's Canadian franchise in Toronto and its successful television spin-off, *SCTV*. Investing along with Alexander were his silent partner, Len Stuart, and Joyce Sloane, long the resourceful mother figure at Second City, who would now finally own a small piece of the action. At first, preoccupied with an effort to establish a Los Angeles branch of Second City, Alexander took a laissez-faire approach in Chicago. Sloane took over as producer and a series of directors, including Sahlins, Del Close, Betty Thomas, and others, alternately took the director's reins. Many cast members felt this "swinging door policy" badly undermined any coherent sense of vision for Second City's work (Sachs 4).

In a thirty-year retrospective of Second City's production history written in 1989, *Chicago Sun-Times* arts reporter Lloyd Sachs characterized the '80s as a struggle: "If, once upon a madcap time, the shows were charged by the intellectual current of the early '60s, the political and sexual upheavals of the late '60s and early '70s, and the me-generation absurdities that followed, they have tended during this uncertain decade to reflect its pragmatic, safety-first climate. Too often, the troupe has swallowed its tail by recycling old bits or seeking inspiration in them, while remaining cutely detached from the pressing concerns . . . that might sharpen its relevance" (4). Sachs notes with irony that many negative comparisons of '80s Second City to its golden days came from people "who couldn't possibly have seen the great shows they claim the new ones fail to live up to" (4). Nevertheless, many in the growing Chicago improv community vehemently agreed that Second City had grown safe, boring, and conservative through the '80s.

With the failure of his Los Angeles project, Alexander returned to Chicago, where he professionalized the Second City organization, replacing favorite veterans with younger and more efficient administrators. In 1986, Alexander also codified and institutionalized the improv workshops, creating the Second City Training Center and Conservatory. He recruited Sheldon Patinkin, an early partner and a true believer in Paul Sills's original vision, to head the school, effectively ousting Jo Forsberg and her Players' Workshop from their long-held status as the first tier of official Second City training.[5] Many of Alexander's other innovations and personnel changes created great bitterness in Chicago's tight-knit improv community.[6] Many old hands felt it was the end of family, the end of idealism, the end of an era.

Both second-wave groups were strongly influenced by the work of British teacher-director Keith Johnstone. Throughout the late '70s and '80s, Johnstone's ideas gained popularity in Canada and the United States, and his teachings about spontaneity, trance, and status were crucial in the development of the second-wave's new attitude toward improv. Second-wave organizational structures were drawn from the sports- and team-based formations of Johnstone's Theatresports.

Johnstone is perhaps best known for his 1979 book *Impro: Improvisation and the Theatre*. He developed his theories in England in the late '50s through the '70s, teaching mask work and improvisation-based playwriting and experimenting with his anarchistic improvisational troupe, the Theatre Machine. Johnstone's initial concern was to unleash "the creative child" inside the socialized adult—to enable artists, playwrights, and actors to be spontaneous and to overcome *blocks* to the imagination. Johnstone encouraged the expression of forbidden, even obscene impulses, saying, "If you improvise spontaneously in front of an audience, you have to accept that your innermost self will be revealed" (111). Many of Johnstone's ideas echoed Spolin's focus on the transcendent potential of spontaneity.

Different from Spolin, however, Johnstone chose not to concentrate on questions of "Who," "What," and "Where" as the basis for improvised scenes, but on exercises designed to explore "relationships between strangers" in terms of the conscious and unconscious maneuvers of *status games* (*Impro* 27). Johnstone worked from the premise that "we are pecking-order animals and that this affects the tiniest details of our behavior" (74). His students learned to invent scenes based on master-servant exchanges and the subtleties of raising and lowering status through gestures and inflection patterns.

Johnstone's focus on masks, trance, and ecstatic rituals impressed many second-wave improvisers. Johnstone emphasized the link between "possession" and the permission to be creative: "We have an idea that art is self-expression—which historically is weird. An artist used to be seen as a medium through which something else operated. He was the servant of the God. . . . Once we believe that art is self-expression, then the individual can be criticized not only for his skill or lack of skill, but simply for being what he is" (*Impro* 78).

Improv-comedy veteran Aaron Freeman gives Johnstone credit for inspiring the second wave's fresh approach to improv. In 1980, Johnstone was hired to lead a two-week workshop for Second City performers. Freeman recalls, "That was when people started realizing that the way they'd been doing it wasn't the only way to improvise. And some people realized that this stuff could actually be important and more spiritual—wild and mystical and neat" (personal interview).

Johnstone's charismatic credo awakened many Chicago improvisers' interest in the process side of improv. The Second City had become a theatre of short, snappy scenes and occasional ad libs. Johnstone's visit was a reminder for some, and a revelation for others, of the magic improvisation could offer.

After moving to Calgary in 1977, Johnstone founded his own troupe, called the Loose Moose Theatre Company, where his actors and students began to present improvisational scenes at half-serious performance/competitions called Theatresports, which soon became popular in the United States.

Players have always regarded improv-comedy as akin to sports, where audience excitement is derived from seeing skilled players challenged by unpredictable combinations of known components. Images from baseball, basketball, and football had long been used by Spolin and other improv teachers to describe the need to be *in the moment*.

Team sports is also the metaphor of choice to describe the group dynamics, the camaraderie, and even the sense of flow that improv players experience. These comparisons have been (and are still) often used to explain women's difficulties with the genre. For example, Second City veteran Avery Schreiber theorized that women's training and upbringing didn't equip them for the kind of sporting teamwork that improv demands. Women, Schreiber opined, don't understand "that moment of chaos just before that mystic thing happens and everyone connects into a cohesive whole for a play," robbing them of the confidence to play, compete, and succeed in improvisation. Instead of rolling with the craziness, Schreiber recalls, the women players he worked with would become "frustrated, angry, hysterical, pensive, or closed" (qtd. in Sweet 301). Schreiber's observation may derive from the fact that, particularly in his day (the early '60s), women improvisers focused on the definition of teamwork as cooperation, while men usually saw team interaction as productive conflict or competition. This tension between competition and cooperation in improv continues to be complicated by gender dynamics.

The narrative of competitive sports also helped organize unscripted improvisations into marketable events where spectators could become fans. This overlay of competition was particularly resonant with '80s sensibilities—rendering the amorphous values of play and free expression measurable in terms of wins and losses. The sports motif also carried with it elements of group identification and belonging—from the idea of team to family, nationality, and even religion—elements that were extremely appealing to many disillusioned baby boomers in the '80s. Over the years, ImprovOlympic and ComedySportz differently foregrounded the tropes of sports, family, and religion to suit their specific goals and modes of expansion.

As the '80s progressed, many fledgling improvisers divided their time between classes at Second City and participation in either ImprovOlympic or ComedySportz (and later, the Annoyance Theatre). Second City offered the scarce commodity of a living wage for its elite troupe of improvisers, while second-wave performers received a kind of club membership in lieu of salary. As the number of student-players increased through the '80s, the cross-pollinated improv subculture became more and more active and improvisers began to vie for relative status and visibility within the larger improv community.

The devotion that many improvisers feel, both for the improv form in general and usually for their particular troupe (or for their own team within a larger company), is part of the basis for my definition of Chicago improv as a subculture. Although most do not make a living improvising, a great number of players see their art form as a crucial element of their identity. As cultural theorist Sarah Thornton writes, "Subcultural ideologies are means by which youth imagine their own and other social groups, assert their distinctive character and affirm that they are not anonymous members of an undifferentiated mass" (10).

Like the youth subcultures studied by Thornton and others, improvisers style themselves as living and playing in a way that is "alternative" and distinct from commercial culture (Thornton 97). [7] For second-wave improvisers, the authenticity that mainstream society lacks is revealed in improv's spontaneity. Group members trade in "subcultural capital," which Thornton defines as a quality of "hipness" or insider knowledge that "confers status on its owner in the eyes of the relevant beholder" (13).[8] ImprovOlympic and ComedySportz both rely on subcultural capital in player-player and player-group dynamics.

The opportunity for players to create new identities and spontaneous relationships within the alternative community of second-wave improv reinforces its status as a meaningful subculture for its members. However, traditional hierarchies of race and gender remain intact and, indeed, are often intensified within subcultural communities. While second-wave improvisers sometimes found playful ways to challenge the status quo, they often acted to reinforce mainstream ideology.

CHAPTER 2

ImprovOlympic:
the truth about improv

Since its inception in 1981, ImprovOlympic has become a powerful and often controversial force in Chicago's improv-comedy community. The company first defined itself in opposition to Second City, which used an improvisational process primarily as a means of developing a comedy *product*. For ImprovOlympic, the process *was* the product.

ImprovOlympic offered what they claimed was a purer and more open form of improvised performance, where immediate and unplanned creation was free from the middleman of director, playwright, or censor (internal or external). Perhaps more important, ImprovOlympic promised the chance to belong, to be one of "us," to student players who paid for its workshops. In fact, for most of its life, the company was supported by class fees far more than by its irregular box office receipts. While Second City sells tickets (the consumption of its product), ImprovOlympic sells memberships (participation in the process).

This philosophical shift had far-ranging implications for second-wave improv, changing its source of income along with its actor-actor and actor-audience dynamics. Much of the company's strength derives from the fortuitous marriage of Del Close's innovative, surreal, and even quasi-religious mode of long-form improv (the *Harold*) with a workable institutional structure organized by his business partner and producer, Charna Halpern. Drawing from the theosophical and educational principles of Spolin, the anthropological and psychological work of Johnstone, and his own countercultural experience, Close created a credo that emphasized improv's transformational, transcendent, and creative potential.

Meanwhile, Halpern adapted the sports-based metaphor favored by Johnstone and others into a business plan. She built a roster of teams, each operating as a semi-independent performing unit of eight to twelve players, and linked them through ImprovOlympic's management and training system. Improvisers are highly motivated to join (and to pay workshop fees) by the frequent opportunity to appear in ImprovOlympic's performance spaces and by the sense of community and identity provided by ImprovOlympic membership.

ImprovOlympic's subculture status is most evident at special events, where the already carnivalesque atmosphere of the troupe's regular shows is heightened to become a playful ritual for the extended ImprovOlympic family. At the 1994 all-company Halloween performance, as at most Saturday night shows, the theatre space (upstairs at the Wrigleyside Bar) was crowded with spectators, many of whom greeted one another and the performers by name. The atmosphere was charged with excitement, and audience members cheerfully shared tables with strangers. Most of the crowd were costumed Improv-Olympic students who enjoyed being recognized and ushered into the show without a ticket.

Halpern, founding co-artistic director of ImprovOlympic, personally welcomed the audience, assuring them that everything they would see would be improvised based on their suggestions and would therefore be a unique experience. She also reminded them of the two-drink minimum, which would "help them enjoy the show" but which was also a requirement of Improv-Olympic's arrangements with the Wrigleyside.[1]

Halpern introduced the *house team* (considered the top team at Improv-Olympic), called "Frank Booth" (pronounced Booooth in honor of the occasion). That night, this group of experienced players was paired with a special holiday squad temporarily dubbed the "Scary Pumpkins." Both teams emerged from the audience, suddenly crowding the tiny stage with almost twenty players. Most of the performers were white men ranging in age from twenty-one to forty-something years old, although the Scary Pumpkins included two white women on its ten-player team and Frank Booth featured two white women and a Latino. Because the Scary Pumpkins incorporated members from almost every team on the ImprovOlympic lineup, the house was crowded with friends and fellow players, all cheering their representatives on the stage.

The show began with Musical Styles.[2] Halpern solicited an audience suggestion for a location (train station) and then explained the rules of the game. Members from either team would start a scene set in a train station. At any point, spectators could call out a specific style of musical performance, and the players would be immediately required to sing in that style—while maintaining the sense of the scene. A funny and fairly impressive performance followed, including a spontaneous rap song, an operatic aria, and a country-western ballad.[3]

For the next game, Halpern invited someone from the audience to tell the assemblage about "her day." A young woman named Kate volunteered and told a mundane story about meeting her sister at the airport. For the next ten minutes, players from both teams improvised "Kate's Nightmare" by free-associating, exaggerating, and recombining elements from her story.

For the main event, each team would perform a *Harold*—the complex, surrealistic long-form improv that is ImprovOlympic's signature game. The Harold was not explained to the audience, but a single suggestion was called for.[4] With Halloween on everyone's mind, someone shouted, "Trick or treat!" Frank Booth took the stage and began to free-associate ideas, words, and memories linked not only to literal trick-or-treating, but to other possible connotations of the words "trick" and "treat." After this prologue, most of the actors left the stage or receded upstage to the back wall, while two players began a scene inspired by one of the ideas mentioned in the opening. After a minute or two, another pair of actors began a new scene inspired by a different association, and the first pair left the stage. Shortly afterward, a third pair of actors began yet a third scene with still a different take on the ideas expressed at the beginning of the Harold. After three such scenes, several actors stepped forward with personal-memory monologues, reminiscing about their own childhood experiences of Halloween and other more serious stories of having been "treated" or "tricked" in different ways.

Over the course of twenty minutes, this pattern of alternating scenes,

ImprovOlympic house team Frank Booth improvises in the newly opened ImprovOlympic Theatre in 1995. In the foreground, Paul Grondy, Lillian Francis, and Liz Allen play a scene, while Kevin Mullaney, Steve Mosqueda (ImprovOlympic's first Chicano player) and guests from another team form the upstage line. Photo: Scott McMillin

monologues, and other group games was repeated twice more, and references from the earlier scenes were increasingly mingled into the later ones until the three unrelated story lines began to merge. When the lights came down on Frank Booth's Harold, it was the Scary Pumpkins' turn to play. This team received a new suggestion (the name of a local Chicago politician) and began with a different technique for free-associating ideas that ranged from politics and trust to the problem of a bizarre, unwanted houseguest. They followed the same alternating pattern of scenes and monologues, adding a game-show parody into the mix. As this Harold drew to a close, the strange houseguest from one set of scenes began to speak eloquently on issues of trust and politics in a way that linked his words to the other scenes, the monologues, and the game show as well. Spectators were thrilled by this deft reincorporation of earlier material, laughing and applauding at each remembered reference.

The most vivid moment of synthesis at this performance, however, came not from a Harold but from the final game of Freeze-Tag, a fast and jokey short-form game popular with improv troupes of every persuasion. While some players disparage Freeze-Tag as an example of the shallow style of improv that ImprovOlympians officially eschew, the troupe often uses it to end a show with a surefire crowd-pleaser. In this game, two players begin a scene based on a suggested opening line of dialogue. The actors perform with broadly physical gestures and body positions. At any point after the scene begins, another player will shout, "Freeze!" The actors on stage must freeze in mid-action, and the new player must replace one of them by assuming his or her *exact* physical position. That player must then begin a new, completely unrelated scene that *justifies* the same physicalizations for both players.

A number of players in the audience who belonged to other ImprovOlympic teams jumped onto the stage on a whim. In this fast-paced game, which depends on aggressive quick-wittedness, the female players were notably less involved. All of the women but one were sidelined for much of the game, although they cheered their fellow players on with enthusiasm and played willingly when they did manage to shout "Freeze" before another player did.

Most games of Freeze-Tag quickly become festivals of pop-culture references. Here, one frozen tableau suggested "American Gladiators," much to the audience's delight, and another was interpreted as Moses with only one tablet—"Moses, there are supposed to be *ten* commandments." The biggest laugh came when one young actor tried to make a joke by stumbling, glassy-eyed and inarticulate, over Clark Gable's famous line as Rhett Butler in *Gone with the Wind*, "Frankly, my dear, I don't give a damn," and another player topped it by saying, "I don't think Keanu is right for this part" (referring to the contemporary young film star known for his vacuous persona). The audience hooted and cheered.

Audience laughter was rarely based on the jokes themselves. Rather, spectators applauded the players' virtuosic ability to recombine new stimuli with well-worn punch lines on the spur of the moment. Patrons also took pleasure in displaying their own, mostly shared, cultural competence and their ability to "get" the allusions in their new configurations.[5] Their enjoyment was enhanced by their level of insider knowledge about the individual players and teams and their understanding of ImprovOlympic's style.

Rules and references are usually subtler in long-form improvs than in Freeze-Tag, and recognizing them requires a real appreciation of the techniques and goals of a Harold. This difficulty threatens to turn audiences away, as Harolds frequently fail to be entertaining by conventional standards. For example, Kate enjoyed the troupe's rendition of her nightmare at the Halloween performance, but she was less enthusiastic about the rest of the show. Kate's sister, Molly, who had been involved in ImprovOlympic in the past, said, "I think it's hard unless you already know the format, which they don't really explain—it's hard for people to understand and appreciate this improv. . . . If you brought a bunch of people in here who had never done improv before, they would have a hard time following it" (personal interview).

Many ImprovOlympic fans and followers hold their ability to decode each performance as a source of distinction and subcultural capital, reinforcing their membership and enhancing their status within the group. Music critic John Corbett argues that jazz improvisation "requires a different kind of listening in which the listener is active, a participant-observer of sorts" (233). Many ImprovOlympians equate their work with the kind of free-form jazz that puzzles the neophyte listener but is enjoyed all the more by aficionados. Theatre critic Sid Smith writes, "[A] Harold is comedy in jazz riff. The payoffs come in fits and starts, if at all, and the audiences, sometimes somberly, sometimes ecstatically, gaze in empathy as these adults manufacture like children at play" ("Funny Business" 24). Artistic director Close claimed, "We've got our audiences so hip, if our actors try to rely on a canned joke, the audience boos" (qtd. in Adler, "The 'How' of Funny").

After the show, players and audience members alike adjourned to the bar downstairs. As performance theorist Richard Schechner points out, this postshow "cool-down" period is as much a part of the ritual of the performance as any warm-up, game, or rule (*Between Theater and Anthropology* 19). The players rehashed successful and unsuccessful moments from the evening's improvisations. Teammates marveled at one another's moments of brilliance, while triumphant performers demurred modestly, "I don't know! It just *came* to me!" Many were eager to talk with a scholar investigating the meanings and purposes of improv-comedy. Articulate and passionate, many Improv-Olympians clearly do a lot of thinking and theorizing about their work.

The bar was crowded not only with that night's players, but with members of many other teams and classes. Performing for so many of one's peers keeps the players honest, according to improviser Keith Privett: "You can tell if somebody is lying or that they're making up a monologue. The more genuine you are, the more the audience likes you" (personal interview). In some ways, improvisers are more authentic in performance than they can be in private life—because the improv setting, especially the monologue format, allows them to express thoughts, memories, and fears that people rarely share with any but their most intimate friends.

Improvisers, as a group, drink heavily, especially after shows. One player suggests, "It's because we're so used to being in an altered state—another reality. It's hard to come down" (Callier interview). Players know they must eventually return not only to reality but to a certain lonely separateness where they no longer feel part of the collective entity of their team and their art form—at least not until the next Harold. For now, no one wants to go home.

The framework of most weekly performances repeats the structure of that holiday show (without the costumes). Audiences almost always include large numbers of student-players and their friends, whose insider knowledge and subcultural competence enhance a key source of ImprovOlympic's popularity—the sense of belonging.

Ironically, the creation and development of ImprovOlympic closely parallels Second City's early history. Both origin stories begin with David Shepherd, the idealistic, impractical "mad genius" who cofounded the Compass Players. In 1981, after decades of working with alternative Compass troupes in various parts of the country, Shepherd returned to Chicago with his newest idea for socially conscious improvisation—the "Improvisation Olympiad." He envisioned an annual event where amateurs and professionals would be able to "get together and interchange new ideas and develop new skills" (qtd. in Fleszewski).

Shepherd was not alone in drawing parallels between improv-comedy and sports. British teacher and director Keith Johnstone began to present Theatresports tournaments in Canada in 1977, using games adapted from his own and Spolin's teaching exercises. It seems likely that, in 1980, Shepherd's idea for an Improv Olympics was inspired partly by Theatresports and partly by his earlier dreams of a proletarian theatre.[6] Shepherd wanted teams of players who would represent various occupations or age groups, which he called "identities." As Shepherd explained, "The rival Greek tribes celebrated their diversity on Mt. Olympus through song and dance as well as sport. So the people of Chicago seem ready to express their identities through drama" (Fleszewski). From his grounding in Marxism, Shepherd believed that people were defined and unified more by their jobs than by any other factor in their lives.

Shepherd's insistence on accessibility, community interaction, and team structures had a lasting impact on the eventual configuration of ImprovOlympic. While later ImprovOlympic players did not come together based on specific occupations or age, they did find a sense of subcultural identity based on their membership in a team. In the third wave, new improv troupes would begin to form around modes of identity that took on some of the political meanings Shepherd once envisioned.

In 1981, Shepherd joined forces with Charna Halpern, an assertive performer-producer who was initially thrilled to be working with this legendary improv pioneer. She acted as producer and publicist for introductory workshops, classes, and demonstration performances—designed more to spread the word about Shepherd's ideas than to make a profit. She accompanied Shepherd to church basements, community centers, schools, and other venues, urging the local press to cover each event. She invited friends and fellow students from Second City classes to form teams that would compete in Shepherd's Olympiad.

Halpern also helped Shepherd recruit identity teams: "I thought, well, this is fun . . . so I called this rabbinical place on Michigan Avenue, and they gave me a team of rabbis, and I called DePaul, and I got a team of psychologists called the Freudian Slippers (the rabbis were called the God Squad), and I called the bar association and got a team of lawyers called the Court Jesters. So I had all these identity teams. I had a team of old people called Acting Up, and I had actors, too" (personal interview).

Perhaps predictably, Halpern had the most success in forming teams not of waitresses or steelworkers, but of educated professionals, managers, information technicians, and other members of the professional-managerial class—players with backgrounds similar to those who had been attracted to the Compass in the '50s. In 1981, however, Halpern had actors, too. Halpern and many of her friends from the Second City workshops were itching to do real improv. According to Halpern, the actors felt hampered by what seemed to them to be Shepherd's misguided effort at social work: "It got to be hard to keep that identity thing going, because I was really into the art of it. It was a good gimmick that got me front page headlines. . . . But it got to be a problem, like the rabbis couldn't do Friday night shows . . . and so I made it more theatrical and David and I had a splitting of the ways—because he did not want it to be theatrical. David was looking for the common man in Berwyn, Illinois, and I was trying to get art" (personal interview).

Thus, in a move not unlike Paul Sills's shift from the Compass to Second City, Halpern rejected Shepherd and took his ideas in another direction. She associates this move with her preference for art over politics, but her choice can also be read as a process-product split, or a distinction between service and success. Without the savvy Halpern to serve as his producer, Shepherd was left once again to return to New York and pursue his impractical dreams.

For the next two years, Halpern struggled to maintain ImprovOlympic on her own. Moving away from identity teams, she fostered several groups of performers who had been yearning for a sense of legitimacy in Chicago improv. Longtime improviser Aaron Freeman recalls, "There had always been little improv groups of Second City rejects. But once the ImprovOlympic happened, that gave you a whole structure, a whole community of people, a way to even make a couple of bucks every now and then, and to get some recognition and to have a forum to exercise your games, your craft, your stuff. So people had an incentive to stay together . . . we weren't just out there on our own. And that was really Charna, of course, that kept all that stuff together" (personal interview).

Freeman belonged to a team called Stone Soup, one of the original actor groups in the ImprovOlympiad. Stone Soup competed with the Oral Majority and other teams in ImprovOlympic tournaments modeled on Johnstone's Theatresports tourneys, an important part of ImprovOlympic's system in the first few years. Each small troupe had its own director and its own approach to the art of improv, as ImprovOlympic had yet to formulate and teach a distinctive style. It was the regular performance–play-off games that maintained them under the aegis of ImprovOlympic.

These were heady times for Freeman, freshly inspired by an improv workshop with Theatresports founder Johnstone. The Stone Soup players were full of hope and energy, and they spent many rehearsals poring over Johnstone's book, excitedly debating, experimenting, and pushing the limits of classic improv technique.[7] Freeman explains, "You'd been freed and liberated by Johnstone to think of [improv] in a different kind of way. And so we sat there and tried to figure out what the hell we were doing and how to do it; what it was about and what it meant to be an improviser; what it meant to achieve a trance state; what it meant to do all the things that we thought were so good and noble and wonderful to do" (personal interview).

Stone Soup's director, Katya Knopf, whom Freeman remembers as "bril-

Annoyance artistic director Mick Napier congratulates Charna Halpern, co-founder of ImprovOlympic, on her group's 15th Anniversary in 1995. The company celebrated with a gala performance hosted by Harold Ramis and featuring videotaped tributes from alumni Chris Farley and Mike Myers. Photo: Keith Privett

liant," left Chicago after spending a year with her little company. In the historical moment between Second City's rules and Halpern's eventual codification of ImprovOlympic's techniques, Freeman and Knopf were important leaders and innovators in the nascent art of improv. After Improv-Olympic solidified its system, women directors were almost unheard of and African American players were rare.

Spirits were high, but Halpern knew that success in improv often depended on the leadership of an inspired teacher like Spolin or Sills, and she made no claims to be one. Then, in 1983, Halpern formed an alliance with Del Close, another mad genius of first-wave improv, whose credentials included early membership in the St. Louis Compass, a long-term association with Second City as performer, workshop leader, and artistic director from 1973 to 1981, and three seasons as "House Metaphysician" at *Saturday Night Live*. Close was widely acknowledged to be a brilliant teacher whose innovations in improv technique included that encounter with alternative reality known as "the Harold"—a new brand of long-form improv.

Close, who had recently departed from his position at Second City over "creative differences," was satisfied to play the guru for Halpern's company and more than willing to leave all production decisions in her capable hands. For her part, Halpern soon found a way to package both the theory and practice of long-form improv and to parlay Close's experiment into a marketable commodity.

ImprovOlympic's popularization of long-form improv was the most significant development in Chicago improv-comedy since the founding of Second City. Although Shepherd and others had experimented with long, scenario-based improvs in the early days of the Compass, Close is credited with inventing a freewheeling mode of play that seemed to capture the ecstasy and sensation of liminality in the improv process. Feeling constrained by short games and sketches, Close had begun as early as the late '50s to conceptualize a more experimental, open form for improv. In the '60s, while working with the San Francisco–based improv troupe, the Committee, Close developed his ideas further, creating an elaborate, amorphous format that at-

Del Close, ImprovOlympic patriarch and guru, had a profound effect on improv technique and philosophy, particularly through his work with the long-form structure known as "the Harold." Photo: Suzanne Plunkett

tempted to combine a variety of improv games and techniques into one unified event.

Close worked with the game's progression from the chaos of free-associated fragments to the order of their reincorporation into themes through the recognition of patterns. Meanings and connections often appeared to emerge unbidden through the game in a way that struck some players as magical, resonating with other elements of New Age spirituality that long-form improv seemed to offer.

After presenting his new form to the Committee, Close invited the actors to give it a name. Somewhat to his dismay, the invention was spontaneously dubbed "Harold" by Committee actor Bill Mathieu—and the name stuck. As the story goes, Mathieu was inspired by the scene in the film *A Hard Day's Night* when a reporter asks George Harrison what he calls his haircut. "Arthur," was the Beatle's reply (Halpern, Close, and Johnson 11). In fact, the whimsical appellation has often been misunderstood by new improvisers, who assume the word must be "Herald" or some other more serious name. Close and the Committee "developed a way to intertwine scenes, games, monologues, songs and all manner of performance techniques" (Halpern, Close, and Johnson 7). According to *Truth in Comedy*, "they came up with one of the most sophisticated, rewarding forms of pure improv ever developed" (Halpern, Close, and Johnson 7). Indeed, the Harold was the progenitor of most long-form structures created by improvisers in Chicago and elsewhere throughout the second and third waves.

Returning to Chicago in 1970, Close continued to experiment with the Harold, first in free workshops at the Kingston Mines Company Store, then at the Body Politic theatre with the Chicago Extension Improv Company (Arbanel). When he was hired as resident director at Second City in 1973, Close brought the Harold along. Second City actor Tim Kazurinski remembers the embryonic form as they played it in the improv sets:

We'd take an audience suggestion and line up against the back wall. Alternately, we would begin coming forward in groups of two, starting scenes that weren't going anywhere yet. Another couple would cut you off, or you would fade to the back wall when you were tiring. You would keep this up for 15 or 20 minutes, until all these little vignettes began to tie up or interweave. . . . When it was really humming, they would all mesh and make a statement that was more of a tableau. Everything that you had done up to that point was synthesized in that final scene or conglomeration of scenes. . . . When it works, it's an amazing thing. And when it doesn't, the audience thinks you're insane. (qtd. in Halpern, Close, and Johnson 19–20)

Actor George Wendt also remembers the early version of the Harold at Second City. He believes that, when done right, "the Harold is the most magical, wonderful improvisational experience you can have, both for the audience and for the company" (qtd. in Halpern, Close, and Johnson 20). For Wendt, the Harold represented a truer and purer form of improv than the more vaudevillian techniques employed at Second City. He enjoyed creating in the moment, working on his feet, without the Second City habit of a backstage planning session including "discussions, qualifications, setups, blackouts and the like" (20). Wendt recalls that "Harold is like jumping out of an airplane! It's like being thrown into the water—you've got to sink or swim. The very intensity of the pressure to create is liberating" (21).

A gifted improviser and compelling storyteller, Close was perceived as a purveyor of alternative realities and a direct channeler of certain ideals of the '50s and '60s. A bonafide Beatnik, he had even recorded a popular comedy album called *How to Speak Hip*. In the years that followed, Close experimented widely with drugs, occasionally (in his own words) "going mad" and dropping out of society for extended periods—including stints with the "Merry Pranksters" and the Grateful Dead in the late '60s (Coleman 245; Arbanel). He was also well-versed in non-Western religions and philosophies, particularly where they pertained to chance, spontaneity, and fate—even making performance and career decisions by throwing the I Ching. Close often cited Krishnamurti or referred to Sufi sayings ("The master weaver incorporated the mistakes of his students into a larger pattern") and Inuit folklore as sources of archetypal truths. Much like Spolin, in true New Age (and arguably postmodern) style, Close drew on traditions from all cultures and religions, detaching them from their cultural and historical contexts and using them to assemble his own belief system.[8]

Through the Harold, Close soon became known as a guru for the ImprovOlympic "cult," a group of intensely dedicated students and performers who still comprise part of the growing improv subculture in Chicago. For many of Close's followers, the Harold was not only liberating, it could induce trance, channel primal creative forces, and forge cosmic connections. Dee Ryan, an experienced improviser in the 1990s, describes the Harold as "primal" and "tribal," comparing it to "dancing by the fire" or a "whirling dervish" (personal interview). Her pleasure in the experience demonstrates the hunger for transformative and communal experience that motivates both men and women to participate in long-form improv.

Freeman disputes the notion that Close was the sole inventor of the Harold, pointing out that long-form improvs had been done at Second City in improv sets and workshops for years.[9] But Freeman admits that Close legitimized this process-oriented game as an art form. Though Johnstone's work was clearly influential, Close clarified the connections between long form and groupthink, connections that released sustained spontaneity. Freeman describes it as a form of faith: "The Harold required of you things that no one had ever asked you to do before. It wasn't like the Second City style . . . this thing required not only that you do a big long-form, but you had to have all this faith. You had to dive out there . . . you can't think your way through it, you've got to just 'faith' your way through it and 'heart' your way through it" (personal interview).

Close was the one, Freeman acknowledges, who made players believe they could give themselves over to this frighteningly free approach to improv and that it was a viable mode for public performance. Freeman asserts, "That's when the long-form became adult and the Harold was something that was worth doing, and a genuine form of its own, as opposed to being the bastard child of Second City improv. And that was all Del" (personal interview).

Yet the endurance and economic stability of ImprovOlympic was based on more than Close's charisma or the Harold's popularity. Despite some controversy over her methods, Halpern's discipline and business sense were vital to the delimitation and dissemination of Close's ideas. When she joined forces with Close in 1983, Halpern writes, "[The Harold's] nascent form was a little too large and chaotic for the stage. The trick would be preserving the chaos on stage while at the same time making it comprehensible" (Halpern, Close, and Johnson 3). Halpern encouraged Close to codify and simplify the Harold into a teachable sequence of elements, incorporating Halpern's own game called Time Dash. Accordingly, a form that had been for many years willfully formless took on a repeatable, saleable structure.

Student improvisers learn to play the Harold in ImprovOlympic classes and workshops. In the earliest, pre-Halpern versions of the Harold, actors were expected to work together spontaneously to explore a single suggestion. Typically, the actors would begin by playing out divergent strands of the idea and end by discovering ways to reincorporate and reweave those strands together. Close had tried his ideas in rehearsal at both the Committee and Second City with highly experienced improvisers who had worked together for years and were extremely familiar with one another's habits, references, and impulses. Yet even these players found the Harold daunting, if exhilarating, and were rarely willing to perform one for a paying audience. The simplified Harold, designed for ImprovOlympic, is both more structured and more intentional.

As it is now played, a team of improvisers asks the audience for a single suggestion, which serves as the initiating idea for a thirty-minute improvised game. The players then begin the Harold with one of a number of techniques to generate potential tangents and directions in which to take their material. Student players are taught a variety of methods for spinning out new threads from the original idea. They may perform personal-memory monologues based on their immediate reactions to the suggestion or play the Pattern Game by free-associating one word at a time.[10] Other methods include the Rant, in which players rail about their pet peeves, or the Invocation, an improvised ritual in which players create and worship a god whose archetypal characteristics will inspire subsequent scenes. Another popular opening takes ImprovOlympic's frequent use of jazz terminology literally, as players lay down a bebop backbeat while their teammates sing, chant, or rap their riff on the suggestion.

These exercises often begin to suggest a theme that is not obvious on the surface of the suggestion, but is several logical leaps removed from it. In one workshop Harold, for example, an opening suggestion of "scissors" was developed through the Pattern Game into themes of conflict, divorce, separation, cruelty, and emotional detachment. As Close says, "[T]he suggestion is the inspiration to discover the theme" (Halpern, Close, and Johnson 147). After the opening routine, players begin to alternate scenes and games that have been inspired by the material created in the first part of the Harold, but which are at first apparently unrelated to one another. ImprovOlympic currently teaches the Harold as a sequence of three scenes, which appear three separate times throughout the performance. A pair of actors will initiate scene A following the opening sequence. After they have established their scene, several other actors may *edit* the first pair by moving downstage and simply beginning to perform scene B. Scene C will similarly edit scene B. The editing itself is a skill that ImprovOlympians practice, learning to assess how long a given scene needs to go on before it is interrupted by the next event.

During the series of small scenes, remaining troupe members, still visible along the upstage wall, often perform sound effects, musical underscoring, or other aspects of a scene's environment, or one may sense that an ongoing scene needs an additional character and so decide to make an entrance. As in first-wave improv, scenes are built through player initiations and agreement. The good Harold performer, Close insisted, is always "a supporting actor," and true improv requires players, above all, to trust and support one another. A crucial skill for the Harold improviser is to "justify, justify, justify" any action that emerges (Halpern, Close, and Johnson 39). No inadvertent reference or gesture is counted a "mistake," but must be woven into the larger fabric of the narrative as if it were intentional. Players say that the best scenes often result from unexpected slips that are inventively justified.

After scenes A, B, and C have each appeared once, the players create a game segment to provide a break, a change of pace, and an opportunity to comment on the themes in a more performative style. Performers may choose a familiar improv game, such as a talk show or song parody—or they may spontaneously invent a game, counting on fellow players to intuit the new rules. At any time, an individual actor may choose to insert a personal monologue drawn from his or her own experience. Halpern and Close admonish, "Players must *remember*, not *invent*. . . . Audiences relate to someone who is telling the truth, and usually know when a performer is inventing" (Halpern, Close, and Johnson 137). These speeches may be nostalgic childhood memories, social commentary, or confessional self-revelation. Monologues provide a forum for individuals to make themselves known on the stage in the context of the heavily group-oriented Harold. Players sometimes take this opportunity to perform a therapeutic expiation of painful or difficult personal issues—including sexuality, loneliness, and alcoholism—for an audience of witnesses. Often, however, the performers merely hope for audience laughter.

In the standard Harold format, scenes A, B, and C appear three times each—and each segment of each scene will have progressed some period of time, this element deriving from Halpern's Time-Dash game, in which scene segments jumped forward in specific time frames, from one second to hundreds of years. Additional games and monologues are interspersed between the recurring scenes. The goal, as the Harold draws to a finish, is for the actors to discover as many patterns and connections as possible within all of the material that has emerged. Citing Johnstone, ImprovOlympians often describe their process as a form of "driving by looking in the rearview mirror" (qtd. in Halpern, Close, and Johnson 23). Improvisers never know where they are going, but do know where they have been. Humor in a Harold is meant to come not from jokes but from the pleasure an audience takes in seeing the performers *call back*, or remember, justify, and weave together elements of earlier scenes to create profundity out of banality and "order out of chaos": "When [the Harold is] properly played, a Harold audience resembles the crowd at a sporting event rather than the audience at a nightclub. A Harold audience will react as if they've seen a Michael Jordan slam-dunk when they watch players remembering each other's ideas and incorporating them back into their scenes. We have witnessed standing ovations when a player pulls together eight different trains of thought in one brief monologue. Those cheers and screams can become even more addicting than laughs" (Halpern, Close, and Johnson 28–29).

Players constantly seek and rarely achieve the kind of "slam-dunk" that Halpern and Close describe. Often, the elements of a Harold never mesh or, conversely, actors are thought to be artificially forcing the connections, trying to be in control of everything or, in ImprovOlympic vernacular, "driving the big rig," as in a truck or bulldozer. Close and Halpern claim that the connections—either comic or cosmic—that emerge in a Harold are simply waiting to be found. But despite official teachings, the pressure can be great for Harold performers not only to *discover* a satisfactory wrap-up for their game, but also to get laughs in sufficient quantities along the way.

Long-form teacher-director Noah Gregoropoulos insists that good players never *make* connections. Rather, they "recognize and pay attention to" patterns that already exist: "You just have to look. You have to open your eyes. It's a way of seeing. Just like any of the arts are. That's what makes it like life . . . you think of your life as a narrative when in fact it's probably a lot more like a Harold. . . . You don't *make* order out of chaos, you see the order within the chaos" (personal interview).

Here, Gregoropoulos echoes the belief in an originary, natural order variously expressed by Spolin, Johnstone, and Close. The artist/improviser, then, is not responsible for the connections he or she makes, but is rather an Eskimo sculptor discovering the shape already inherent in the bone. While this notion helps to unleash spontaneous creativity, it also serves to reinforce and even to *justify* conventional roles and relationships and absolves individuals of any obligation to look beyond stereotypes.

In performance, Harolds end with a blackout of the stage lights—often cued by Halpern herself, or by another director, coach, or teacher in the house. Ideally, the lights are taken out at a high point, or slam-dunk moment, after twenty to thirty minutes. But, especially with younger and less experienced teams, the lights may simply put a stop to a long and inconclusive set of personal monologues, vague and surrealistic scenes, and half-baked parodies of popular culture, a combination that often leaves the audience confused and anxious.

Over the years, ImprovOlympians have experimented with a number of variations on the Harold. Close himself began to invent and teach new structures, including the Movie, in which actors announce framing shots and edits as the improv progresses, and the Deconstruction, which begins with a single scene (or monologue), then uses various techniques to dissect the characters, situations, and themes found within it. The Harold's hodgepodge structure can be tailored to suit a specific team's strengths and preferences. In fact, to distinguish themselves from other teams and to keep play interesting, groups often invent their own versions of the Harold.

As a matter of honor, ImprovOlympians never plan or discuss scenes and games during a Harold performance. Many players are scornful of Second City, where players often take a long intermission to plan scenes before they "improvise" them. But ImprovOlympic scenes are rarely satirical in the way more scripted or planned scenes can be. As Shepherd discovered in the early days of the Compass, collectively created impromptu scenes tend to gravitate toward shared references and social observations without any larger point or message. It takes the distanced stance of a commentator—the Brechtian actor's alienation, the political comedian's attitude, or the writer's time-lag—to point the satire. In a Harold, the drawn-out time factor does give actors a chance to make connections and to underline the incongruities and social ironies that emerge in the scenes. Indeed, Harolds often seem to make a progressive statement about the differences between appearance and reality in American society. But, Gregoropoulos insists, these themes are organic and thus cannot and should not be wielded in any particular cause.

In lieu of planning time or script writing, ImprovOlympic relies all the more heavily on such classic improvisation building blocks as groupmind and agreement, *"the one rule that can never be broken"* (Halpern, Close, and Johnson 47). While these basic concepts are taught at Second City and elsewhere, they are all the more critical in the Harold's more open framework. In Improv-Olympic's rhetoric, groupmind is seen as far more than a technique for generating comedy. Rather, it is seen as a goal in itself, particularly as a means to achieve altered and ostensibly higher states of consciousness or to discover cosmic, universal truths.

According to one ImprovOlympic brochure, "The Harold reaches out from within us, bridges gaps between us, and sharply defines our similarities." But many of the elements that make ImprovOlympic attractive as a source of subcultural identity and connection—agreement, groupmind, and the reliance on so-called universal truths and archetypes for narrative closure—have widespread implications for the suppression of difference within its workshops and performances.

ImprovOlympic's commitment to improvisational authenticity and process was a hard sell at the box office, making it difficult for the group to sustain itself. By the 1980s, Second City was a stable comedy institution with dependable box office income, despite being criticized by purists for selling out on its improv ideals to please middle-class audiences. But a theatre based on experimental, long-form improv could not bank on support from well-heeled patrons seeking surefire entertainment. To circumvent this problem, Halpern focused her attention on alternative means of income—a shift from selling improv as entertainment to the manufacture and marketing of improv as subculture. Subcultural capital became the currency that has kept Improv-Olympic in business.

Halpern's strategies for economic survival and her managerial techniques worked both deliberately and in unpredictable, sometimes uncontrollable ways to foster the development of subcultural ideologies and identities among the improvisers. Many of ImprovOlympic's official organizational structures, such as its teams and required classes, are presented as integral aspects of the artistic mission. Other practical considerations—the need to match income to expenses, sell tickets, attract and hold onto students, retain and encourage the most talented players, increase the level of professionalism, and maintain a high profile in the local press—were often at odds with the egalitarian, supportive, spiritual philosophies espoused by Close.

As ImprovOlympic grew in size and prestige in the late '80s and early '90s, some participants began to accuse the company of betraying its own ideals through favoritism, economic exploitation, emotional manipulation, cliquishness, spiritual pretensions, and suppression of difference (recalling similar charges of hypocrisy at Second City). Dissatisfaction was particularly high among women. Close was often heard to assert that women were simply "not funny" and many ImprovOlympic players and students followed his lead.[11] Yet, many of the company's philosophies and practices served to bind scores of players (including some white women and a few people of color) to the company with something akin to religious fervor.

Halpern was determined to build the company into a prosperous institution and was willing to bear harsh criticism from those who believed her policies were ruining the very art form she claimed to be promoting. Notably, Close himself virtually never reproached Halpern, perhaps recognizing that her machinations were exactly what made his purist position possible.[12]

ImprovOlympic's major source of income is the tuition of hundreds of student players who are willing to pay to play. While Second City's conservatory program is a secondary, if important, source of revenue for the troupe, ImprovOlympic's program has been its primary breadwinner since 1984. The company was and continues to be run more as a school or club than as a professional troupe. Actors are almost never paid for their performance work. Tuition, bar, and box office income has been used to pay modest salaries to Close and Halpern, for performance space, for advertising and production costs, and to support additional member-generated projects at the theatre. Most ImprovOlympians have day jobs, and some even have demanding full-time careers—yet they make time for improv as their primary avocation.

A striking proportion of ImprovOlympians is young, white, male, and heterosexual, as indeed is the case in most improv-comedy troupes and classes throughout the Chicago area and elsewhere. Throughout the '90s, the average team included two white women and seven white men, with a tiny handful of black, Asian, and Latino performers—mostly male—scattered across the roster. Players tend to be well educated and middle class, often members of the professional-managerial class or of the "cognitariat"—information workers and computer jockeys. Still, there is often quite a range of backgrounds and goals represented within one team.

Many players see the privilege of performing and belonging to the company as its own reward. Student improvisers are encouraged to attend performances (free of charge), where they make up a large percentage of each night's audience. ImprovOlympic fans are mostly cognoscenti—friends or relatives of the performers, other improvisers, and sophisticated improv aficionados. Gregoropoulos suggests two possible explanations for this phenomenon: "One is that nobody else likes it but other improvisers, the other is that people don't watch improvisation very long without getting involved in it" (personal interview).

Throughout the '80s and '90s, students were required to take several beginning and intermediate classes, taught by Halpern and other teachers, to qualify for Close's advanced class. Halpern's focus on success sometimes led to odd contradictions. According to one former player, Halpern encouraged wit and cleverness in the beginning and intermediate workshops she taught and heavily favored talented young comedian-types, such as Chris Farley and Mike Myers, who both studied at ImprovOlympic before going on to Second City and *Saturday Night Live*. Close, on the other hand, was contemptuous of jokes, asserting that laughter derives from the truth of a scene. Close even went so far as to deny that ImprovOlympic is creating comedy, insisting that theirs is a serious art form: "It is easy to become deluded by the audience because they laugh. Don't let them make you buy the lie that what you're doing is for the laughter. Is what we're doing comedy? Probably not. Is it funny? Probably yes. Where do the really best laughs come from? Terrific connections made intellectually, or terrific revelations made emotionally" (qtd. in Halpern, Close, and Johnson 25). In fact, Close encouraged surrealistic scenes and appreciated the bizarre. The difference in approach between the two teachers was rarely acknowledged but was clearly manifested in performances.

In the early '90s, ImprovOlympic used two performance venues, a cabaret space upstairs from the Wrigleyside Bar and a tiny proscenium theatre space, on Clark Street, that also served for classes and workshops. In the Wrigleyside performances, Halpern incorporated short, audience-pleasing games and tacitly encouraged jokey performances—often drawing large crowds that included a number of outsiders. The smaller, more formal theatre was reserved for experimental, Close-inspired performances, and the atmosphere was quite different: no alcohol, fewer laughs, and far fewer spectators. Halpern walked a fine line, balancing the cachet of Close's spiritual work with the box-office benefits of more conventional comedy.

Students are often attracted to the ImprovOlympic training program because it provides an early opportunity for public performance. Unlike Second City's training center, which teaches basic skills, object work, character development, and sketch writing, ImprovOlympic classes focus on the discovery of connections, patterns, and humor through groupmind.[13]

Usually by the third or fourth round of classes (and sometimes earlier), students are assigned to performance groups by Halpern. An advanced player will then rehearse or coach the new team and public shows are scheduled. However, students may participate in team rehearsals and performances only as long as they remain tuition-paying members of a concurrent class in the training center.

Halpern herself programs the weekly performance schedule and decides which teams will appear when and how often. In the early days of Improv-Olympic, Harolds were presented as a "sporting event and a theatrical competition" where audiences voted for the winner—much as in Theatresports or ComedySportz (Halpern, Close, and Johnson 8). The top teams were selected through tournaments, with judges recruited from Chicago's theatre and comedy community. Halpern eliminated tournaments in the early '90s, saying that competition distorted the "family" feeling of cooperation (personal interview). Yet some ImprovOlympians suggest competition has not been eliminated, but driven underground—and the contest is for Halpern's approval rather than for quality.

In the late '80s and '90s, shows still featured a pair of teams, but rather than competing, an inexperienced group was often coupled with a veteran team to balance the evening's entertainment (weeknight shows often featured three teams). The ImprovOlympic Teams Roster expanded rapidly, from nine teams in 1992 to fourteen in 1994 and twenty-six in 1999—each with seven to eleven members. Halpern struggled to provide the promised performance opportunities to the ever-increasing number of players. She scheduled two shows on weekend nights, added mid-week performance spots, and was finally driven to find a building ImprovOlympic could call its own and could schedule at will.

Beginning in 1992, Halpern began posting new team rosters and performance schedules every four to eight weeks. Through these announcements, individual players might find themselves added to a group, shifted from one team to another, or dropped completely. New teams of promising students were formed, and existing teams dismantled, based on Halpern's assessment of their talent and viability. Student players often awaited each new posting with great anxiety. For many, Halpern's mode of quality control was antithetical to the ethos of support and solidarity that ImprovOlympic taught. As one former ImprovOlympian pointed out, "[Y]ou can't learn in fear, and you can't trust in fear" (Semelsberger interview).[14]

Once formed, groups jostle for position within the ImprovOlympic hierarchy, hoping to be named by Halpern as a house team, or resident company—a status that entitles them to regular, prime-time performance dates. Among other privileges, house-team members may be offered paid positions as coaches or, eventually, teachers in the training center. These coveted positions are often doled out as a means of keeping restless but important players in the fold. In the early years, Halpern rarely promoted women players to the rank of teacher or coach, a policy that changed in the late '90s when she invited Annoyance mainstay Susan Messing to teach. By 2000, Halpern had warmed considerably to her sister improvisers, appointing women to as many as one-third of ImprovOlympic's coaching and teaching positions.

Members of a house team are also the only players exempted from paying

ImprovOlympian Rachel Mason (center) improvises a heroic song, supported by Ali Davis (left) and a chorus including Don Bardwell, Bob Dasse and Bob Kulhan. Their ensemble, Baby Wants Candy, specializes in improvised musicals based on a Harold structure. The group reigned as an important ImprovOlympic house team throughout the late 90s and early millennium. Photo: Amy Seham

for classes while on a team and from bearing the additional cost of chipping in to pay a team coach. Any other student who cannot afford either the time or the money both to take classes and to perform with a team must drop off the team. Despite these requirements, ImprovOlympic provides the most immediately accessible performance opportunities for the most players in the Chicago improv community.

Halpern's use of a pyramidal, team-based management structure reinforces improvisers' tendency to form tight-knit relationships. Over the years, she has blended the language of family and team with ideas about loyalty and belonging in order to organize large numbers of student performers and motivate them to work together for the good of all. While the strategy of team identification strengthens ImprovOlympic as a whole, the idea can occasionally backfire when players develop more affinity for their team than for the larger company. Arbitrary as the combinations of personalities may be, sometimes these groups gel into something more than the sum of their parts, while in other cases, individuals may believe themselves trapped in an unsupportive team. Relations between successful individuals, popular teams, and ImprovOlympic management are particularly strained when issues of money and professional advancement arise.

For example, in 1990, the restaurant hosting ImprovOlympic offered the popular house team (Blue Velveeta) an arrangement independent of Halpern's organization. Eager to graduate from perpetual student status to that of paid professionals, Blue Velveeta took the deal. Halpern viewed their defection as the worst kind of betrayal. Student players were told that Blue Velveeta had stolen resources that rightly belonged to "us." Blue Velveeta's key players soon left the team for career opportunities at Second City, Hollywood, and New York. The mantle passed to the Family, an all-male house team that became Close's favorite vehicle for exploring long form's outer reaches. Close directed them in such experiments as *Dynamite Fun Nest* and *Three Mad Rituals* before Family members, too, began to get offers from Second City, *Saturday Night Live,* and elsewhere.

Halpern worked hard to keep talented players committed to the company, both by emphasizing the family nature of the group and by creating opportunities for faithful favorites to produce original shows with ImprovOlympic backing. A dedicated core of performers stayed with the troupe for years. But she had a hard time insisting on player loyalty in the face of paying opportunities. In a 1995 interview, Halpern recalled being bitter and angry when actors left for "greener pastures," especially when Second City reaped the benefits of ImprovOlympic nurturance of performers. In later years, however, Halpern resigned herself to the inevitable graduation of some players, taking pride in their success as evidence of their excellent ImprovOlympic training (personal interview).

Throughout the '90s, ImprovOlympic continued to attract hundreds of students each year to its classes, teams, and performances. In 1995, Halpern was finally able to fund the complete renovation of a new performance space dedicated to ImprovOlympic work. It included a cabaret space, with tables, chairs, and a bar, and the formal Del Close Theatre, designed for more serious or experimental work.

Improvisers often talk about improv as a way of life, or philosophy, that guides their interactions with the world offstage as well as on. Improv, they assert, teaches them to say "YES*and*—" to life—to take chances, go with the flow, connect and collaborate with others. ImprovOlympic mimicked a New Age religion, or even a cult, through its rules and beliefs governing human interaction; rituals and ceremonies; offer of community linked with personal growth; promise of transcendence; and system for creating meaning and truth out of the seeming randomness of life. Halpern writes that when she proposed they collaborate on a book, coauthor Close was at first reluctant to commit his philosophy of improv-comedy to paper because "it would be as much work as writing up a religion" (Halpern, Close, and Johnson 4).

According to Johnstone, improvisers need a guide if they are genuinely to cross the boundaries between the conscious ego and subconscious sources of imagination: "Students need a 'guru' who 'gives permission' to allow forbidden thoughts into their consciousness. . . . They are people who have been into the forbidden areas and who have survived unscathed . . . a teacher who is living proof that the monsters are not real, and that the imagination will not destroy you" (84). Close took on the guru's role at ImprovOlympic as he had for the Committee in the '60s; "In his canon . . . the risks of improvisation had to get higher and higher and the players had to learn to fly without nets" (Coleman 292).

Theorist Schechner asserts that only "artists, shamans, conmen [or] acrobats" can maintain the balance between the flow of ordinary time and the flow of performance time to achieve "the 'present moment,' synchronic ecstasy, the autotelic flow, of liminal stasis" (*Between Theater and Anthropology* 113).[15] Indeed, Close was called artist, shaman, and con man throughout his career for his attempts to create liminal performance experiences through the Harold. Players in every wave seek the "high" or the ecstasy that group improvisation can sometimes provide. This phenomenon of intensified community and spontaneity can be analyzed, if not perfectly explained, from a variety of perspectives, including anthropology, psychology, and cultural studies. ImprovOlympic's claim to have the formula for this kind of threshold experience is the key to its charismatic appeal. For young improvisers in the '80s and '90s, Close's work with the Harold hearkened back to the old days of the Compass, where improvisation was seen as "a doorway into something" (Adler, "The 'How' of Funny" 17). Many flocked to ImprovOlympic hoping Close would lead them through that doorway.

Close teaches the Harold by first urging players to overcome their egos in order to give way to their subconscious or inner voice, then to access the collective unconscious through groupmind. In performance, this process enables groups of performers to enter surreal and dreamlike scenarios, tapping their subconscious minds or childhood memories as they play. It often results in grotesque recombinations of memories, objects, or cultural references and gives players and audiences a sense of entering a liminal space where, as anthropologist Victor Turner writes, "the bizarre becomes the normal, and where through the loosening of connections between elements customarily bound together in certain combinations, their scrambling and recombining in monstrous, fantastic, and unnatural shapes, [they] are induced to think . . . about cultural experiences they had hitherto taken for granted" (*Ritual* 42). Much of ImprovOlympic's humor comes from these bizarre juxtapositions.

At one level, this kind of Harold experience can work to undermine the current order by denying rules, norms, and hierarchies and encouraging groups to play with alternative realities. On another level, through his insistence on groupmind and the immutability of patterns, Close shut off many of the avenues his techniques might have offered for questioning society's status quo.

ImprovOlympic players claim to avoid jokes in favor of the laughter that comes from a sudden insight into the true nature of the world, derived from our "innate *in*ability NOT to make patterns" (transcript of class 1994). According to *Truth in Comedy,* the ImprovOlympic manual, this insight derives from the successful working of groupmind, which links improvisers to "a universal intelligence, enabling them to perform fantastic, sometimes unbelievable feats" (Halpern, Close, and Johnson 93). Close naturalized both the structure and the content of each Harold's discoveries. The patterns, he claimed, are innate, and the Harold's movement from chaos to order reflects the laws of physics or biology. Close believed that actors "needn't worry about things like structure—it's already there. The 'Rule of Threes' is a deeply ingrained biological phenomenon" (89).[16] According to Close, groupmind creates "Supermen" with minds wired together, "releasing higher and greater powers of the human being. That is what we mean when we say that Harold 'appears.' A melding of the brains occurs on stage. When improvisers are using seven or eight brains instead of just their own, they can do no wrong!" (89). This approach fosters the New Age–like pleasures of community and spontaneity but is quite unlikely to challenge conventional gender roles or other stereotypes.

In his cultural-anthropological study, *From Ritual to Theatre*, Victor Turner discusses ways in which shared liminal or borderline experiences create a sense of *communitas*—or community, connection, and the "direct, immediate and total confrontations of human identities" (*Ritual* 46). With reference to anthropologist Arnold van Gennep's work on human "rites of passage," Turner describes the three phases of these rituals as separation from the established order, eventual reincorporation into that order, and the transitional margin, or ambiguous "social limbo" between those two poles, that Turner calls the "liminal space" (*Ritual* 24).[17]

In their pure form, the rituals Turner describes exist only in preindustrial, tribal societies, where liminal performances "invert but do not usually subvert the status quo" (*Ritual* 41). Turner writes that in industrial society, entertainment genres such as parody and burlesque may use an unstructured, nonnormative performance to question or undermine the central values of society. These activities, according to Turner, are "liminoid" rather than liminal because they are not integral to the life and work of the community but rather set aside as play or diversion. Still, Turner believes there is value in liminoid expressions as they demonstrate the possibility of alternative paradigms.

As for a modern sense of communitas, Turner writes, "it is within leisure, and sometimes aided by the projections of art that this way of experiencing one's fellows can be portrayed, grasped and sometimes realized" (*Ritual* 46). He describes three forms of communitas: spontaneous, ideological, and normative. Spontaneous communitas is the "magical" feeling of connection shared by groups of people who "become absorbed into a single synchronized, fluid event"—perhaps such as neighbors piling sandbags against a flood, strangers sharing food and jokes in a snowbound airport—or improvisers swept up in groupmind (48).[18] Ideological communitas is a set of theories that try to explain and describe spontaneous communitas. Most relevant to this study is the third category, normative communitas, defined as "a subculture or group which attempts to foster and maintain relationships of spontaneous communitas on a more or less permanent basis" through structures, rules, and institutions that can often destroy the original spontaneity (49).

Many improvisers describe good Harold play as not unlike the synchronous, fluid event of spontaneous communitas, and ImprovOlympic's team structures give players their own tribes with which to strive toward these symbiotic experiences.[19] Within this subculture, then, ImprovOlympic stages a space where participants can enact rituals of separation and reintegration in ways that resonate with Turner's description of tribal ceremonies. Improv-Olympic works, both artistically and institutionally, to manage the chaos represented by improvisation—first by celebrating chaos as free play, then by discovering the universal patterns and connections that order that chaos. This focus on the myth of universal meaning can strengthen the sense of spirituality and community within the group, while audiences are simultaneously reassured by the company's ultimate assertion of coherent narrative in improvised scenes.

Many players form deep, unspoken connections with teammates, and they often speak of finding *the zone*—a state of unselfconscious awareness in which every individual action seems to be the right one and the group works with apparently perfect synchronicity. A number of players consider the zone to be a high that is, in comedian Jim Belushi's legendary words, "better than sex." Cultural theorist John Fiske identifies groups of sports aficionados, or of Elvis fans, who forge both individual and group meaning through shared peak experiences. For fans, cheering for a team or screaming for a rock star can allow the full engagement of their minds and bodies in the pleasures of the present moment, often described as a "sense of release [or] loss of control" that feels like freedom—or even madness (Fiske 89). ImprovOlympians describe the Harold experience in much the same terms.

Like Schechner's description of an ecstatic performance, improvising in the zone achieves what psychologist Mihaly Csikszentmihalyi describes as the experience of "flow": "In the flow state, action follows upon action according to an internal logic that seems to need no conscious intervention by the actor. He experiences it as a unified flowing from one moment to the next, in which he is in control of his actions, and in which there is little distinction between self and environment, between stimulus and response or between past, present and future. . . . Games are obvious flow activities, and play is the flow experience *par excellence*" (21).[20]

Players do not experience flow or the zone in every performance. In fact, it is fairly difficult to accomplish—and all the more desirable and addictive for its rarity. Performers often call groupmind magical and believe it has a spiritual dimension in which players virtually channel a truth beyond their own conscious reasoning. Yet, the never-satiated desire to achieve the zone, combined with the pressure to produce successful performance products, often results in the naturalization of mainstream values, forced conformity, and strained relations among players—especially along the lines of gender and race. Many women and people of color are deeply committed to the experience of flow within improv. But, as in first-wave improvisation, these spontaneous performances often serve to validate unexamined archetypes and given truths.

Audiences, too, can be caught up in the powerful flow of groupmind. Lisa Trask, an ImprovOlympic performer and the first woman team coach, describes the zone this way:

> When you're in the zone . . . the people on stage are saying things a second to three seconds before the audience comes up with it. And the reason that happens is you've got eight minds working on it at once, instead of just one. . . . And I firmly believe that the audience can be in that groupmind too—they're only a few seconds behind you. We get people screaming "Yes!" because it rings true with them . . . because they knew it. They don't know how they knew it—but when we said it, it was so. And that's why it's so gratifying for an audience member to see it. [When they] see a good improv show, the audience walks out just as high as the performer does. (personal interview)

Trask reveals the connection between groupmind, the zone, audience and player pleasure, and the essentially conservative nature of second-wave improv. The question must be asked: When the group works as one mind, whose mind is it? How does the seeming rightness, inevitability, and spontaneity of improv mask the unmarked power of hegemony?

With the support of their aficionados, ImprovOlympic built a successful improv theatre to stand beside Second City. But the increasing intrusiveness of Halpern's rules and structures, and growing competition among the teams, chipped away at the spontaneity of the group's atmosphere—precipitating the departure of a number of players who went on to create third-wave (and possibly even fourth-wave) companies.

With ImprovOlympic's reclamation of improv process as a public performance mode, a number of women believed that the slower pace and the more thoughtful, more dramatic, and more personal style of long-form improv finally gave them a chance to play to their strengths (and gender training). ImprovOlympic officially discouraged joke-telling, insisting that humor would emerge naturally from character interactions and the recognition of incongruities—ostensibly a more feminine approach to comedy. ImprovOlympic's expanded troupe structure also created more opportunity for women to participate. And despite Close's public skepticism of any woman's comic ability, Halpern's powerful presence at the helm seemed to make this company a woman-friendly alternative to Second City.

Yet, while some women feel very comfortable at ImprovOlympic, others have quit the group in frustration. Despite the rules about mutual support and trust, much ImprovOlympic performance places a premium on speed, assertiveness, and conventional joking, making some women feel outgunned. Groupmind's propensity for "rediscovering" archetypes and mythic narratives often results in stereotypical gender roles in the Harold. Many players and ex-players also claim that the ImprovOlympic's subculture is that of a boys' club and that Halpern has been less than encouraging to women improvisers, perhaps preferring to be one of the boys herself. Then there was the master and his ambivalence about funny females.

At the Wrigleyside Bar after a show in 1994, Gwyn Ashley, one of three women in her eleven-member ImprovOlympic team, Faulty Wiring, and Kevin Mullaney, from the long-running house team Frank Booth, discussed gender issues in improv:

Mullaney: It's really odd. It does affect the chemistry of a team. There was a team that Gwyn was on, Mr. Blonde. Last year they had a lineup of four men and four women, and the house team at the time, the Family, was all men. And I remember going to see Mr. Blonde, and the chemistry, or the feeling, the style of it, felt very very different than the Family's, who are very good, but it was very much a testosterone team—
Interviewer: There are those who argue that improv is a testosterone art form.
Ashley: Because improv is a very initiative-heavy art form, and so guys are usually the ones who are more likely to edit someone and jump out. They're more likely to interrupt something and—
Mullaney: Get in the way.
Ashley: No, no, no, I mean they're more likely to go "oh" and jump out, whereas the women are more likely to hang back and say, "Oh well, let's see how this plays out," or "Let them develop that character a little more." But the guys'll say "oh!"—which is why when you have them both working together, when it's more of an equal team, it creates more interesting things than if it's all one or all the other. I don't like all-women teams either. (personal interview)

While Ashley enjoyed the different power relations between men and women on the teams, other players have felt more inhibited by them. Men still initiate far more scenes, games, and monologues than women do. Once again, women, following the rules of agreement, frequently find themselves defined as girlfriends, wives, and mothers, and far less often as central agents in a scene or set of scenes. Women themselves sometimes participate in this process of marginalization. In girlhood, many have internalized the social training that reinforces conventional gender norms. Ingrained habits make some women hesitate to take up space, take focus, or make strong initiations. Thus, in the pressured interactions of improv, some female players automatically give away power on stage, effectively compelling teammates to take the lead.

The short-form tendency to stereotype is perhaps an even deeper problem in the Harold when the image is validated as an archetype and, thus, an abiding truth. In one Harold, for example, described in *Truth in Comedy,* the scene began and ended with the woman as sexual object and symbol of degradation. As the Harold draws to its slam-dunk: "the innocent high school boys reading the bathroom wall to discover how many classmates had screwed the same woman [from the first scene], is reflected in the scene of the vet reading the names on the Viet Nam Memorial. The woman becomes the symbol for America when it becomes apparent that the vet is still reading on the wall the names of men who have been 'screwed' " (Halpern, Close, and Johnson 145). While this metaphor might be read in a number of ways, the woman herself was never given voice or subjecthood, reinforcing the perception that she merely represented "screwed-ness."

Women at ImprovOlympic often find themselves second-class citizens off stage as well as on stage. Improviser Mary Fahey described the typical Improv-Olympic party as a festival of one-upsmanship, in which men joke and women laugh appreciatively (personal interview). As at Second City, some women ally themselves with high-status male players, often both sexually and socially, in order to find their place in the ImprovOlympic community. Theorist Sarah Thornton notes that, despite the rhetoric of freedom and equality in many subcultural formations, "the social difference along which [subcultural capital] is aligned [most] systematically is, in fact, gender" (13). Like the club culture Thornton analyzes, improv-comedy is often invested in the feminization of the mainstream. Some (though not all) male improvisers equate the libertarian self-expression of improv-comedy with roguish masculinity, while women are made to represent both the obstacles to freedom and the objects of desire.[21]

Female improvisers are caught in a double bind. A passive support player might be regarded as talentless, but an assertive woman is just as likely to be criticized. In her experience, Fahey says, "I do think that as a conscious feminist in improv you are going to find resistance and be considered a bitch. And I also think you probably couldn't do as good work, because being a conscious feminist is considered having a personal agenda—it [means you are resisting] 'groupmind.' You're going to have the same backlash as you would have in life" (personal interview). Some women, such as Fahey, feel most comfortable with the traditional role that women played in first-wave improv, focusing on acting skills and creating reality-based characters and relationships. Those who take this approach can find some outlet at ImprovOlympic but are often frustrated with that company's focus on surreal twists and unexpected edits.[22]

Women seeking a voice in second-wave improv have had a variety of responses to the problems they encounter. While most women improvisers would refuse the contested label "feminist," their different tactics and strategies resonate with the distinct categories of feminist theatre practice—liberal, cultural, or materialist—articulated by feminist theorist Jill Dolan in *The Feminist Spectator as Critic*. Most of the successful women at ImprovOlympic take the liberal approach—working to show that they can be just as assertive, just as funny, and just as uninhibited as the men are. Others, who might be compared to cultural feminists in this taxonomy, believe that women are best able to embody Close's teachings on process, support, and spirituality. However, these players are rarely influential on stage. Finally, in the materialist vein, a few women find ways to critique and comment on the improv system as a whole, even within their own performances. But these players risk being seen as bad improvisers who self-consciously plan or think too much on stage. For the most part, any political belief or agenda—any identity position that is marked as "other"—is considered inappropriate to the agreement-based work at ImprovOlympic and is certainly seen as an inhibitor to the collective achievement and organic truths of the zone. Yet any real challenge to society's status quo requires conscious thought and the deconstruction of normative values—a task quite difficult in the context of groupmind and long-form improvisation.

Trask defends ImprovOlympic and long-form improv as the one style of improv-comedy that does allow you to think before you speak. The problem, she says, is in equalizing male and female timing and combating society's gendered behavior patterns: "When I see the women letting the men do a lot of the talking, I stop them and I tell them both—I say to the guys, 'Are you talking without thinking first? Because you're talking an awful lot. Slow down. Let the other person get a word in edgewise.' And to the women I say, 'Are you waiting for him to tell you something, or do you have something to say and you're waiting to speak? Because if you're waiting to speak, as soon as he stops for breath, start talking.' I tell them they've gotta move quick. You know—and everybody has to move quick" (personal interview).

For many, improv is based on "no-mindedness"—speaking without thinking. But Trask insists that audiences have more patience than they are given credit for and that "ImprovOlympic is the place where you can take your time and think before you speak" (personal interview). ImprovOlympic does teach a certain amount of zenlike patience and intelligent choice during improv play, although Close and Halpern are very clear that ideas must emerge spontaneously and should never be preconceived (Halpern, Close, and Johnson 64). Unfortunately, as Trask is forced to admit, the theory of taking one's time does not translate into gender-equal practice, especially during high-pressure performances.

Despite its challenges, the Harold does provide some potential for voicing difference, particularly through impromptu monologues, which may be inserted at will almost any time in the game. The only element of long-form improv that is not group-oriented, the monologue can be used to explore the intersection of the personal and the political. Women and people of color sometimes express a dissenting view of the emerging themes in a Harold, and a number of gay male players have even used monologues to "come out of the closet" to the often homophobic improv community. Gay improvisers find ImprovOlympic far more tolerant and supportive than most troupes in Chicago. The company tends to value outsider sensibilities, especially when those sensibilities are expressed in personal, rather than political, terms, thus generating original material that can then be recuperated into universal truths.

Individual teams sometimes find new ways to experiment with gender roles and conventional truths through their own variations on the Harold. The Deconstruction game has been a popular mode of playing with stereotypes, and other games, such as Movie, use an epic, narrated style that allows for Brechtian distancing.

In 1996, a group of women at ImprovOlympic formed their own all-female team, called Jane. Their action was highly irregular, as Halpern usually reserves the right to assemble the teams, distributing players as she sees fit. Nevertheless, Halpern finally accepted (and even began to take credit for) Jane's success—shortly promoting them to the coveted status of ImprovOlympic house team.

Jane was the brainchild of improvisers Katie Roberts and Stephnie Weir, who had made their way onto high-powered teams in the ImprovOlympic system but felt that they were missing out on the intense camaraderie their male counterparts seemed to enjoy. Weir valued her time with the Lost Yetis, a team she describes as consisting of "six boys and two women." The Lost Yetis were a good, skillful, and even cooperative group. Weir says her teammates made her feel welcome to play along with their roughhousing boys' games. But she remembers thinking, "I want what they have. I want a girl thing" (personal interview). Weir knew that she was forced to translate her own experience into a male language in every improvised scene. She explains, "The white male lifestyle and experience is so on the forefront of everyone's mind, TV, everything in our lives, that everyone has that common experience.

The first all-woman ImprovOlympic team, Jane broke through many of the barriers facing women in Chicago improv, providing an important role model for women who followed. Pictured are Jane's founding members. In the back row: Stephnie Weir, Tami Sagher and Abby Sher. Middle: Abby Schachner, Monica Payne, Bina Martin. Front: Molly Cavanaugh, Sue Maxman. Photo: Suzanne Plunkett

We all know how to support that. 'Oh, that's familiar, I can heighten that' " (personal interview).[23]

Weir and Roberts wanted to create a group in which female experience was the common denominator, and where the mention of Judy Blume received the instantaneous recognition that sports figures did in the Lost Yetis. They wanted a venue where women could work to conquer the self-censorship and self-doubt that was engendered when their references and initiatives were not recognized—a place, says Weir, that would help "remind you that your voice is legitimate" (personal interview).

They called the new team Jane in honor of Jane Doe, Jane without Tarzan and without Dick; Jane, the underground abortion network; Jane, the everywoman. Weir and Roberts invited six other women from various ImprovOlympic teams to add the new troupe to their other performance commitments. They chose women who were strong and talented, but who they also believed would benefit from their experiment. In fact, they deliberately chose not to include several women they saw as "tough, run with the boys" players who seemed not to want or need this kind of sisterhood (interview). The women they did contact eagerly accepted their offer. Weir and

Roberts quickly explained that there was no political agenda or anti-male sentiment intended. They just wanted to see what it was like to feel more fully supported in their choices and to explore performance options not open to them in their coed teams.[24]

Their Jane experience taught these players to lead as well as follow, to make strong initiations, to take more risks, and to trust their own impulses. Dislodged from their safe, familiar positions as support players, the women soon learned that constant deference or passivity in improv was just as damaging to the ensemble as bulldozing and that sometimes the best way to support the scene or the troupe is to lead.

One of the important pleasures and benefits that Jane provided its members was the frequent opportunity to play male roles. In a mixed improv team, outnumbered women very rarely attempt male impersonations, although male players are known to present a variety of female impersonations with relative frequency. When women do initiate male characters, they can often be misread and ignored in the midst of improv play and simply endowed with a female name, called "honey," or asked to take a letter.[25] Jane member Jennifer Bills suggests that it is more fun for an audience to see a man lower his status to play a woman than to see a woman play a man. "A woman as a guy is not as wacky," she explains, "it's a character" (personal interview). Here, Bills uses *status* as a familiar improv term derived from Johnstone. In concept, status describes an improviser's freely chosen decision to play a dominant or a deferential character. In practice, however, performance status usually replicates offstage status, and women are far more likely to play low while men play high—especially in relation to women.

Because women played all the roles in Jane's scenes, the company produced a fascinating commentary on gender roles and improv. Gestural, physical, and verbal indicators of gender were starkly foregrounded through the female body—a reversal of the more common female impersonation in many comedy genres. It was sometimes unclear in a romantic scene, for example, whether the women were playing a lesbian relationship or whether—when she took on an aggressive posture, commanding voice, and confident attitude—one of the players was doing a male role.

Unlike most drag performances, the women of Jane wore one basic, casual costume and made no attempt to disguise their sex. Moreover, improv performance is unscripted and, especially in ImprovOlympic's long-form style of improvisation, flows from scene to scene with actors playing multiple roles. Players often do not know what gender they will be until a teammate endows them with a name, calling for "Bob," or shouting, "Hortense, we're out of licorice." This uncertainty helps pose the question of intrinsic maleness and femaleness in all improvised representations. Jane's audiences could observe the process by which each improviser put on and discarded a variety of gendered personae, while remaining clearly identifiable as a woman throughout the performance.

Performance theorist Rhonda Blair suggests that "Cross-gender performance can use stereotyping deliberately to emphasize the nature of character-as-construction" and that both males and females who perform across gender develop "theatrical codes . . . a particular gender vocabulary and hierarchy for each piece" (292). Each of the women in Jane defined her own techniques and methods for playing male characters. They approached the task in one of several ways depending on the demands of the scene. A broadly comic sketch might allow a player to indulge in a ball-scratching stereotype or to exaggerate the characteristics of the aggressive "alpha male." For Weir and her teammates, poking fun at the classic bad date, macho barfly, or self-important geek makes use of women's unique set of shared references and creates a refreshing comedy of instant recognition for the women in their audience. Stereotypes or not, says Weir, "these are men I know" (personal interview). But Jane was even better known for its slower, more thoughtful, and more detailed scenes. In these, the actors often worked with the blurred edges of gender, looking for the commonalities as well as the differences between their characters and their selves.

Many improvisers base all their characters on highly visible body language designed to communicate quickly and efficiently to teammates and audiences. According to Judith Butler, gender "must be understood as the mundane way in which bodily gestures, movements, and enactments of various kinds constitute the illusion of an abiding gendered self . . . an act . . . which constructs the social fiction of its own psychological interiority" (270–71, 279). Every woman in Jane discussed using strong physical choices as the key to creating both the outer impression of and a certain inner identification with maleness. Perhaps surprisingly, only Bills mentioned working with the image of "something between [her] legs" (personal interview). Far more critical for most of the players was the notion of expanding their use of space and weight.

Founding Jane member Abby Sher confides, "A lot of my men are a lot more confident than my women are. They try to command attention or command women, though I do play other kinds of men as well. For me, the delicious part of it is taking on the confidence. That kind of attitude sticks out if you don't play a man" (personal interview). Tami Sagher, another original member, summarizes her male characters as "slower, heavier, deeper, and higher status." A woman of normal weight, the twenty-four-year-old Sagher freely admits to having serious body-image problems, even using her fear of fat as material for her improvisations. She confesses, "If I'm feeling yucky about my body, I play a man" (personal interview). As a male character, weight is permissible. As an attractive, date-able, castable female, the same weight is not. Sher and Sagher are intelligent, independent, motivated, and successful young women. Yet their equation of maleness with a greater entitlement to space and weight, a more relaxed demeanor, and a sense of confidence speaks volumes about the way femaleness is constructed in our society.

Many of the performers were particularly interested in exploring the borderlands of gender and sexuality. For example, Sue Maxman enjoyed portraying adolescent boys in the midst of struggling with masculine identity. Moreover, in Jane's impromptu performances, actors sometimes began a scene in one gender, only to be endowed in mid-gesture as another. This misrecognition occurred less frequently among the members of Jane than it did in coed groups, but it was not uncommon for characters initiated as men to shift into lesbians or vice versa. A character in the midst of a conventionally feminine gesture could suddenly be called Herb. The Janes reveled in these moments of incongruity, moments which helped to keep scenes interesting. The key is not to reject the seeming error in proper gender performance, but to incorporate it as an integral part of the character in process. These are the moments when improvisation can interrupt the constant repetition of gender norms.

Although none of the women in Jane identified herself as lesbian, the troupe quite often played romantic scenes between women without a male character in sight. While it was sometimes difficult for audience members to read the difference between the actors' physicalizations of male and lesbian roles, Sagher, Schachner, and teammates are clear that there is a distinct difference for them in terms of interior motivation, attitude, and mannerisms. Interestingly, the theatrical code for lesbian also tends to be less constricted and less self-deprecating than those of most heterosexual female characters.

The newfound confidence and power of their performances transformed the group and its individual members into hot properties. Shows were sold out, reputations soared, and almost every player took on coaching responsibilities with newer troupes. Second City producers, often heard to bemoan the scarcity of "funny women," quickly recruited Jane members for touring companies and the e.t.c. troupe. In 1998, Weir and Sagher were cast for the Second City mainstage. Weir acknowledges, "I do think it was because we were able to make ourselves seen and our voices heard; we were getting some acknowledgment for the work we were doing" (personal interview). For several months, Jane accepted eager replacement players, but the chemistry was not the same. The team disbanded in 1999; but they had done much to redefine the role of women throughout the improv community.

Several of Jane's newer members soon formed an independent all-female troupe called Sirens, while another women's group, Red, became a founding company in the Playground (an improv co-op).[26] The players in these troupes were from the next generation of improvisers—less experienced in the art form than Jane had been, but also with less to "unlearn." Weir admits that Jane's improvisation often served as therapy, a chance to confront insecurities and to practice self-confidence. The Sirens didn't seem to have "the neuroses we had" (Weir interview). But Sirens player Sara Gee gives the credit to Jane: "We had much more solid role models—women who were kicking ass in improv that we could come to Chicago and see" (personal interview).

Veteran ImprovOlympian and founding Jane member Lillian Francis helped to coach both Sirens and Red, directing them to "play like a boy," choosing success, rather than "like a girl" who gives away her power—a tendency still too common among women. "No more pathetic victim characters," Francis insists, "win that spelling bee" (personal interview). Once again both troupes insist there is no political motive behind their choice to play

Sirens, an independent, all-female improv troupe, was inspired in large part by Jane's example of strength and mutual support. Founded in 1999, the group organized fund-raising efforts for cancer research through Gilda's Club. Clockwise from far left: Celeste Pechous, Erin McEvoy, Jacqueline Stone, Lindsey Harrington, Molly Erdman, and Sara Gee. Photo: Rue Robbins

together—only an artistic one. They wanted the opportunity to create material from a new and different perspective. Most of the Sirens had recent memories of the college improv circuit, where each had struggled as the only female player in her troupe. In Sirens, they suddenly realized, "you don't have to be Wonder Woman any more, you don't have to cover twenty bases, you don't have to fight for your ideas . . . you can relax—you can breathe (Stone interview).

Founding Siren Jackie Stone believes that working with an all-female troupe has made her a stronger improviser: "It's a psychological shift. Part of it is how you perceive and initiate things on stage. It opens your mind, expands your possibilities—you're more likely to pick different kinds of characters than you would in a mixed group. Now, even when I am the only woman on a team, I don't play the same way I used to. My Sirens experience becomes my ammunition—it's in my system" (personal interview).

With Jane's success, women gained prestige and visibility at ImprovOlympic, and their numbers rose slightly in classes and Harold teams. But the theatre was still a male clubhouse in the subcultural life of late-night improv jams and parties.

In the 1990s, women, though still outnumbered, were increasingly evident on ImprovOlympic stages and were beginning to be more assertive in Harold play. However, the number of people of color remained extremely low, with no more than a handful of black, Latino, Asian, or Native American players in a hundred. Ironically, Chicago improv, like many other countercultural movements, is primarily in the business of giving middle-class whites a mode of escape from the rigidity, rationality, conformity, and order associated with whiteness. At ImprovOlympic in particular, Close described the hipness, spontaneity, and spirituality of improvisation in terms of cultural and racial "others" through the language of jazz, sports, and New Age religion.

Close focused on the hipness of ImprovOlympic performers and audiences, linking the practice of improv to everything the Beats and the avant-garde admired about African American life and music. As Norman Mailer wrote in "The White Negro," "It is no accident that the source of Hip is the Negro for he has been living on the margin between totalitarianism and democracy for two centuries. But the presence of Hip as a working philosophy in the sub-worlds of American life is probably due to jazz . . . the music of orgasm" (278–79).

As I have mentioned, ImprovOlympians speak often of riffing, jamming, and bebop, though they rarely acknowledge these and other aspects of jazz as derived from African American culture. As cultural theorist Kobena Mercer writes, "[T]he trope of the White Negro encodes an antagonistic subject-position on the part of the white subject in relation to the normative codes of his or her own society" (433). The spontaneity and self-expressiveness of Chicago improv has always been linked to African American forms of expression. Whether they recognize it or not, many white players are drawn to improv, jazz, and hipness as a means of disaffiliating themselves from the constraints of conventional white identity.

Race is also a factor in ImprovOlympic's frequent use of sports imagery. Close described the ideal Harold finale as a "slam-dunk," but, more precisely, a "Michael Jordan slam-dunk" (Halpern, Close, and Johnson 29). Chicago improvisers clearly admire not only Jordan's skill, but his spontaneity and style on the basketball court—qualities again associated with blackness. Close, however, recognized that his notion of patterns can be used to justify negative racial stereotypes as well as positive ones. For example, in a 1994 class, the guru told his students, "If you've been beaten up by black people six or seven times, you're probably going to extrapolate that—if people beat me up again it's likely to be blacks. So as I say, man has a tendency—we have an absolute built-in instinct—to make patterns" (transcript of class). While Close acknowledged to the class that this kind of assumption was ultimately false, his work with the Harold could too easily fall into this kind of stereotype.

Still, the Harold format does allow for some comment and resistance on this score, if the actor is quick enough on his or her feet. In one performance I saw, an impromptu game show was created to fill in between two sets of scenes. A single Native American player (the only one on the entire roster) jumped in to quiz the contestants. "Name an American sports team with a racist name," he asked. The white player was bewildered (whether his character or the player himself was stumped was not entirely apparent). "Give up? The Atlanta Braves. Next question—name another American sports team with a racist name." In a few minutes (after moving through the Kansas City Chiefs, the Washington Redskins, and others) the player had made his point. Whether he could be accused of imposing a preconceived political agenda on the game is not clear.

In the second half of the '90s, the tempo and atmosphere of ImprovOlympic began to change. Increased expenses for the new building and the ever-increasing number of students vying for performance time made the company more and more concerned with product, quality, and entertainment. Halpern expanded the number of classes required of each student from three levels to five—postponing the coveted opportunity to work with Close. The company's output was separating into two distinct modes of play that some have termed "upstairs" and "downstairs" improv. Upstairs, Close coached favored players in experiments with new structures and worked with advanced students in levels 5A and 5B to create original shows for performance. Nightly audiences, composed almost entirely of other improvisers, were quietly attentive to every subtlety. Downstairs, players competed with the whirring frozen-drink machine and a rowdier crowd. According to Francis, ImprovOlympic cabaret shows had become "very fast and very funny. . . . It's like Harold on speed" (personal interview).

As the number of teams tripled, the company-wide sense of communitas dissipated (though team loyalty remained strong). A larger percentage of the students were just moving through, focused on comedy careers beyond Clark Street. When she played with Frank Booth, Francis remembers that "the crown passed from group to group, but everybody was still very friendly and we were all peers. It's so large now that the competition is much fiercer" (personal interview). But the theatre still provided an instant social group and nightly hangout for many, and students continued attending shows in enthusiastic droves.

ImprovOlympic's prestige rose throughout the '90s as Halpern continued to publicize the growing number of alumni who had made it in television or film. Big names included Chris Farley, Mike Myers, Andy Richter, Upright Citizens Brigade, and others, although most of these were also Second City alumni.[27] Chicago improvisers began moving to New York and Los Angeles in increasing numbers—all hoping for that big break. In 1996, a group of displaced ImprovOlympians in Los Angeles proposed the creation of a West Coast branch where they could continue their work with long form. With Halpern's cooperation, players from the Tribe and several other teams opened ImprovOlympic West, a space that has become a home base for expatriates from both ImprovOlympic and the Annoyance Theatre.

On March 4, 1999, Del Close died of emphysema at the age of sixty-four. In his last days, a stream of disciples, former students, and fellow travelers came to his bedside to express their admiration and affection. A few days before his birthday (March 9), many old friends gathered for a kind of "living wake." Ever the performer, Close was energized by the celebration. He enjoyed the telegrams, the music, and the attention, and with a true sense of timing, made his final exit the very next day.[28]

When they heard the news of Close's death, the cast of Second City (all his former students) tacked his photograph above the mainstage so Close could continue to watch over their work. At ImprovOlympic, students improvised a Del-style ritual in his honor and constructed an impromptu shrine to his memory in the lobby of his eponymous theatre. The memorial features photos from Close's childhood, family, and early career along with Close's favorite toys, awards, and a book-shaped urn containing Close's ashes. There is also a highball glass into which students regularly place, or from which they borrow, cigarettes. Close was remembered in a special service at Second City and in outpourings from a "Who's Who" of improvisers. Ted Flicker declared, "It was Del who brought the truly unknown into the improvisations of the St. Louis Compass" (qtd. in Arbanel). Arts critic Jonathan Arbanel called Close "one of three 'titans' of improvisational theatre who (with Spolin and Sills) put it on the map, refined it, and turned it into the fixture of comedic and acting technique which it has become" (6).

Under the terms of his will, Close bequeathed his skull to Chicago's Goodman Theatre, where he had once played Polonius in a production of *Hamlet*. Now, as one final absurdist joke, he was determined to play Yorick. Halpern promised to honor his request and, weeks later, presented the skull to Goodman artistic director Robert Falls in a formal ceremony at the ImprovOlympic theatre.

ImprovOlympic had long depended on Close's guru status to attract prospective students, but the company's alumni believed his power would not be dimmed. "I see it growing," predicted Weir. "I definitely don't see him fading away from the picture. I don't see him being forgotten or his teachings falling by the wayside at all" (personal interview).[29] One tender moment stands out in the accounts of Close's last days. Bernie Sahlins, former producer and artistic director of Second City and famous cynic on the value of improv, made a visit to his dying friend: "The last thing he said to me . . . I took his hand, and I even kissed him, and he said to me, 'It's an art form.' I said, 'For today, Del, it's an art form' " ("Close Friends" 28).

ImprovOlympic created new structures that strove—on both the artistic and the institutional level—to reclaim Chicago improv's commitment to spontaneity and community. Their efforts were instrumental in reviving the inventiveness and energy in Chicago improv and in greatly expanding the number of participants in the Chicago improv community and subculture, though some (particularly some women and people of color) still felt marginalized by the company's policies.

ImprovOlympic's long-form improv remains extremely influential for improvisers in Chicago and elsewhere. But it was ComedySportz that moved out of the Midwest to sow the seeds of improv-comedy in over twenty cities across the United States. In the next chapter, I examine the other side of the second wave and its somewhat different interpretation of spontaneity and community.

CHAPTER 3

ComedySportz:
play's the thing

On page two of his three-hundred-page manual for team managers, Comedy-Sportz founder Dick Chudnow defines his creation: "ComedySportz is a sport. It is a competition for laughs" (2). In fact, this second-wave company is a highly popular vehicle of improv-comedy and a national business that licenses ComedySportz teams in more than twenty cities throughout the United States. Like ImprovOlympic, ComedySportz marked a return to "live" improv instead of improv-based revues and saw itself as an alternative to Second City and to Johnstone's Theatresports models. It also implemented distinctive structural innovations—both institutionally and artistically—that set it apart from either ImprovOlympic or Second City. Beginning in the mid-1980s, ComedySportz took advantage of the national comedy boom to establish a lucrative and wide-ranging improv empire. ComedySportz franchise teams soon radiated out from its home base in Milwaukee, Wisconsin—reaching as far away as New York, Los Angeles, and Austin.

Although the company is based in Milwaukee, the Chicago ComedySportz team has been an influential troupe in that city since the mid-eighties. Young improvisers from ComedySportz teams across the United States arrive in Chicago each year hoping to parlay their regional experience into comedy careers in improv's version of the big time. While the effect of ComedySportz in the second wave was to disseminate certain ideas about improv throughout the nation, Chicago later experienced an influx of ComedySportz-trained improvisers, from regional teams, who played a large part in the development of Chicago's third wave.

Artistically, ComedySportz' approach is virtually the opposite of ImprovOlympic's ethos. While both second-wave companies make use of sports-based organizing elements, such as teams, games, and rosters, the troupes have quite different ideas about the sports metaphor. Del Close was never fond of the name ImprovOlympic, which he inherited from David Shepherd's early endeavor. Nevertheless, the original ideals of Olympic sports resonate with

79

Chicago ComedySportz involves the audience in every performance. Pictured clockwise from center: Referee Jay Sukow, Kevin Colby, Lori McClain, artistic director/co-owner Dave Gaudet, co-owner Jill Shely, volunteer Juliet Curry, Marvin Howard, Katie Caussin and Dr. Jim McDonnell. Photo: Joey Edmonds Agency

Close's philosophy about improvisation: the audiences are elite aficionados, the game itself is ennobling and artistic, and the players are pure amateurs.

Close was fond of basketball terminology and often referred to the "slam-dunk" as the phenomenon "when some really terrific insight happens and the audience is really empathizing with you to the point of even body-Englishing you through the work you're doing up there . . . it's more like the audience at a sporting event than 'Yeah, like tell us another sick joke' " (ImprovOlympic class, 11/94). For Close, the slam-dunk implied an epiphany for both audience and actors not unlike the catharsis in ancient Greek drama, an idea that reinforces their Olympic designation.

ComedySportz, on the other hand, is modeled on pro sports. It does not demand an audience of cognoscenti but is marketed to the mainstream, family audience. In Milwaukee in particular, seats are often filled with high school groups, Little Leaguers in uniform, and families with children. As with professional sports, ComedySportz is also especially popular with young men. Chicago and Milwaukee are both cities with loyal and committed sports fans. ComedySportz' philosophy and its commercial success were both connected to that energy, as were many of the difficulties women improvisers have faced throughout ComedySportz history.[1]

Improvisation is a risky performance genre with no guarantee, indeed little prospect, of consistent success in terms of marketable, mainstream entertainment value. Producers and directors have created a variety of strategies designed to eliminate, valorize, or minimize improv's risk while still claiming the benefits of its spontaneity. Although producer Bernard Sahlins viewed improvisation as audience-worthy only after extensive scripting and polishing, Second City continued to be marketed as an improv-comedy theatre. ImprovOlympic, by contrast, seeks to develop an audience that appreciates its performance of the process itself. ComedySportz (and its precursor, Theatresports) took another tack, developing what could be seen as an exoskeletal structure in which the improvised performance seems to remain free-form and spontaneous, but within the confines of a highly codified sports event.

ComedySportz mimics a sports model, according to founder Chudnow, primarily in order to make improv into popular, accessible entertainment. Echoing Shepherd's early intentions for the Compass Players, Chudnow was determined to create "theatre for the masses" (Gagné interview). Feeling that much improv and theatre in general was lifeless and boring, Chudnow subscribed to the Brechtian notion that "the theatre must acquire . . . the same fascinating reality as a sporting arena during a boxing match" (Brecht 233). Chudnow superimposed the familiar and exciting narrative of competition over the indeterminacy of improv to give theatre-goers the enjoyment fans experience in the bleachers of a ball game.

Chudnow wanted not only to use the metaphor of sport, but also to create a performance event that could be recognized by audiences as a legitimate sport in itself. He constructed an entire alternative language to translate the elements of theatre and comedy performance into sports terminology. As Chudnow describes it in the ComedySportz manual, "A 'show' becomes the 'match,' an 'audience' becomes the 'fans,' the 'theater' is an 'arena' or 'stadium,' the 'intermission' becomes 'half time,' and instead of 'actors,' there are 'actletes' or 'players' " (2). Improvisers have long referred to games and sports as cognates for their art. ComedySportz has literally put the AstroTurf on the stage.

At the company's home base in Milwaukee, the ComedySportz experience begins in the parking lot, where a young man in a tutu offers fans "Free Ballet Parking." While this joke does not serve to further the sports motif, the comi-

Mark Redlich, Tim Higgins, Jason Denusek, and Jake Rasmussen pirouette from Milwaukee ComedySportz' High School League. Redlich and Higgins both graduated to the big league mainstage company by the late '90s. Photo: Pat Goetzinger

cal parking attendant pokes fun at ballet as high culture, while offering Comedy-Sportz as popular culture. A sign in the Milwaukee lobby reads, "This is ComedySportz—If you want art, go to a museum."

Temporary arenas in Madison and Chicago were decorated with team photos and sports paraphernalia, but Chudnow's home team in Milwaukee has the advantage of its own full-time stadium. There, elements of a sports arena are juxtaposed with those of a comedy club. The bleacher seats are labeled in large letters as sections A, B, and C, recalling the signage in most baseball and football stadiums, while a number of small cabaret tables bridge the distance to the AstroTurf *playing field*. The field is marked with white lines like football zones and features the outline of a penalty box where players may be sent later in the show. On each side of the stage are benches or dugouts, and a stadium-style scoreboard with blinking lights hangs overhead.

The Milwaukee ComedySportz arena gives audiences a more fully articulated effect than did the makeshift shared venues in Madison or Chicago. In the early 1990s, Madison ComedySportz performed in the upstairs dining rooms of a Wendy's fast-food chain restaurant and a Rocky Rococo's Pizzeria (finally moving into a tiny space of its own in 1997). Meanwhile, the Chicago team performed at a variety of venues before moving to the TurnAround Theatre in 1995 (and their own renovated space in 2000). The pre-performance and performance activities were similar in all three cities, emphasizing the sports metaphor at every opportunity. Before the action begins, the familiar sound of Sousa marches and ball-game–style organ music is piped through the sound system. As game time nears, the ComedySportz players begin a series of activities to warm up the audience, including sing-alongs and the aggressive vending of peanuts, ComedySportz T-shirts, and ridiculous items such as toilet seats—cueing the spectators to engage in interactive stadium behavior rather than passive and silent theatre behavior.

Before the game actually begins, the referee appears (announced with a fanfare from the sound booth), dressed in the familiar black and white striped jersey worn by baseball referees, complete with whistle and clipboard. Much like a cabaret host, the ref welcomes the crowd and presents a *Refspiel*. Each ref develops a personal style, but all must cover the same basic points. To open, the ref explains to any first-time spectators that ComedySportz is competitive improv that depends on audience suggestions to create scenes and games and uses audience laughter and applause to determine a winning team of players. Audience input is "your proof that everything we are doing is completely and totally improvised [and] your guarantee that no matter how many times you come to see ComedySportz, you will never see the same show twice" (Chicago Refspiel).

ComedySportz games are officially restricted to four minutes or less and require frequent interaction with the spectators. The audience is trained for its increased role in the performance both vocally and physically. The ref commands everyone to sing "Take Me Out to See Improv" (to the tune of "Take Me Out to the Ball Game") and sometimes even has the crowd perform a "stadium wave." These warm-ups are usually followed by several practice rounds of suggestion making as the ref steers spectators toward the appropriate method of shouting out ideas and the types of suggestions needed.

The ref then catalogues the three main ComedySportz fouls, insisting that fans repeat the name of the foul after him and do the hand gesture. The *waffling foul*, with a two-handed wavy gesture, means that the scene is stuck and going nowhere. The penalty may be for the offending team to be waved right off the stage. The *groaner foul*, with two hands crossed under the chin in a choking or gagging gesture, means that a joke is just too bad or obvious to be tolerated. The individual perpetrator is sent to the penalty box to apologize to the audience and beg forgiveness. Finally, the *brown bag foul*, with a gesture showing a bag being placed over the head, means that a player or audience member has said or suggested something lewd, crude, or offensive by ComedySportz standards. The offending player or spectator is then actually required to wear a brown paper bag over his or her head for the remainder of that game. The referee goes to great lengths to let the audience know that ComedySportz is a family show in which nothing off-color is officially permitted.

At last, an amplified offstage voice proclaims the official opening of the match: "Ladeez and Gentlemen! The ComedyLeague of America proudly presents ComedySportz!" The spectators are given "the starting lineup," featuring real players' names, joke nicknames, and positions: "At Half-Wit Position—Brian Judkins. At Right Dead-pan, Joe 'Terrible Two' Thompson" (Madison ComedySportz performance). The players trot onto the field dressed in ComedySportz baseball-style jerseys, coordinated pants, and caps. One team is dressed in blue, the other in red. Teams vary in size from three to six players. There is rarely more than one woman per team (if that), and there are very few players of color.

When the players have all reached the field, slapping five and posturing like professional athletes, the announcer proceeds with the traditional ritual opening of a baseball game: "And now to honor America, please rise right

Improviser Brian Green leaps into action, supported by teammates John Podlesnik, Carol Hirschi and Joe Cortese. At home, Milwaukee's players are divided between the Dendrites and the Sparklers. For away games, they all play under the Milwaukee Cheezeheads banner. Photo: Courtesy Milwaukee ComedySportz.

out of your seats, doff your headgear, face the flag, and join us as we sing the National Anthem" (Madison ComedySportz performance). In fact, a flag is unfurled, and the players turn to face it. Spectators rise, many of them bewildered and wondering if this, too, is a joke. Some join in singing "The Star Spangled Banner," which is rendered very quickly but with fairly straight faces by the performers. ComedySportz player-manager Mike Rock's "Notes for Players" cautions, "The National Anthem should be sung seriously. No hats, no monkeyshines. You are very visible up on stage and this is the first impression the audience has of you as a player" (4).[2]

The team captains toss a coin for the first challenge game of the match, and the winner decides whether to initiate or receive the challenge. The elaborate presentation of this sports framework creates immediate cultural competence for most audience members—drawing them into active and enthusiastic involvement. Before the game itself has even begun, the ComedySportz rituals and audience warm-ups present sports, mainstream morality, patriotism, and capitalism rolled into one spontaneous performance.

As the typical evening continues, the referee chooses from the audience three judges who will hold up red or blue signs to determine the winner of each round of play. The referee whimsically assigns arbitrary points for each game and deductions for any fouls. The referee is constantly active—keeping time checks, goading spectators to call fouls, and eliciting suggestions throughout the show. For most games, teams take the field separately and are judged for their relative success in the performance, although in Elimination Rounds players compete individually on their team's behalf. The performers work with conventional, popular improv-comedy games, including Changing Emotions, Dr. Know-It-All, Musical Styles, and Dubbing.[3] In the first game, or Warm-up Round, players go head-to-head in elimination games, such as What Are You Doing? or Story, that require players to concentrate and think fast or be sent back to the dugout.[4] The exciting sudden-death quality of these games makes them popular as openers or closers for the show.

The match then moves to a Challenge Round, in which the opposing team selects a game supposedly difficult for its rivals (although players admit these are often agreed to beforehand), and the Audience Challenge, in which spectators choose a game from a list of over sixty possibilities listed on the two-page program. The program lists are categorized by type—musical games, word games, physical games—and referees often curtail audience choice to a certain area in order to ensure variety in the show.

The half is often concluded with a high-energy *gimmick* game or guessing game, in which a single player is sent out of earshot while the referee elicits from the spectators suggestions that the returning player must then decipher with the help of his or her teammates. Gimmick games are used by some troupes as a way to display their performers' skills in mime, gibberish, rhyming, memory, and group intuition or communication, and they adapt well to the sports-based competition. These trials of skill dispense with any pretense at creating scenes or characters, concentrating on the pleasure audiences feel in seeing the performers' virtuosity. While gimmick games were part of the repertoire of many early Chicago improv troupes, ComedySportz is one of the few companies that still regularly play this kind of game. More serious troupes such as ImprovOlympic are frequently disdainful of their use.

The two most popular gimmick games at ComedySportz are Five Things, where the audience creates five absurd, surrealistic phrases, which the team may then only communicate in mime or gibberish, and Catchphrase (sometimes called Torture the Actor), in which the absent player must return to guess a popular slogan or proverb suggested by the audience. In this game, the guessing improviser's teammates invent short dialogue exchanges or activities that suggest key phrases in the proverb without using any of its actual words. As the guesser throws out possibilities, spectators are encouraged to cheer when the player gets closer to the right phrase and to boo or groan when he or she takes a wrong turn. Audiences express almost as much glee when players fail as when they guess correctly. Joe Thompson, player/manager of the Madison ComedySportz troupe, says, "Failure is funny—as long as you fail with 110 percent commitment" (personal interview).

After the gimmick game, the typical ComedySportz match pauses for halftime, and spectators are urged to eat and drink until play resumes. Another gimmick game usually opens the half, followed by a Team Choice round. The match typically winds up with a Catch-up Round, where teams can rack up points as their players survive elimination games like Story or get the most individual laughs in a joke-based game. One favorite here is 185, in which players must invent jokes based on the old standard "185 ducks go into a bar. The bartender says, 'I'm sorry, we don't serve ducks here' and the duck says 'just put it on my bill.'" With an audience suggestion to replace "duck," players step forward to float newly minted puns on the old pattern.

The match concludes with a recap of the score and the performance of the thrill of victory and the agony of defeat from the players. The competition is, of course, merely a pretense—although it may reflect actual success and failure on the level of audience pleasure and preference, and thus can have an impact on player status within the group.

At ComedySportz, although the content of the games and scenes and even the nature of competition are presented in a parodic, irreverent tone in a carnivalesque atmosphere, any sustained critique or subversion of mainstream values must take place in the individual spectator's perception rather than on the playing field. Chudnow claims that his sports format is apolitical and that audience laughter is far more important than any content or message that might emerge. Chudnow proudly asserts that ComedySportz, in contrast to ImprovOlympic, is not art, nor indeed is it even authentic improvisation. Acknowledging that his insistence on time limits and his willingness to allow repeated jokes and bits conflicts with a purist idea of improvisation, Chudnow calls his technique "comprovisation," saying, "It's a new term. And what I like to think that is—in my wildest dreams—is a combination of comedy styles and methods of getting an audience to laugh and that includes comic acting, it includes improv, it includes mime, it includes acting, burlesque, slapstick—whatever you have to do" (personal interview).

Although Chudnow means "comprovisation" as a blending of the words comedy and improvisation, the term also sounds like "compromise," reflecting Chudnow's own recognition that many of the ideals of improvisational process are sacrificed in his sports and comedy product. The comprovisation is fast, funny, and uncomplicated. But, despite Chudnow's disclaimers, his sports format has far-reaching political implications. For many audiences, the recognizable sports rituals, unexamined stereotypical humor, and overarching narrative structure all serve to reinforce conservative ideology. At the same time, many ComedySportz players firmly believe in the spiritual qualities of improvisation, especially as expressed in such sporting terms as team spirit and flow.

Sports sociologists describe the category of games as "less codified, more changeable" than that of sports, which are described as needing specialized training and as more likely to be played before an audience (Harris and Park 3). The shift from Spolin's theater games to Johnstone's Theatresports did involve a further formalization of the rules governing the mode of play. In many ways, sports was an obvious structuring device for improvisation, maintaining the excitement of improv's immediacy while creating external goals for its open-ended exercises and imposing win-loss results on its indeterminacy. Johnstone began presenting Theatresports tournaments in 1977 in Calgary, Canada, where his Loose Moose Theatre Company continued into the millennium as a center for his work.

In Theatresports, two teams compete with the same series of games (performance variations of both Johnstone's own and Spolin's exercises) and are then judged by knowledgeable improv or theatre insiders who give each team points for their improvisational skills. An MC calls for suggestions from the audience for various scenes. The individual games, however, can still be fairly process-oriented. Johnstone used the idea of a sports tournament as a structure for involving the audience and creating a shape to the performance, but he was also interested in telling stories and pushing boundaries. Chudnow's ComedySportz, by contrast, used the sports analogy to structure foolproof entertainment.

Chudnow was a comic actor and writer who cofounded the Kentucky Fried Theater with several fellow students, including Jim Abrahams, David Zucker, and Jerry Zucker, at the University of Wisconsin–Madison in the late 1960s. Kentucky Fried Theater used informal improvisation and written sketches to create vaudevillian satires of popular culture. The troupe's outrageous parodies are examples of "Boomer humor." From the '60s to the '80s, according to historian Tony Hendra, boomer humorists created comedy that was "peculiar to the post-war or Baby Boom generation . . . at various times described as 'black,' 'radical,' 'underground,' 'tasteless,' 'sophomoric,' 'gross,' 'Communist,' 'anarchist,' . . . and 'sick' " (2).

As students in the late '60s and early '70s, Chudnow, Abraham, and the Zuckers enjoyed a certain reputation of radicalism as their pointed social satire reveled in such taboo subjects as sex, venereal disease, and excrement. Successful in Wisconsin, the Kentucky Fried Theater headed for Hollywood in the late 1970s, where Chudnow broke with his colleagues over artistic differences, ironically, on the eve of their success with *Kentucky Fried Movie.* Despite their youthful iconoclasm, however, neither Chudnow nor his former colleagues would pursue comedy as a platform for political satire, even at the relatively mild level of their contemporaries at Second City or *Saturday Night Live.* The Zucker brothers went on to make the slapstick comedy *Airplane!* and other film projects, while Chudnow looked for a new outlet for his comic muse.

After a halfhearted stint as a stand-up comedian in Los Angeles, a job he called "one of the loneliest in the world," Chudnow returned to his home in Milwaukee to join his father's family business, Chudnow Iron and Metal (Blinkhorn). He was teaching some informal improv workshops and looking for a fresh start in comedy when Chris Keane, a friend from his university days, introduced him to Theatresports. Chudnow had always enjoyed the spontaneity and troupe/audience interaction of improvisational comedy, the basis of much of his favorite work with the Kentucky Fried Theater. He saw both great potential and serious problems in Johnstone's concept. As he remembers, "I think we saw it in Vancouver first; there was a tournament, and I remember thinking, 'This is really interesting, but it's not a show'—it's like you're watching a workshop and two teams, competing for points, that are very serious about improv. They're judged on their improv skill, not their entertainment [value]" (personal interview).

But the energy of the competition excited him. In 1984, Chudnow and several colleagues decided to put together their own interpretation of the sports format in Milwaukee. When Chudnow called Theatresports organizers in Canada to ask permission to start his own Theatresports troupe, the Canadians gave the new team their blessing. They immediately invited the Milwaukee players to participate in an upcoming Theatresports tournament in Toronto, where teams from Seattle and several Canadian cities would compete on a large scale. But in the months before the tournament, Chudnow and company developed their own brand of competitive improv, making it at once more theatrical and more of a real sport than the Canadian version: "I knew if I did it here [in Milwaukee], I'd have to change it drastically because audiences here wouldn't accept that it was improv—they never heard of that—it's a sports town, so we'd have to make it a sport" (personal interview).

Chudnow wanted to preserve the thrill of improv's spontaneity and presence while transforming the image of its performance style from amateur workshop/games/process to professional entertainment/sports/product. He devised a sports-based overlay that was far more comprehensive than the competitions of Johnstone's Theatresports. He introduced new terminology, uniforms, a uniformed referee, an AstroTurfed stage, and audience-initiated "fouls." But these trappings were only the most superficial changes. Chudnow created extensive rules governing the speed and duration of scenes and designed to keep the action interesting. He dispensed with purist notions about serious, authentic improv and was frank in his deliberate focus on comedy. Moreover, he created a show with a narrative structure, giving spectators a social drama to enjoy. As Chudnow told the *Daily Cardinal* in 1986, "In Canada the show is all middle. They don't have the sports analogy that we do. Here we've got a beginning, a middle and an end" (Olson 6).

Chudnow acknowledges that in 1984 his timing was finally right. In Chicago, ImprovOlympic had already established a firm foothold, and a number of other small improv troupes created in Second City's image were flourishing. Stand-up comedy was proliferating in comedy clubs throughout the United States, but there was no regular comedy performance available in Milwaukee. Chudnow's packaging of comedy with the wholesome, all-American trappings of a ball game appealed to the conservative Reagan-era values particularly prevalent in much of the Midwest. Many Milwaukeans who had never attended live performance in a theatre were comfortable with the idea of attending a sports event. And Chudnow was careful to market his comedy as clean, family entertainment.

The tone of Chudnow's new enterprise was rambunctious, but much more conservative than his earlier work with Kentucky Fried Theater. For Chudnow, this shift reflected less a philosophical change than a pragmatic one.

Ever the showman, Chudnow knew his Midwestern audience and was determined to respond to their tastes and desires.

Chudnow launched his altered version of competitive improv-comedy in the back room of Kalt's, a Milwaukee family restaurant. The new company consisted, Chudnow recalls, of "anyone who showed up to the first meeting," including Karen Kohlberg of Friends Mime Theatre and actor Jon Banck. Calling themselves TheatreSportz, the hodgepodge group of actors and amateurs concentrated on keeping the action moving and the spectators involved—and hit upon a winning combination. Chudnow credits their early success to the new format: "We were sold out almost right away from the very start—because even if the show didn't work, the format worked. And that's the problem with improv. If the improv doesn't work, you're dead. . . . People want to come out and laugh—they don't want to see death. So even if the improv didn't work, it only didn't work for three minutes—and you were on to another game" (personal interview).

Excited with his success, Chudnow took his group to the Theatresports tournament in Toronto, where he urged the Canadian players to make similar adjustments to their style of play: "I said, 'You guys gotta change this and do it the way we're doing it. You can make money doing this!' And they looked at me like I was nuts. They said, 'You can't. You can't make money doing this.' And I didn't know if they meant 'You can't make money doing this because it's not morally right or philosophically right' or 'It's just too hard to make money doing this.' I never knew what they meant, but they didn't want any part of it" (personal interview).

Johnstone's players probably did have a philosophical problem with Chudnow's frank commercialism. Loosely organized, Theatresports never achieved the commercial or institutional status of ComedySportz, although Theatresports groups are active in an increasing number of cities in Canada, Australia, Europe, and the United States. With the exception of the Loose Moose theatre itself, and a handful of professionalized endeavors in the United States, Theatresports remains an ad hoc amateur or educational activity for most of its players. For many Theatresports aficionados, amateurism is a conscious choice. These players retain their claim on pure and authentic improv precisely by resisting some of the modifications Chudnow made to achieve financial success.

Chudnow and his team returned to Milwaukee and changed their name from TheatreSportz to ComedySportz (immediately copyrighting both the name and the format). Chudnow says he added the *z* because "we in Milwaukee drink Blatz and Schlitz . . . and we have ComedySportz" (qtd. in Cole 4). The next year, when the Milwaukee group wanted to compete in the Theatresports tournament, they were rejected as being too different from the official style to participate, and Chudnow was on his own.

Even before the name change, Chudnow sponsored a separate Theatre-Sportz team, in Madison, Wisconsin, which was well received by the community. Starting with midweek performances at bars and restaurants such as the Hoffman House and Zinger's (where they sold out the house), they later moved to the upstairs dining room of a local Pizza Hut, where the troupe was able to set up a semi-permanent arena. As in Milwaukee, the ComedySportz team would take the gate or ticket income from shows, while the hosting restaurant would receive all the income from the sales of food and drink.

While many on the Milwaukee team were hobbyists—players included a lawyer, a Marquette University psychology professor, a social worker, and a teacher—Madison players tended to be students from the University of Wisconsin with a strong interest in theatre careers (Rath). Early audiences reflected the differences in personnel and venue. In 1986, Chudnow described his Milwaukee audiences as "yuppies" attending a cabaret, while the troupe at Zinger's played to a much younger, student bar crowd (Olson 6).

Like Shepherd's original vision for Improv Olympics, Chudnow's dream was that ComedySportz would someday catch on as a real sport, with teams and leagues throughout the country and at all levels. Madison's first team manager, Mike Rock, articulated the expansionist idea, asserting, "Eventually, I'd like to see it in high schools with the forensics team, drama club and TheatreSportz team" (qtd. in Wilcox). In 1986, Milwaukee business entrepreneurs Pat and Maureen Riordan went into partnership with Chudnow, investing in the ComedyLeague of America (CLA), a corporation designed to syndicate ComedySportz teams throughout the United States. In the first phase, the CLA set up teams in seven cities. But this sudden growth proved to be too much, too fast. Chudnow recalls, "[The Riordans] hired managers in different cities, and it was unmanageable. We had seven different cities, and they all would send their money to us, and we were supposed to pay all their players. We had hundreds of employees. It was totally unwieldy. We didn't know the managers we hired—they'd come in for one interview, and they were running this team, and some of them were nuts. It was just a mess" (personal interview).

Chudnow bought the Riordans out in 1988, eliminated several of the cities deemed too far away to be supervised or too badly managed, and started sending his own experienced players to manage other cities. Often, when Milwaukee players had to leave town for business or personal reasons, Chudnow would encourage them to start a team wherever they were going. Fed up with the cumbersome centralized administration of income and salaries, Chudnow created a franchise system, "So each [manager] owns it as their business and they pay us a royalty, just as you would pay a royalty if you performed 'Arsenic and Old Lace' or whatever play you were doing" (qtd. in Cole 4).

Chudnow uses the term "royalties," but his actual arrangements with satellite teams resembled those of the franchise restaurant chains, such as Pizza Hut or Wendy's, that often hosted those teams' performances. ComedySportz teams agreed to use a common name, to receive training, guidance, or assistance from the parent company, and to pay a fee to ComedySportz. Some paid a percentage of their income, while others were charged a flat fee.

Chudnow unashamedly linked the dissemination of his brand of improv to business and profit making. In this way, ComedySportz diverged still further from the ethos of Theatresports, whose teams were philosophically but not financially connected to Johnstone's group in Canada. But ComedySportz players also shared the wealth—routinely getting paid a percentage of ticket income. As with any chain, Chudnow worked to systematize his process and homogenize the ComedySportz performance product. But improvisers were not always easy to control, especially from a distance.

By 1990 there were fourteen ComedySportz teams nationwide. Chudnow posed for a photograph in the *Milwaukee Sentinel* in front of a large map of the United States, with red pins marking teams from San Jose to Dallas to Washington, D.C. "I've always wanted a map with colored pins stuck in it," he told the reporter. "I think about this day and night. I dream about it. . . . Every city is going to have a ComedySportz. And the headquarters will be—Milwaukee!" (qtd. in Blinkhorn 8). By 2000, there were twenty-six pins on Chudnow's map.[5]

Although Chudnow resists taking financial responsibility for his offspring, he tries to supervise the consistency of the ComedySportz style and philosophy. Each potential franchise owner must persuade Chudnow that he or she is capable of running the business. The new owner then receives the three-hundred-page manual in a large loose-leaf notebook. This ComedySportz bible details every aspect of ComedySportz style and procedure, listing games, rules, and fouls and outlining the roles of referees, managers, and "actletes." The manual also contains an extensive discussion of ComedySportz philosophy about improvisation, comedy, and business. Prospective managers who are not known to Chudnow are required to make the pilgrimage to Milwaukee to attend performances and rehearsals. In addition, they usually must pay the transportation costs to have Chudnow, or one of his assistants, come to their city to approve the casting of the first team and to spend a week training them and helping to set up ongoing workshops. Chudnow also gives managers helpful hints, urging them, for example, to start at a small venue, so that a handful of spectators would make the room look full. Above all, he tries to be sure the managers and players "have the best interests of the show at heart" (qtd. in Cole 4).

But the franchise expansion had its own growing pains. Most new managers had little or no business experience, and teams often faltered without financial support from Milwaukee. As the number of teams proliferated, it became increasingly difficult for Chudnow to supervise artistic decisions or troupe dynamics. Moreover, each new city presented a unique financial and entertainment context that could not be provided for by any uniform set of policies.

Each franchise became the personal project of a committed owner/manager who sometimes doubled as artistic director. Richard Gardner, the owner of the Raleigh, North Carolina, franchise, had no training in theatre or business. He was a chemical engineer who was inspired to launch a troupe after seeing the Kansas City team perform. It took eight months for Gardner to convince Chudnow to give him a franchise. But once the team was started, he says, Chudnow was extremely helpful, assisting with training and even visiting Raleigh twice a year to "keep tabs" on the new company (Cole 4). Madison improviser Jay Patrick had a lot of theatre training but little business experience when he struggled to launch his franchise in Hartford, Connecticut, in 1987. But Patrick, a stranger in Connecticut, found it difficult even to gather a cohesive team, and the Hartford franchise soon folded. Patrick then moved to Boston, where the venture managed to take root. "I'm not living off this yet. I still have a day job," he told the *Milwaukee Sentinel* in 1990. "But all my players are getting paid something and we all have the same vision, to make this a full time thing" (Cole 4). Later, Chudnow personally recruited a replacement manager in Boston when Patrick became ill.[6]

The Chicago ComedySportz team came onto the field in 1986. True to form, the new franchise was initiated by Milwaukee-trained improviser David Paul "DP" Knudson. But, unlike other franchises, which often introduced the idea of professional improv-comedy to a city, the Chicago team had to find a niche in the home of Second City. By 1986, Chicago hosted a burgeoning group of small Second City clones—including offshoots from the Player's Workshop, ImprovInstitute, and the already important ImprovOlympic. Liz Cloud, an early member of the Chicago ComedySportz team, believes that the support system from ComedySportz central in Milwaukee was far from adequate. She remembers, "DP kind of thought he could just come here and ace Chicago . . . but it was an incredible uphill battle . . . he had no business training, he had sort of a science background—and improv. He was launched in Chicago, and it was kind of 'Go ahead. Rock Chicago.' But he really had no support—he had to do it all on his own" (personal interview).

When Cloud joined the company as an original member in 1986, Chicago's ComedySportz team appeared in three separate locations in one year, undermining their efforts to build a following. This constant shifting was partly a result of ComedySportz' national policy never to pay rent for performance space, but to find a gate and food and drink split with a local bar or restaurant. But this Milwaukee-based business approach did not work as easily in Chicago. By the mid-eighties, there were so many small companies in Chicago vying for space and attention that such arrangements were difficult to find. Once in a space, if a troupe did not immediately produce lucrative crowds, the restaurant's management was likely to ask to the company to make room for a fresh source of entertainment.

Cloud believes that the undercapitalized nature of the ComedySportz assault on Chicago had an adverse effect on both the artistic output and the gender relations in the company. As talented an improviser as Knudson was, he was suddenly thrust into the multiple role of artistic director, business manager, and marketing director. A director who is so overextended, Cloud explains, tends to "fall back on expediency. You're just trying to make it work; you don't have any time for anything else" (personal interview). Cloud felt in particular that Knudson did not pay enough attention to the power dynamics and locker-room atmosphere of ComedySportz, factors that often intimidated the women players. She retired from the team—temporarily.

Throughout the '80s and much of the '90s, ComedySportz teams in many cities were dominated by young, white, heterosexual men who often created such a powerful locker-room culture that women felt shut out. During her time at Chicago ComedySportz, Cloud says that the boys' club atmosphere made her feel she simply was not talented at improv and that "the women kind of cowered in a corner a lot." She describes the ambiance this way:

First of all, it means that all the guys really get along well, and they all talk this lingo. They have this buddy-buddy thing, and they do this joke thing—not all of them, but the core, the influential group does. If you're a woman, you can be a "snotass" and try to zing it right back—[but] I'm a nice girl and nice girls don't do that. Nice girls are just nice. I don't know how to speak that language . . . I felt like an intruder. And I felt like I didn't really have much voice. If I happened to be beautiful, that would have been one thing; I would have been given honorary permission to enter. But I wasn't beautiful. I wasn't a babe. (personal interview)

Women who survived in this atmosphere, says Cloud, were "women from the Southside" who were "tough" and willing to act in ways that many perceived as masculine (personal interview). In many ways, this came down to an issue of class. "Southside" is code for working-class and often minority neighborhoods. White, middle-class women often have the most trouble overcoming their training in "ladylike" or "good-girl" behavior in order to compete or bend the rules.

In 1990, Knudson threw in the towel, abruptly informing his team that the game was over. But the players, led by popular comedian David Gaudet, were eager to continue. Gaudet agreed to take artistic responsibility, but the group needed a financial backer. Together with business partner Jill Shely, Cloud returned to purchase the Chicago franchise, hoping her investment would help change the "frat boy" control of the company. The new owners moved the team to the Congress Hotel, where it performed successfully for several years. Because she did not feel qualified to direct the troupe, Cloud counted on Gaudet to provide leadership. Determined to create and market a success-

Gary Kramer, manager of the San Diego team, looks on as Chicago manager Dave Gaudet hoists ComedySportz founder Dick Chudnow. ComedySportz players from all over the United States gathered with celebrity guests for a 1998 benefit for Gilda's Club. Photo: courtesy Chicago ComedySportz.

ful comedy product, the young director ignored Cloud's desire to create a safer process. Gaudet was having fun with ComedySportz and found it hard to understand why anything should change (personal interview). From his viewpoint, Cloud was "like an opera singer in a rock group. She didn't connect with the ComedySportz audience" (personal interview). Unable to transform ComedySportz culture, Cloud finally sold out to Shely and Gaudet in 1991 and later became a founding member of the Free Associates, a woman-friendly third-wave troupe.

Since 1990, ComedySportz has been a solid and comparatively well-paying fixture of the Chicago improv-comedy scene. Moreover, quite a few of the leaders of Chicago's third wave of improv-comedy have emerged from the ComedySportz national franchise system. Many young actors throughout the United States are introduced to the basics of improv performance through local ComedySportz teams. Those who become serious about improv as an art form and yearn to explore it further often migrate to Chicago. A number of regional ComedySportz players arrived in the late '80s and '90s, only to abandon the limited ComedySportz format as soon as they were able to take advantage of Chicago's varied and sophisticated improv community.

Jill Shely, owner/partner and Joey Meyer referee at Chicago ComedySportz. Inspired by Johnstone's status hat games, the frequent use of silly hats to create improv characters is unique to ComedySportz and Theatresports. Photo: courtesy Chicago ComedySportz.

Stepping up his efforts to supervise teams in more than a score of cities, Chudnow formalized the ComedyLeague of America and instituted national meetings, conventions, and annual tournaments hosted by a different team each year. In 1999, for example, eighty-four representatives (nineteen female and sixty-five male) from twenty-two cities converged in Portland, Oregon, for a tournament that featured workshops, performances, jam sessions, social activities, ComedySportz songs, and merchandise.[7]

A sporadic ComedyLeague newsletter also announces the invention of new games, new locations, inspirational quotations, and even births, engagements, and weddings among its constituents. Despite these efforts at enforcing a unified vision, regional teams began to evolve in distinctive ways, even bending or breaking Chudnow's rules to fit their own preferences.

Milwaukee ComedySportz prospered and grew at a steady pace. In 1992, Chudnow was finally able to open his own facility on Jefferson Street. A large brick warehouse was converted into a stadium with two playing spaces, a game room with a pool table and video games, and a fully equipped bar/restaurant that sells "Comedy Cuizine."

The Milwaukee team became more professional over time, with players receiving salaries based on a percentage of the ticket income, usually 3 or 4 percent of the gate per player. Still, for most team members, this was not a living wage. Some players make additional income teaching in the Comedy-Sportz Training Center, where high school students and adults can take beginning, intermediate, and advanced classes in the basic skills of improvisation and comedy performance, including mime, object work, scene building, and the specific techniques needed in various games. Chudnow extends the sports connection to the ideal way of learning and rehearsing these techniques: "We run our practices like sports practices: we drill. You have to drill on these things; you can't expect people to go up and do these games without any training or working on these skills. You can't get up and bunt without working on bunting and doing it and doing it and doing it and doing it" (personal interview). ComedySportz players also study the foundational concepts derived from Spolin and Johnstone, including agreement, teamwork, groupmind, status, and flow.

In Madison, Chicago, and most other cities, ComedySportz teams offer classes both as an important source of income and as a method of cultivating new players in a farm team or minor league. Promising students are placed on teams that present exhibition games, and may then be drafted onto the mainstage teams.

For all improv troupes, the biggest challenge is often to reconcile pressing economic needs with the artistic goals of the company. Chudnow recognized the duality of his enterprise from the very beginning. In the ComedySportz franchise manual, the first page bears the ComedySportz vision and philosophy. Chapter 1 begins this way:

> There are two basic facts to remember when thinking ComedySportz:
> COMEDYSPORTZ IS A SPORT
> COMEDYSPORTZ IS A BUSINESS
> If it is run as one, to the exclusion of the other, its days are numbered. (Chudnow)

It remains Chudnow's goal fully to professionalize his Milwaukee company, allowing players to spend their days practicing instead of working at day jobs. He tries to supplement player income by marketing touring performances designed for business functions and characters that can be hired as individual entertainers. A marketing brochure announces, "We've custom tailored shows for anything from national sales conventions, training seminars, banquets, holiday parties, even company picnics [sic]. What's more our show is completely portable—we've played arenas, theaters, restaurants, hotels, cafeterias, gymnasiums, even living rooms. All in the name of good business" (brochure copy). At the bottom of the brochure, a list of satisfied customers includes Apple Computer, Intel Corporation, IBM, Hewlett Packard, Club Med, Microsoft, and the Bernstein Bat Mitzvah.

In 1987, *Milwaukee Magazine* reported Chudnow's plans for creating surplus commodities, including "hats; shirts; pre-game betting (if gambling is legalized); CSZ cards, a variation of baseball cards; and laugh bucks, coupons bearing actlete's mugs and good for CSZ merchandise. Soon fans will be able to purchase laugh insurance, too" (Ratay 39). By 1996, the hats and shirts were available, along with pennants and sweatshirts (though not the cards or insurance yet).

For most teams outside Milwaukee, a rent-free venue depends partly on the conspicuous consumption by ComedySportz fans of their hosts' food and drink. In Madison, for example, players and programs expressly encouraged audiences to buy Wendy's refreshments when the team played in its dining room. As part of the *Refspiel*, the fans were asked to sing this:

> Take me out to see improv
> Take me to CSZ
> Buy me a "FROSTY" and let the jokes fly
> I don't care if I laugh 'til I die . . .

A variety of Wendy's products were substituted for "Frosty" at each performance. In Milwaukee, ComedySportz touts its own Comedy Cuizine, which includes both family fare and alcoholic beverages. Chudnow told one reporter, "We'd like to be recognized as the McDonald's of entertainment" (Holmstrom 14). Business success is more than just an expedient for Comedy-Sportz players; it is an integral part of its vision and spiritual philosophy.

In *Sport, Society, and the State,* John Wilson summarizes the Marxist argument: "The capitalization of sport means the separation of the worker-player from the means of production and the transformation of the fan into the customer. Sport becomes a business" (18). According to Wilson, Marxist and Weberian theories demonstrate that sport, "so popularly associated with the notion of agency (of individual freedom, spontaneity, and impulsiveness) is highly structured, if not administered, behavior" (18). This interpretation of professional sports undermines improvisers' frequent reference to sport as an analog to the freedom and spontaneity of play.

As the founder of ComedySportz, Chudnow sees no contradictions among the goals of capitalism, sports, and improvisational comedy. He deliberately uses a sports motif to help commodify the playful, gamelike qualities of improvisation. In fact, Chudnow is eager to maximize the capitalist implications of sports in his comedy context. The ComedySportz franchiser's manual admonishes, "As grandiose as it may seem to you now, let's believe we are in the forefront of the new wave of entertainment. You are part of a budding business. A growing corporation. A coming phenomenon" (Chudnow 10).

In a comic spirit, but seemingly without irony, ComedySportz players incorporate the idea of selling into their concept of playing. Each performance begins with the audience-interactive game of Vending, where players mingle in the crowd in imitation of hotdog or peanut vendors in a ballpark. Chudnow feels that vending is a crucial way to get spectators into the participatory mood: "I go right for someone who's sitting with their arms folded and looking ticked that someone brought them there . . . and I don't leave that person 'til I get them to smile. And that's my goal in going out and vending—it's to get to those people" (personal interview).

In his five-page "Notes for Players," Rock instructs his team members on the similarities between vending and performing: "We are salespeople. We have to believe in what we are selling. We have to believe the reality. If we don't believe it, no one will" (1). Performer-spectator interaction takes the overt form of a business transaction. Consumption is the clear means to cultural participation and inclusion.

Sports sociologist Richard Lipsky writes, "Sports, as a social drama . . . is an analogical world that dramatizes the dominant values in an arena that excludes much of what is problematic in real life. . . . The sports aesthetic can be seen as facilitating the internalization of the 'proper' attitudes towards mobility, success, and competition. In this way, sports is the *symbolic* expression of the values of the larger political and social milieu" (83). While the improv-comedy context might imply a satirical critique of mainstream society, ComedySportz almost always presents dominant values concerning capitalism, religion, and nation as well as race, gender, and difference—in the naturalized package of an all-American ball game.[8]

ComedySportz performances are competitive on several levels. Officially, the competition itself is primarily a performance for the audience's benefit. "Notes for Players" insists, "Don't be afraid to fail. It's part of the games. Remember 'We want to win, but we don't mind if we lose' " (Rock 4). Since the referee may assign points and fouls at random, actual scoring is clearly not serious in these games. But, despite Rock's assertion, winning can be. Spectator judges vote for the winners of each game, and, unofficially, teams and individuals can be said to score laughs in performance. This laughter operates as ComedySportz currency. Because they believe successful comedy leads to bigger audiences and better income, laugh-getters at ComedySportz achieve status and power within the group. Despite the emphasis on team play, individual stars emerge as audience favorites. Moreover, the competition for laughs can sometimes become less a conceit of the sports analogy and more a genuine rivalry among players.

The power of comedy currency is reflected in the aggressive male dominance in ComedySportz, particularly because many male players believe that women are *not funny.* Liz Cloud remembers that her actual ownership of the team bore little weight in her interactions with players because she was still perceived as a weak and effeminate performer. When she negotiated with artistic director Gaudet, hoping to make ComedySportz operating procedures more nurturing for inexperienced and intimidated (mostly women) players, Cloud says she interpreted the thought process behind Gaudet's reaction this way: "She's sucky at ComedySportz; why should I pay any attention to her? It's working fine for me. What is she talking about, and what does she mean by 'nurture'? If they can't cut the mustard, why are they here?" (personal interview). Gaudet ruefully admits rejecting Cloud's idea: "In the beginning . . . I was twenty-three years old, I had just gotten out of school and knew nothing other than the fact that I was really good at making audiences laugh. I had never been in charge of anything like that. I was this BMOC fraternity guy. I was the poster child for everything that Liz is saying, I guess" (personal interview). But Gaudet adds that he has learned a lot since then.

ComedySportz rhetoric is full of the ruthless positivism associated with motivational speakers—often sports and business figures—who insist that success is a simple matter of mental attitude. For ComedySportz, the credo of

"Yes" is more than the improv-comedy rule of agreement; it is a pervasive philosophy. Chudnow's manual asserts,

"No" is the stopsign of life.

"YES" sets things in motion. If you believe in the art, the science, the religion of improvisation, you know nothing moves until someone says: "YES . . . and. . . ." (Chudnow)

Chudnow proclaims, "Nothing . . . no one . . . can stop us from achieving our goals . . . from what we want to do. Except ourselves" (Chudnow). And Rock's "Notes" are filled with such aphorisms as "Be positive. Don't let a negative thought enter your head" (1).

ComedySportz managers often distribute inspirational materials showing sports figures and others who have succeeded in the face of adversity. One packet for the Madison team included a quote from Christian Larsen's "Creed for Optimists" (which tells how you can be *"somebody"* by always looking on the "sunny side of everything"), several poems about the power of positive thinking, and a story about the day Michael Jordan "cried behind closed doors" but still did not give up (Jordan had been cut from his high school basketball team).

The message of all of this material is the same—success in sports, in comedy, and in business is a matter of individual commitment and determination. Much of ComedySportz' rhetoric echoes the language of "prosperity activities," the translation of New Age self-spirituality into empowerment in the marketplace (Heelas 62). Historian Paul Heelas notes that New Age leaders from Werner Erhard to Deepak Chopra have offered seminars, books, and training techniques designed to help followers "attain success and abundance through spiritual growth" (64).

Critics of New Age individualism point out, "When personal consciousness is the single determining factor in social change, then all social problems, including the specters raised by racism, imperialism, sexism, and homophobia, are seen as the result of personal failures and shortcomings. Individual consciousness becomes the source, rather than a major site of socially oppressive structures, and the opportunities for a radical humanism is lost" (Ross, "New Age" 546).

But ComedySportz takes the position that social conditions are merely obstacles that can be overcome by hard work and fearlessness. Many of the company's attitudes and practices reinforce the conservative values of individual over social responsibility, even while they valorize groupthink and teamwork. In a related way, the qualities of competitiveness and toughness prized in sports and business reinforce aggressive approaches to ComedySportz, often intensifying the difficulty women find in being included.

Chudnow is a laissez-faire producer, but his personal politics are fairly liberal (improviser Gagné calls him "a gentle, granola kind of refugee from the '60s"). The founder is sometimes dismayed to hear how conservative the values of his players are and has even spoken against the worst homophobia and sexism in the extended company (Gagné interview). Nevertheless, Chudnow insists the ComedySportz format is apolitical.

Unlike the more elitist and leisurely ImprovOlympic, ComedySportz is known for its quickness of play. This speed has a significant impact on the content of its comedy. Chudnow's manual proclaims, "VISION: THE COMEDYLEAGUE OF AMERICA IS DEDICATED TO ENRICHING LIVES AND TRANSCENDING ALL BOUNDARIES BY CELEBRATING THE CREATIVE IMAGINATION OF THE HUMAN SPIRIT . . . IN FOUR MINUTES OR LESS" (Chudnow). The speed and intensity of ComedySportz is entertaining, but it erases shadings and subtleties in representation much the way sports does. Sociologist N. Offen explains, "Sports is a world speeded up and a world of absolutes. There is good and bad, black and white, right and wrong. It's not gray and tentative like the real world. It is hyperlife under glass" (qtd. in Lipsky 87).

Zoe Beckerman quit the Madison team in 1994, offended by her teammates' performances of racist and sexist stereotypes. Fellow players explained that these images emerged "spontaneously" and were virtually impossible to censor given the speed of play (personal interview). Speed and spontaneity are often used as a rationale for the performance of stereotypes. Many ComedySportz players and audiences are convinced there is an implicit truth to these representations because they seem to be intuitive references to popularly held and recognizable beliefs. More often than not, spectators applaud scenes in which their suggestions produce the expected jokes and relationships rather than original or innovative ones.

While gimmick games are extremely popular with audiences, they are particularly susceptible to stereotypes—the mainstay of much popular humor. When Madison player-manager Thompson was assigned to communicate the country of Japan to a fellow player—as only a small part of a long and complex guessing game—he did a three-second sketch of a bowing, slant-eyed samurai. What would have been the three-second sketch of Africa or of Native Americans (or of the United States, for that matter)? Yet, these images do communicate, and often with thrilling immediacy, both to a player's teammates and to the audience.

Cultural theorist Michael Omi explains that "the necessity to define characters in the briefest and most condensed manner has led to the perpetuation of racial caricatures" as many racial stereotypes have long served as shorthand for the producers of television and film (115). Because popular culture is the source of most improvisers' references, these stereotypes are repeated and revalidated by audience laughter and recognition. As Omi points out, "This process is often unconscious; we tend to operate off of an unexamined set of racial beliefs. . . . Ideas about race, therefore, have become 'common sense'—a way of comprehending, explaining, and acting in the world" (113). Players tend not to question the representations that emerge through spontaneous improvisation because, in that moment, they seem like commonsense truths.

Cultural critic and sociologist Pierre Bourdieu sees "the game" as an illustration of the multiple levels of consciousness at play in social interaction. Consciously, social actors may master the overt rules of the game—whether in baseball, improv-comedy, or the "social game" (*Other Words* 63). Yet a player's "feel for the game," a facility which seems to be instinctive or like "second nature," is based on lifelong training and layers of learned habits which are no longer conscious but have become that player's engrained "habitus" or "society written into the body" (*Other Words* 63). Multiple social constructions, including class, race, and gender, define each player's performance in the field, even as he or she makes conscious choices. Bourdieu writes, "Nothing is simultaneously freer and more constrained than the action of a good player" (*Other Words* 63). The good improv-comedy player, too, is always negotiating with both the spoken and unspoken rules beneath the apparent spontaneity of the improvised game. This theory may explain why many women considered good players continually demote themselves to subordinate support roles that seem, in the improvised moment, to be "natural."

Spontaneity is clearly improv's primary selling point. Chudnow describes spontaneity as "almost a meditative state. When you're really doing improv you're just powered by some other force—it's a great feeling." On the other hand, he insists, "we use improv because of its spontaneity. When you're spontaneous, people laugh. . . . It's a vehicle. It's just a vehicle" (personal interview). Cultural theorist John Fiske writes that "the tension between improvisation and structure is a tension between bottom-up and top-down control which has become . . . a legitimated source of pleasure in our culture" (62). Audiences enjoy believing that they are watching something dangerous and risky, in which something uncontrolled or subversive really could happen. Chudnow acknowledges that improvisational performance is historically associated with liberal or even transgressive politics. But ComedySportz, through its sports overlay, not only disallows transgressive performances, it actively produces normative ones.

Chudnow describes the ComedySportz referee as a means of controlling the audience by giving them exactly what they want: "The referee has to reflect the audience. The referee is the audience, so that if the audience isn't liking the scene, the referee should not be liking that scene also. . . . That's pretty much how the audience has to be controlled" (personal interview).

Thus, the spontaneity of the audience is simultaneously encouraged and controlled by the activities of the ref. Moreover, the figure that disciplines the players is clearly in league with the audience. In this way, spectators are encouraged to identify with the official, rather than with the most carnivalesque elements of the performance.[9] While there are two teams on the field, the competition for laughs could also be understood as pitting the audience against the players, with the referee disciplining both.

The illusion of spontaneity and audience control is thoroughly managed through the teaching and practice of "fouls." This procedure can be seen not only as responding to standards of good or bad performance or acceptable subject matter, but as actually creating those values. Much in the way children learn the rules of good and bad behavior in kindergarten by memorization or repetition and then learn to help enforce those values, ComedySportz fans enthusiastically participate in keeping games short, fast, and clean. The question remains, however, whether learning to name and judge the fouls has actually *caused* the audience to look for and reject social transgression (brown bag) or narrative deviance (waffling) where they might not have noticed them before.[10]

Rigorous censorship is overtly acknowledged at ComedySportz through the brown bag foul. Chudnow's manual instructs, "If a Player, or Audience member says something offensive to the Referee or Audience, the Referee should throw the red flag, call the foul, and place a brown paper bag over the offender's head. . . . The audience suggestion, 'sex' should always be bagged. Bag most diseases. Ignore 'aids' [*sic*] and other sensitive suggestions that are better off left alone" (112). Because the action of brown-bagging a suggestion actually draws attention to the subject mentioned, making it an object of teasing and fun, referees ignore subjects they consider too sensitive to produce the illicit laughter that "sex" provides.

Responding to the perceived values of the audience, the referee will immediately stifle any idea he or she considers unacceptable. At a Milwaukee match, for example, a suggestion of the phrase "queer as a three-dollar bill," was rejected with an unusually terse "No." In fact, any suggestion relating to what some would call controversial lifestyles is avoided rather than being *bagged*, as players have been instructed not to engage with these issues at all (though the vagaries of audience suggestion and impromptu performance often result in allusions to forbidden topics.)[11] On the other hand, racial and gender stereotypes are often not officially considered offensive in this context.

For their parts, players are usually self-censoring. They tend to perform comedy designed to appeal to the mainstream values they assume prevail among the majority of the spectators. For example, Jay Patrick, a gay performer who worked in ComedySportz in the early days, states, "If I have to play a 'love' scene with another male player—whether he is defined as a woman in a wig and dress or not—I always play the embarrassment and weirdness of the situation. And it gets a laugh. And that's my job" (personal interview). [12]

ComedySportz is advertised as a family show, as wholesome and all-American as any real sports event. But the awarding of a brown bag foul is often the moment of greatest hilarity and pleasure for the spectators—who frequently test the boundaries of a referee's tolerance for double entendre or toilet humor. Players, too, will flirt with the edge of propriety, often encouraged by audience laughter. In a strange symbiosis, the brown bag foul both protects conventional family values and allows transgression to be all the more titillating. While the spontaneity of improvisation often works to absolve performers of full responsibility for what emerges in a joke or scene, most ComedySportz players are very much in control of their performances, always weighing the entertainment value of scatological humor against the potential offense for each specific audience.[13]

Regardless of the censorship and control mechanisms, Chudnow firmly believes that ComedySportz helps free spectators and performers from their worries and inhibitions. "If I were to rewrite [my] vision statement now," Chudnow said in a recent interview, "it would be 'ComedyLeague of America is dedicated to making people—or allowing people—to have fun and play.' Because people lose their sense of play, they don't play any more. But if you can create a format for people to play, I think that's as beneficial as creating a format for people to think deeply about philosophical and political things" (personal interview).

Religious imagery abounds in rituals that bracket each ComedySportz performance and in the materials that players use to psych themselves up to play. In addition to the biblical aphorisms which appear both in the Milwaukee stadium and in ComedyLeague of America Newzletters, "Notes for Players" exhorts performers to trust themselves, believe in the group, and "Make it easy on yourself. You have suffered long enough. Eliminate your justification of fear. . . . The more style you have, the more you are you. Amen" (Rock 2). The religion of sports blends with the religion of improv and the (New Age) religion of self-improvement, and all these are connected to the American dream of business success through pluck and determination.

Jody Amerling, a ComedySportz performer, athlete, and successful businesswoman, links the spirituality of ComedySportz to the deep sense of flow she feels as a runner. Moreover, she asserts, "Some people go to church on Sunday; they have these belief systems, and through the week you must use [them] in your daily life. ComedySportz is the same way . . . we've got these philosophies. These are religion. These are laws. And if you make these everything, and if you strive for these laws to be a part of your everyday life, things are so much better" (personal interview).

The most important ComedySportz law is "YES*and*—." For many players, this philosophy is a powerful and positive commandment to have courage, take risks, and believe in yourself. Chudnow also admonishes,

The actlete should sacrifice for the good of the team.
The actlete should sacrifice for the good of the match.
The actlete should sacrifice for the good of the show. (11)

For some women who have worked in ComedySportz, the intersection of a sports ethos and the philosophy of "YES" is riskier. While men may be drawn to the team spirit of improv performance as a sport, women performers often must choose continually to sacrifice their own ideas in support of the men, to fight for equal time, or simply to not play.

A number of women say they are more comfortable giving support than taking initiative or focus for themselves. According to Beckerman, women are socialized to be "this supporting thing in the background [who] never takes center stage." Beckerman was a good team player, but shied away from initiating scenes. Her own timidity surprised her: "In any other venue I have not been that kind of performer. But my place was very ingrained when I got there. And I also had no female role model" (personal interview).

"Notes for Players" tells the reader to "Accept all offers. If someone points up, look" (Rock 1). However, giving and receiving offers depends on players' ability and willingness to read each other's signals. Amerling found that her offers were frequently denied by certain players. When she, or her teammate Mary, tried to initiate male roles with a husky voice or muscular walk, teammates would simply endow them as conventional women. Confronted about this, the men explained that they had not understood or recognized the women's signals. Several years before Chicago improvisers would form all-woman troupes like Jane, Amerling mused, "I think it would probably be different if we had an all-woman troupe. Then we could play any character and the audience would see it as normal" (personal interview).

Much of this dynamic may indeed be unconscious and a result of imperfect communication. But when there is a deliberate power play on stage, women who follow the rules of agreement may find it difficult to resist. Those who *deny* conventional gender roles are often ostracized from the group. Beckerman recalls a teammate who was considered too feminist and "shrill." "Every time she came on stage, she'd get 'shot.' And of course, she'd have to die. But I'll give her credit, she kept on trying to get on stage" (personal interview). This phenomenon is not unique to Madison (or to ComedySportz). Canadian Theatresports player Linda Rosenfield remembers, "There's a real lack of trust in women's choices and . . . women's talent. So what happens is you get kneed and elbowed out of scenes, you get killed a lot, asked to exit, sent out. . . . I have learned to survive in my league by playing stereotypical roles—because you get squelched for playing a really strong female role" (Foreman and Martini 135).

The religious, nationalistic, and spiritual imagery surrounding sports makes it all the more difficult for women to be received as comedians within that context—an arena where many feel women do not belong in the first place. Fiske discusses sports fandom as a powerful and pleasurable source of connection and communitas, but notes that it is primarily a masculine formation (86). Women, Fiske suggests, tend to relate to masculine sports fanaticism with mockery, "a valuable tactic in women's strategies for coping with patriarchy in general" (87). "Funny woman" and "sports" are dissonant concepts. A striking example is the infamous incident of comedian Roseanne's comic rendition of the national anthem at a baseball game:

> Baseball is not merely a game, something that is played, but a collective, public, and masculine ritual, a quasi-religious reaffirmation of patriarchy, patriotism, and the myth of our nation's Edenic history. . . . [Roseanne] staged a joke that reframed that ritual event and turned it into something else—a carnivalized moment of leveling, mockery and inversion. By exceeding the limits of play tolerated on that diamond, parodying the gestures of the Boys of Summer, and singing the national anthem less than reverentially—in effect, by being who she was, a comedian, joke-maker, and unruly woman—she violated the space of that ritual. (Rowe 53)

At ComedySportz, funny women have often been viewed with great ambivalence and sometimes with outright hostility.

As Rowe discusses, team sports are linked not only to masculinity but also to national culture and identity. Sports act as "anchors of meaning" in a rapidly changing global culture, and "sport occasions are viewed as counterpoints to change . . . closely connected to the invention of traditions that attempt to bind the past and present together" (Jarvie and Maguire 152–53).

For many Americans, rooting for the home team is the most tangible, recognizable way they can express national consciousness, particularly in a country that is not unified by ethnicity, race, language, or religion.

In 1972, Title IX regulations required gender equity in men's and women's sports programming in federally funded education. Implementation of this law has been slow and incomplete; still, women's place in sports has visibly grown. Girls coming of age in the '80s and '90s had far more opportunity to participate in sports than their older sisters (or mothers) had, though still far less than boys. These levels are mirrored in ComedySportz participation. Until the late '90s, women were outnumbered in most ComedySportz teams by a ratio of more than six to one. In recent years, a few teams have approached gender balance, though nationwide it is still unusual to see more than one woman on the ComedySportz playing field at a time. Despite some progress, the model of competitive sports can still serve to reinforce improv's tendencies toward male dominance.

According to sports psychologist Don Sabo, traditional sports are a significant medium of male socialization, teaching "conformity to patriarchal values" and shaping "men's individual and collective behavior and consciousness along the lines of male dominance and sexist values" (qtd. in Oglesby 129). For women, on the other hand, sports are "negatively encoded in female gender appropriate schemas . . . the domain of boys and tomboys" (Oglesby 130). Girls often shift away from sports at puberty, when many are anxious to demonstrate their "date-ability." Sports, comedy, and improvisation all challenge rules for acceptable femininity in terms of their aggressive verbal and physical behavior. Sandra Bartky writes that society disciplines women through "a regulation of the body's size and contours, its appetite, posture, gestures and general comportment in space, and the appearance of each of its visible parts. . . . Feminine movement, gesture and posture must exhibit not only constriction, but grace and a certain eroticism restrained by modesty: all three" (67).[14]

Canadian Theatresports player Barbara Scott speaks from personal experience: "Funny women are scary. Because they tend to be bigger, not necessarily like you have to be fat to improvise, but they present themselves—they have a bigger aura, a louder voice, and that intimidates. [But] when guys are funny, it's sexy" (qtd. in Foreman and Martini 141).

As Chudnow interprets it, "women may be a little less comfortable with their bodies in doing improv." Recent advances in comedy notwithstanding, he concedes that "women were taught that they shouldn't be funny, they shouldn't be silly, they shouldn't be clowns—you shouldn't make yourself look funny. I think that's a carryover and it's probably changing now" (personal interview).

Chudnow points with pride to the large percentage of women "in the pipeline" (personal interview). More women than men take the ComedySportz workshops, and the numbers of girls and boys in the high school program is roughly equal. At the Madison high school workshop I visited in the mid-nineties, while girls were still outnumbered, most of the girls who played seemed generally confident and self-assured. All three girls I interviewed at this workshop were also very active in their school sports programs—two in track and one in swimming.

Ironically, during my 1994 interview with Chudnow at ComedySportz' Milwaukee headquarters, just as we were discussing the gender issue, a teen-age girl from one of the improv classes came over to us. She submitted to an impromptu interview:

GIRL: It's so much easier for men to do comedy—because I think, like, the women suck compared to men. Because the men are so less restricted and uninhibited and a lot less self-conscious. Because you know women are worried about their hair, their nails, their looks and men aren't worried about anything. They're so young, they don't have one bald spot, they don't have to worry about anything. They're physically and mentally loose, and lucid.

Interviewer: And so for you it's harder to forget about how you look when you're up there?

Girl: Oh no, I don't think about me when I'm up there. I just think about everybody else and how much better the guys are than me.

In our spontaneous exchange, this young woman (who never gave me her name) responds as she might in an improvisational scene on stage. Working to appear smart and appealing in the presence of Chudnow, she performs herself as a stereotype, glibly reinforcing the cliché that all girls care about is their looks. Yet, she does not question the underlying social forces that cause girls to value themselves primarily in terms of appearance. She is not yet at the point where she can think of improv as a means to challenge those values.

Despite these hurdles, opportunities for women and people of color to find expression in ComedySportz increased steadily through the 1990s. Growing numbers of women began to emerge in the powerful positions of referee, director, and manager. Quite a few female players are particularly drawn to the referee's somewhat Brechtian ability to stand outside the action, critiquing or commenting on the images and choices the improvisers present.

Throughout the decade, individual teams around the United States also developed their own codes for interaction and their own variations on fouls, rules, and agreement. Boston, for example, has a far more liberal policy on references to "alternative lifestyles," and the women from Boston Comedy-Sportz were often more assertive than those in the Midwest. Teams in Texas, California, and Oregon moved away from the "boys' club" atmosphere sooner than others, welcoming women, a number of gay men, and several players of color. Not coincidentally, ideas about sports and who gets to play were themselves slowly beginning to change in American society.

In Chicago, Gaudet and his team fought to define a style of playing that would both succeed with the audience and help to build a strong ensemble. From 1993 to 1995, the troupe performed at the Improv, the Chicago branch of a series of nightclubs that featured stand-up, not improv-comedy (its name a source of much genre confusion for comedy fans). Audiences expecting to hear jokes about sports would often boo the ComedySportz players when they tried to present Chudnow's format. Gaudet recalls, "We changed our show so that every second of it was funny—it was a frenetic pace" (personal interview). The strategy worked, but the speed and pressure exacerbated gender tensions in the company. Dismayed by accusations of sexism and the departure of several key female players, Gaudet began to realize that he could no longer "foster growth within the group" without addressing gendered issues of playing style, communication, and backstage behavior (personal interview).

Co-owner Shely and veteran performer Joanie Cloonan helped guide a number of candid conversations among the players, while Gaudet made a real effort to move beyond his own "frat boy" attitudes. Gaudet acknowledges that improv can be emotionally vulnerable for both women and men who walk onto a stage with nothing but one another's support. To repair and preserve the all-important feeling of family in his troupe, the director and the other men in the company worked to become more aware of the emotional life of the ensemble.

While Gaudet does not claim the group has entirely solved its problems, he believes Chicago ComedySportz has "gotten a lot better and is a lot better than most in terms of providing a level playing field for women to perform" (personal interview). From the mid-nineties onward, the Chicago team fielded almost as many women as men, and women had a strong presence in management as well. By 1995, Chicago was one of the few national teams with a gender-balanced roster. Gender issues have been raised sporadically at ComedySportz conventions, where women tend to be greatly outnumbered, but there has been little national leadership for addressing the issues. Chudnow's credo is simply "Be Nice," and Gaudet calls the ComedySportz founder "the kindest, gentlest man I've ever known"(personal interview). But Gaudet also wishes that the ComedySportz owner's manual gave instructions on how to manage the power dynamics involved in forging an improv ensemble.[15]

After its rocky start, Chicago ComedySportz began to enjoy some measure of success in that improv-saturated city in the mid-nineties. Gaudet began to focus his energy on marketing the group to corporate clients for parties, training sessions, and industrials. The company's mainstream style was suddenly its biggest asset, as it made improv safe for such companies as Intel, Ameritech, Motorola, Kraft Foods, and Club Med. ComedySportz performers could earn more in a season (up to three hundred dollars per outside show) than their counterparts in Second City touring companies. And ComedySportz did not require players to pay for classes in order to perform (the way Improv-Olympic does).

In the late '90s, the troupe hired part-time artistic directors, including Jim McDonnell, Randy Smock, and Matt Kaye, who (alternating with Gaudet) coached weekly shows at the TurnAround Theatre, and two full-time staff people to manage the marketing, corporate bookings, tours, and classes. But ComedySportz still had an image problem—they were "doing short-form improv in a long-form town" (Semelsberger interview). Some in Chicago's community of improv elitists see short-form improv as inferior and gimmick games as lower still. Other players defend short form, acknowledging that basic games are at the root of all improv and that short form is more accessible and entertaining to a general audience than the Harold—and thus more profitable. The popularity of television's *Whose Line Is It Anyway?* has provided a significant morale boost for ComedySportz players, whose short-form skills most closely match the entertaining mimicry, physical humor, and quick-thinking comprovisation evident on that show.

Nevertheless, the Chicago team members did make several modifications to the ComedySportz format, partly to prove themselves to their artistic colleagues and partly to accommodate local audience taste. Chicago eliminated the "vending" segment, they stopped singing "Take Me Out to See Improv," and—perhaps even more drastic—they no longer covered the stage with AstroTurf. They also added more scene-oriented games to their performance list and deliberately allowed some scenes to go longer than Chudnow's time limits suggest.[16] Keli Semelsberger, a veteran of ImprovOlympic, Comedy-Sportz, and several independent groups, explains, "We really try to do good scenes, but some of the [ComedySportz] games are not about good scenes. They're about failure and pimping. If you take yourself seriously it will kill you. You'll shut down. You've got to enjoy the failure of this game" (personal interview). In improv terminology, *pimping* refers to the deliberate manipulation of a player (forcing him/her to do something embarrassing or difficult) for a laugh. Discouraged in many improv settings, pimping is an accepted part of many ComedySportz games. The audience almost always responds with delight.

DeWaegeneer, associate producer and performer for the Chicago team makes no apology for ComedySportz' popular style: "I like the fact that our show stands for entertainment for the audience. We're not trying to entertain each other. I like when I look out to our audience and I see that it's 90 percent John and Joan Q. Public. I like the fact that I can take our show anywhere—to a corporation, to a church group, to a high school, to any audience—and know that we're not going to offend anybody. ComedySportz is almost always a guaranteed product—complaints are rare. That's nice" (personal interview). DeWaegeneer is unperturbed by the notion that these "inoffensive" perform-ances may affirm a conservative worldview, but concedes, "I like being able to make political and social satire in my classes at Second City" (personal interview).

In 1999, Chicago ComedySportz rented and began to renovate the former Touchstone/Organic Theatre, a two-hundred-seat theatre in the three-story building that once housed the prestigious Steppenwolf Theatre company. The new space opened to the public in 2000. The Chicago team also filed for corporate status and awaited a similar move by the national organization. ComedySportz was going corporate and would soon be reorganized as Come-dySportz North America. According to DeWaegeneer, "The big joke at the national tournament a couple of years ago was to run around chanting 'We are not a cult.' Now it's 'We are not a cult; we are a corporation' " (personal interview).

ComedySportz had a wide-ranging impact on improv-comedy in Chicago and throughout the United States. The franchising system vastly expanded the number of regional audiences and performers involved in the genre, and even provided a mechanism for improvisers to circulate in and out of Chicago and from state to state. At the same time, ComedySportz' aggressive style and macho subculture caused a large number of players—especially women, gay men, and people of color—to seek alternative improv communities. Third-wave improv emerged from perceived gaps between the rhetoric and practice of the second wave, much as the second wave rejected the compromises of first-wave troupes. While the second wave focused on community and spon-taneity, third-wave improvisers questioned improv's claims for free expres-sion and reconsidered the notion of identity teams.

the third wave

Like much late '80s and '90s culture, third-wave improv coalesced not as a radical break from the past, but as a recombination and reinterpretation of ideas from many decades of improv technique and theory. Rather than developing revolutionary artistic ideas, the third wave realigned the structures, goals, and membership of their new companies.

First- and second-wave theatres remained powerfully active throughout this period, but many third-wave players had come to believe that early improv's all-encompassing ideals of spontaneity and community did not, in fact, include them. Unwilling to give up the pleasures of improv, they sought to redefine its workings in terms of newly foregrounded identity positions based on gender, race, sexuality, and generational sensibilities. They addressed improv's power dynamics at the level of player-player interactions on the stage, but, even more important, they recognized the significance of the organizational, economic, and administrative structures of their companies in shaping the very meaning of their art form.

In less than a decade, Chicago had changed from a city hosting a single improv-based comedy theatre to the home of more than a hundred improv troupes. Throughout the '80s, the Second City Training Center and second-wave troupes with their training programs spawned a series of offshoots and imitators. The training center, in which "Level Five" students created their own shows, unintentionally encouraged a number of these students to form groups of their own. (One fairly long-running company even dubbed itself "Level Six.") ImprovOlympic's team system assembled scores of semi-independent troupes that occasionally broke away from the home base. At the same time, players from ComedySportz franchises in Boston, Texas, Milwaukee, and other cities began to migrate to Chicago. Chicago theatre listings showed more than one hundred improv-comedy offerings each week, with troupes on the first- or second-wave model along with emerging third-wave companies. This golden age proved short-lived, however, as the market became saturated and audiences began to dwindle in the early '90s.

The glut of new improv companies vying for attention from the mid-eighties onward made novelty imperative. Troupes had to find a means of distinguishing themselves, particularly if they wanted to be recognized as separate from ImprovOlympic's large stable of teams or from the scores of Second City imitators. Despite the increasing competition, hundreds of would-be improvisers continued to flock to Chicago from around the United States each year, most to enroll in the Second City Training Center, which continued to shape and influence the improv community. Many young improvisers in the '80s and '90s saw Second City both as a career opportunity and as an example of ideals forsaken and vision lost. Developments in Second City's management and methodology had a significant impact on the emergence of the third wave.

In 1990, Andrew Alexander intensified his changes to the Second City organization. He started a Business Theatre wing, which tailored comedy shows and workshops to the needs of local corporations. By 1994, the Business Theatre, also known as Second City Communications, Corporate Comedy, or BizCo, had begun to generate sizeable earnings for the company (W. Smith B22). Alexander also systematized casting and production procedures for Second City's three touring companies (RedCo, BlueCo, and GreenCo) and for the additional resident companies, Second City e.t.c. Stage (opened 1982) and Second City Northwest (1988–95) as well as Second City Toronto (opened 1973) and Second City Detroit (opened 1993).[1]

The Second City Training Center also became a significant income source for Second City, processing thousands of students each year. Sheldon Patinkin handed over the training center reins to Martin de Maat, a director and teacher deeply committed to Spolin's philosophy and trained by Jo Forsberg, Spolin's chosen surrogate. With this renewed emphasis on Spolin's technique, Second City continued what improv critic Adler dubbed a "de-Sahlinization process," slowly trying to recoup its claim to spontaneity on stage.

The absence of a controlling figure as powerful as cofounder and former producer Bernie Sahlins opened the door to other innovations. Many beginning improvisers began to study at more than one place—at Second City, ImprovOlympic, ComedySportz, and other, smaller companies simultaneously. This multiple affiliation encouraged some developing improvisers to compare philosophies and techniques, to use one approach to critique another, and to feel entitled to construct their own approaches to improvisation rather than follow any one method religiously.

Del Close's innovations had changed the landscape of Chicago-style improv and greatly influenced a new generation of improv performers and directors. Many third-wave improvisers were driven by a desire to recapture the original first-wave ethos and to expand the possibilities of second-wave structures. But the Harold was no longer the newest frontier. Players were becoming more ambitious, and local audiences were increasingly sophisticated about the art of improvisation. Aaron Freeman, participant in both first- and second-wave Chicago improv, attributes the emergence of a third wave to this maturation of both the city's improv community and of the genre itself. Third-wave improvisers, Freeman says, are "stealing as much as they can from their parents and grandparents" and reshaping it for their own purposes (personal interview).

As the genre itself matured, the population of Chicago improvisers grew younger. With first- and second-wave companies churning out graduates, the number of players multiplied, and the tastes, values, and experience of a new generation began to influence the output of all Chicago improv companies—most particularly the independent troupes of the third wave. Many believed that second-wave improv, like Second City, had become institutional, hierarchical, and exclusive. Women, people of color, and gay men were now improvising in larger numbers, and many were increasingly unwilling to tolerate their marginalized status not only in the dominant first- and second-wave companies, but in the scores of satellite troupes that comprised mainstream improv in the '80s.

The third-wave surge of independent, alternative improv can be traced to the 1987 founding of the Annoyance Theatre, a company dedicated to high-risk, no-guilt, no-rules improv. In a review of the troupe's long-running original musical comedy, *Co-ed Prison Sluts*, *Chicago Tribune* reporter Sid Smith calls the show "a post-Letterman, post-'Saturday Night Live,' post–Second City, post–*Rocky Horror* entertainment misadventure. . . . [*Sluts* is] part of a package of weekly offerings at Annoyance that seems to be feeding a young, nontraditional theater audience with a new kind of live offering. The aesthetic—raunchy, outrageous, free-for-all and deliberately messy—may be a kind of latter day Second City, the anarchy of its early days somewhat restored, with updated consciousness, for a new generation" ("Beyond the Fringe").

Third-wave improv-comedy includes more than an aesthetic shift; it engages with the complex and critical relationship of structure, power, and identity in improvisation. For Shaun Landry, artistic director of Oui Be Negroes, "third wave" means the crack in the wall that long excluded minority performers from participating in improv. For her, Aaron Freeman's performances at Second City, also in 1987, inspired other performers of color to see this brand of improv-comedy as an option for them.

Anthony Adler, a journalist who has written extensively on improv in Chicago, marks the expansion of long-form improv in the early '90s as the defining feature of a "new wave" of improvisers in Chicago who are "dead serious" about improvisation (" 'How' of Funny" 14). Adler defines this movement as a rejection of Second City's commercially comic short-form approach and a reworking of the spiritual elements of ImprovOlympic's Harold: "After more than three decades during which audiences and entertainers alike came to think of improv as another word for skit-style comedy à la 'Saturday Night Live,' a younger bunch of artists has begun to emerge here with a very different—and much larger—sense of what the form can be and do. . . . For them, improvisation isn't simply a means to a punchline; it's a kind of walking meditation, and process of discovery . . . a way to get at and disclose everything they didn't know they had in them—funny and otherwise" (" 'How' of Funny" 14–15).

Writing in 1993, Adler noted that "most of the new wave has percolated through [Del Close's ImprovOlympic] workshops at one time or another" (" 'How' of Funny" 19). Under Charna Halpern's influence, however, ImprovOlympic, like Second City, was focused on producing marketable entertainment. The new wave of independent troupes resisted Halpern's organizational strategies as well as her financial goals.

The Annoyance Theatre was a pioneer in this new focus on exploration and experiment, while groups such as Jazz Freddy and Ed captivated critics with their commitment to improvisation as a pure art form. Ed soon disbanded, however, and Jazz Freddy disintegrated when core members were cast by Second City's talent-hungry comedy machine. By 1995, only the Annoyance remained.

A crucial factor in the emergence of the third wave was the gradual shift in generational affiliation both of the improvisers and of the audiences who were drawn to the small clubs, bars, back rooms, and theatres where new troupes performed. The founding members of second-wave companies were, for the most part, from the latter half of the baby boom generation, influenced by the societal goals, cultural references, and experiences of that age group. By the mid- to late 1980s and early 1990s, improv-comedy in every wave was increasingly influenced by the age group known to some as "Generation X."

Dubbed "13th Gen" by the authors of one book that tried to define the group, these young people, born between 1965 and 1985, had never known a time before television (Howe and Strauss 23). Their media-saturated lives made them approach live, impromptu theatre with a different hunger for "realness" and an increased skepticism about the possibility of finding it. By 1987, the first crop of Generation X college students graduated from college. A few, like the founders of the Annoyance Theatre, moved to Chicago looking for a way to create their own brand of improvised theatre.

In 1992, a commentator for the *Village Voice* suggested, "The difference between earlier incarnations of hedonists, cynics, and gallows humorists and

[Generation X writers] is one of mainstreaming. What used to be the pessimism of a radical fringe is now the shared assumption of a generation" (Anshaw 25). Writing in the *Drama Review,* Susanna Speier both objects to the term "Generation X" and works to define it: "Generation X is too smart for a manifesto. When I say 'smart' this is what I mean: Post Watergate; Post Family; Post-Post. Foundations are to be doubted. Uncertainty is omnipresent. We have remote control and can flip channels continuously. We've grown up in multiple realities. . . . Trojans are ancient warrior condoms. Mars is a candy bar, descended from a planet named after a Roman adaptation of a Greek god. We are trained to suck up info. We are trained to deconstruct. . . . We contextualize and recontextualize" (3).

Because improv material is dependent on the performers' own experiences and references, this description of Generation X reality helps to explain the pastiche style and cynical tone that characterize much third-wave improv. Third-wave Chicago improv is distinguished by a new intensity, an ambivalent style of humor, and an almost ubiquitous habit of cannibalizing, parodying, or rewriting older forms of entertainment. While most third-wave improvisers still hang onto traditional notions of presence, connection, and originality, they clearly make use of postmodern techniques of double-coding, or a paradoxical approach that "uses and abuses, installs and then subverts, the very concepts it challenges" (Hutcheon, *Poetics* 92).

The postmodern, Generation X influence was felt least, of course, by Second City, which continued to cater to audiences of well-to-do, middle-aged tourists. Dependent as it is on scripted material, the content of Second City shows is also slower to be influenced by a new generation. Yet, in the '80s and '90s, the students who populated Second City's training center and who performed in its touring companies were frequently in their early twenties, and even Second City's mainstage style began to show signs of change. Second-wave theatres, still run by boomers, responded more quickly to the spirit of their younger players. Frequent references to MTV and such Generation X television shows as *The Real World* abounded in ImprovOlympic's sets and ComedySportz' tournaments.

Some players began to dissect the very root of the genre itself—the game. Improviser Dee Ryan, whose improv experience spans all three waves, says that performers started to experiment with "calling the game" on stage (personal interview). Instead of maintaining an illusion of realism layered over a structure or pattern of interaction, actors began to challenge one another by naming their own devices—forcing the action to another reflexive level. For example, a scene might be established where one character is trying every angle to get money out of another, while the second character resists. In an earlier mode of improvisation, once both improvisers realized that this cat-and-mouse interaction was the internal "game" of the scene, they would heighten and enhance the pattern until it reached a dramatic climax and then cooperatively bring the scene to a conclusion. Many teachers urge players to "find the game" of every human interaction.

Later improvisers, however, realized that the audience is often one step ahead of any such classic premise. For the hypothetical scene above, for instance, one of these actors might choose to say—in character—"I see what you're doing. I know you're going to try everything in the book to get that money. I'll tell you right now. There isn't any." In an earlier day, this response would have seemed like bad playing, denying an offer, and undermining the reality of a perfectly good scene. But many later improvisers have enjoyed playing a kind of meta-improv. When an easily predicted pattern is interrupted, the performers are forced to find another angle and may even make calling the game into the new game of the scene.

"Calling it on stage" can also be a useful defensive tactic when a female player feels bulldozed or silenced by a teammate. When complaining backstage proves ineffective, women have encouraged one another to mark or *call* actor-to-actor power abuses right in front of the audience. For example, in a scene with a selfish player, a woman might say—in character—"Gee, I can't seem to get a word in edgewise here," making her experienced reality part of the reality of the scene—an idea much praised in improv teaching. She also puts her scene partner on the spot—and on notice.

Ryan believes this playing with structure and levels of reality is "very postmodern." She explains that this technique is a means of breaking down the reality of a scene by "going in in back" of the representational facade of a performance. Yet, even as this practice may challenge theatrical reality, Ryan believes that "calling the game" is actually truer to real life, because "you're calling attention to what's *actually* happening—which I think is like a postmodern play" (personal interview).

Ryan may be too quick to label this new approach to improv as postmodern. Certainly Brecht and other modernist directors have foregrounded the structures and material reality of artistic production in contrast to the illusions of realistic theatre. But in many ways, the improvisers' motivation bears some of postmodernism's world-weariness. Ryan and her colleagues call the game not to shock complacent bourgeois audiences into recognizing the material labor involved in production, nor to force them to think instead of feel the effects of a melodramatic situation, as Brecht might have done. They do it as a means of grappling with the fragmented world around them.

Elements associated with postmodern cultural expression, including the values of process, indeterminacy, and mutability, can be seen in first- and second-wave improv as well. In particular, ImprovOlympic's Harold creates a semblance of chaos and playful citation. Much of ImprovOlympic's New Age rhetoric is detached from its cultural specificity, as the group reuses archetypes and myths in new combinations. But for ImprovOlympians, there is a definite metanarrative, an original truth that they strive to reconstruct by rearranging fragments of meaning into discoverable patterns. Thus, despite their apparent postmodern style, ImprovOlympic maintains a solid grounding in modernist—even premodernist—ideas of meaning. In fact, it is common for young improvisers to want both the freedom of fragmentation and the reassurance of fixed meaning. They celebrate the fractured nature of a postmodern narrative, but cling to a belief in an essential self, soul, and spirit.

The Annoyance Theatre, however, is more likely to create performances that question the stability of meaning, rejecting the underlying mythic universals so important to ImprovOlympic. For the most part, Annoyance players remain incredulous of the metanarratives that once legitimized social norms and conventions (although the group also has moments of retrenchment from this position).[2] As theatre historian Marvin Carlson summarizes, "[The postmodern] orientation . . . shifts attention from . . . the determination of a general truth or general operating strategy to an interest in 'performativity'—activity that allows the operation of improvisatory experimentation based on the perceived needs and felt desires of the unique situation" (138).

This unfettered, experimental, even post-structural approach is indeed what the Annoyance Theatre wants to explore. They believe, with cultural critic Natalie Crohn Schmitt, that improvisation's emphasis on the moment allows us to "view the world as something that we make at each moment, as we make ourselves. . . . We are not tied by our past, by our future, or by definitions of our identity" (122).

Most third-wave improv troupes, including those in the Annoyance Theatre and the Free Associates, have found success in radical reworkings of mainstream genres. The Annoyance has made its mark with improv-based film and television parodies that take familiar formats to absurd lengths, while the more refined Free Associates came to Chicago's attention with its improvised takeoffs on Tennessee Williams plays. Oui Be Negroes concentrates on deconstructing stereotypical images of blacks on television, film, and in the news media.

Students graduating from colleges in the '80s and '90s were influenced by the changes their baby-boom professors and administrators had wrought on the university system. While many third-wave improvisers did not personally experience '60s activism, they nevertheless were strongly affected by its legacy.

The energy of broader civil rights and feminist movements had for the most part been turned inward, fueling a personal-is-political movement and an identity-politics focus that resulted in academic programs designed to redress the former exclusion of marginalized groups. Women's studies, Afro-American studies, Chicano studies, Asian American studies, and other specialized courses were available—sometimes even required for many college students.

In the same period, as Carlson notes, there was a growing interest in the political and social function of performance, despite a more general postmodern anomie. A surge in performance art was populated mostly by performers "normally excluded by race, class, or gender from consideration by the traditional theatre" (144).

Cultural theorist Stuart Hall writes that the stylistic shift toward the postmodern and postmodernism's "deep and ambivalent fascination with difference" have combined to allow "cultural life, above all in the West, but elsewhere as well, [to be] transformed in our lifetimes by the voicing of the margins" (23). The emergence of African American culture on its own terms and in its own voice can be seen in the '80s and '90s as part of the "cultural politics of difference" (West 204).[3]

Chicago improv, too, was caught up in this movement. At Second City, Alexander and his directors began a focused effort to include people of color in first-wave improv. The "minority male" position that Aaron Freeman had established in the mainstage company was filled by Tim Meadows, an unthreatening, mild-mannered member of the troupe, until 1991.[4] He was joined for a short time by Judith Scott, the first and, until that time, the only African American woman to play the Chicago mainstage.[5]

On Meadows' departure, the mainstage show reverted to an all-white cast. The mainstage minority slot was downshifted to the second-string e.t.c. troupe and cast with local improviser John Hildreth in 1994.[6] There were issues, however, of difference and power in improv that a lone token player could not address. In 1992, Second City established a Minority Outreach Program that recruited a number of players for its touring companies and eventually for the e.t.c. Stage. Additional integration efforts continued into the millennium with varying degrees of success (see chapter 6 for more detail).

As with many performance and political groups in the '80s and '90s, however, some marginalized improvisers were no longer willing to subscribe to the utopian universal truth claims of mainstream improv, but sought to use their own improv performances for more specific ends of self-definition and social commentary.[7] Independent groups, including Oui Be Negroes, Stir-Friday Night, GayCo Productions, ¡Salsation! and Black Comedy Underground, began to emerge as identity-based improv troupes.

Second City's 1989 revue, *The Gods Must Be Lazy*, featured the company's first African American woman, and was the first show to include more than one person of color. Pictured in the front row: Holly Wortell, Joel Murray. Middle row: Chris Farley, Judith Scott, Joe Liss. Back Row: Tim Meadows, David Pasquesi. Photo: Courtesy Jennifer Girard/Jennifer Girard Studio

But for these and other groups just beginning to find their voices through performance, the instability of postmodernism posed a particular problem, undermining the basis from which marginalized people might stage their resistance to dominant ideology. On the one hand, as cultural critic Philip Auslander explains, postmodernism provides opportunities for performers to challenge the legitimacy of all representation and, therefore, to reject the prevailing stereotypes and archetypes that often entrap them. On the other hand, a resistant postmodern performance is, "of necessity, an elusive and fragile discourse that is always forced to walk a tightrope between complicity and critique" (Auslander, *Presence and Resistance* 31). Third-wave improvisers work with parody, masquerade, and camp simultaneously to claim and to comment on their identity positions.

In delineating a third wave of improv-comedy in Chicago, I have focused on troupes that define themselves in opposition to mainstream companies modeled on first- and second-wave rules. Many third-wave improvisers are those whose re-formation of improv structure reflects an interest not only in personal discovery, but in equal opportunity. Freeman's work at Second City and ImprovOlympic blazed a trail for improvisers of color to create their own identities in improv groups like Oui Be Negroes. The tenacity of women improvisers such as Ryan encouraged some women to "call the game" of sexism in other troupes. In a larger sense, the third wave was created by improvisers whose impassioned pursuit of improv's promise of free self-expression had been thwarted in other groups. In fact, most significant third-wave companies conceive of their troupes as havens for players who are misfits— both in the improv community and in the larger society.[8] Whether their inability or unwillingness to "fit" stems from philosophy or identity, most still see improv as a means of finding expression and belonging.

CHAPTER 4

The Annoyance Theatre: carnival of misfit toys

In 1993, the six-year-old Annoyance Theatre company added several new productions to its repertory of original, improv-based comedies and musicals. One of these, *Dumbass Leaves the Carnival*, seemed, despite its title, to be more serious than the others. In fact, it appeared to be a rather dark allegory of the Annoyance troupe's own artistic and financial struggles. This theatrical fable, directed by Annoyance founder Mick Napier, begins with a troupe of carnival performers and freaks who perform joyfully together with such disregard of money that they allow greenbacks to drift unnoticed across the stage. Into their midst comes the evil Coffee, a former playmate who left the carnival years ago and now returns, wealthy, powerful, miserable, and determined to teach these happy misfits the value of money.

One by one, throughout the play, the carnival performers are seduced into trading their pleasure and nonconformist self-expression for another conventional plot and another pile of dollars. A puppeteer must change her idiosyncratic animal characters into the sitcom staples: a heterosexual couple and a wacky neighbor. The midget freak-show operator begins to treat his charges, including a half-man/half-lizard and a dubiously flexible character named Stretch, as commodities rather than friends. All of the performers learn to see their work as a daily grind made of drudgery instead of dreams.

In his review of *Dumbass Leaves the Carnival*, *Chicago Reader* arts critic Jack Helbig compares the play and its message to serious political works by Brecht, such as *The Caucasian Chalk Circle* or *Threepenny Opera*. He writes that "*Dumbass* is clearly Napier's anguished protest against a system that teaches talented comic actors to buckle down, play the game, and perform not for the joy of it but for the chance to make a pot of money on a network TV show" (*Brainwarp/Dumbass* review).

The story can be seen as a parable for the Annoyance Theatre's struggles

123

on many levels. The troupe's dogged commitment to risk, permissiveness, and process has resulted in brilliant comedy performances, critically acclaimed original works, the intense devotion of fans, and a tight-knit family of performers. Indeed, the Annoyance became the vanguard for an emerging third wave of improv-comedy in the late '80s and '90s. Yet, over the years, their no-holds-barred approach has also led to painful schisms and defections, fickle critics, economic hardships, and accusations of cultlike exploitation of players. The Annoyance has also been charged with sexism—yet its women members are among the most assertive and accepted in the city.

The carnival and the freak show are also apt analogies for the Annoyance Theatre's company, once dubbed the "Island of Misfits" by Second City performers (Adler, "In Your Face" 93). The troupe was founded in 1987 by a group of improvisers seeking asylum from the conventions and competition at both Second City and ImprovOlympic. Their idea was simple—to build a utopian improv playground free from the commercialism, rules, hierarchies, rivalries, and fears that marred the pure process of improv in first- and second-wave institutions. Resonating with Russian literary theorist Mikhail Bakhtin's description of carnival, improvisation at the Annoyance Theatre is aggressively practiced as "the suspension of all hierarchical rank, privileges, norms and prohibitions, [a feast] of becoming, change and renewal . . . hostile to all that was immortalized and completed" (10). The Annoyance Theatre embraces "carnival" in all its disorder and earthiness.

Napier intentionally emulates Brechtian theatre in a number of ways, but he and the Annoyance are entirely unfamiliar with Bakhtin. Still, the troupe's distinctive performance style embodies a key aspect of Bakhtin's notion of carnival, the "grotesque," which leaves the body "unfinished and open . . . not separated from the world by clearly defined boundaries" (26). The Annoyance revels in the grotesque through the constant mutation of their material, the physical shape-shifting of their characters, and, perhaps most importantly, their celebration of everything lewd, crude, and socially unacceptable. The Annoyance carnival leaks off the stage to include the audience, as patrons smoke, drink, and lounge on the theatre's decrepit sofas and armchairs. The troupe's symbiotic relationship with its cadre of passionate fans creates another element of carnival, the permeable boundary between performer and spectator.

Their carnivalesque refusal of anything complete, finished, or official pervades not only Annoyance performances, but the company's business and internal dealings as well. The Annoyance leadership eschews titles or official job descriptions. They teach against the rules and structures most improvisers learn at Second City, and they reject conventional measures of success when choosing or creating material. As unhinged as their actions appear, there is an underlying method to the Annoyance madness. As Napier, who would be the Annoyance artistic director if the troupe used such titles, once told a reporter, "We take seriously not taking anything seriously" ("Theatres Take It to Limit" 16).

In his "Director's Notes" for their popular, long-running show *Co-ed Prison Sluts,* Napier expresses the credo of his company in three words—"to have fun": "Let us have fun. Let us laugh. Let us smoke cigarettes and drink alcoholic beverages. Let us be stimulated by an experience on stage. Oh God, let us have a party and invite the world. That is why it is called a 'play.' It is not called a 'bore,' or a 'tedium,'" or a 'too long.' It is a play. So let us play, let us play so hard our tits fall off" (*Co-ed Prison Sluts* Program).

Napier's play on the word "play" underscores his insistence that the process and action of playing take precedence over the finished product. As a completed work of art, a play can all too easily become calcified, boring, and tedious. This simple idea is a determined philosophy that the troupe has fought to maintain since their first improv-based performance in 1987.

As they illustrated through *Dumbass Leaves the Carnival,* the Annoyance Theatre struggles with a central issue that has plagued improvisers over the decades—the relationship between pure artistry and commercialism, between process and product. For many years the Annoyance has taken a stronger stand than most against the forces of fixity. Napier sees the idea of "product" built into every rule and structure of conventional improv play in Chicago. "The improv game itself has product implied," he asserts. "You plug in the process to the product that's already there. The success rate is much higher" (personal interview). To combat the ascendancy of product-based values, the Annoyance struggles to redefine success. The troupe strives for unconditional acceptance of one another as performers and as people. Core member Ellen Stoneking insists, "Failing [at the Annoyance] is virtually impossible. Certainly it's possible to have bad shows, to go on stage and not do quite as well as you wanted, but failing in the sense of 'You are wrong, you are bad; go sit in the corner'—is virtually impossible" (Adler, "In Your Face" 93).

To maintain their purity of motive, Annoyance members are never paid to perform. They remain amateurs in the classic sense of those who love what they do. After an extended interview with the company in 1992, theatre critic Anthony Adler concluded, "What the misfits want more than money is to experience the mystic paradox that's printed *on* the money: *E pluribus unum*—out of the many, one. They want to explore the possibility of finding absolute creative freedom within the context of a group. 'Process over product,' Sutton [a core member of the troupe] said. 'We're more concerned about the way we do things and the effort and the joy that we get out of doing them. We just subscribe to the notion that if we keep doing that then everything else will take care of itself.' And in a lot of ways it has" (Adler, "In Your Face" 92).

Napier, Stoneking, Mark "Howard" Sutton, and the others believe that the intrusion of product over process in improv is an expression of fear—fear of the unknown, the emotional, the uncontrolled; fear of being judged; and fear of both artistic and commercial failure. In his teaching and directing, Napier disdains the accepted rules of improv as crutches for the weak of heart, saying, "I started in my teaching to figure out—how do you have to rearrange your behavior in order to transcend that space of fear? Because I believe that rules are only a consequence of that behavior—that the rules themselves are bull-shit" (personal interview).

Yet, as I have shown in earlier chapters, some of the most attractive and compelling qualities of pure improv—the mutual cooperation, the idea of agreement, spontaneity, comedy, and the unity of groupmind—can be used to reinforce conventional gender roles and other power relations rather than to circumvent them. Napier, a charismatic performer/director who presents himself alternately as gay, bisexual, and pansexual, asserts that the problems of marginalized people in improv lie not in the genre's anarchy but in the individual's own fears and "baggage." But Napier and the Annoyance often ignore systemic and political sources of that individual behavior. The absence of rules and structures can likewise create a very uneven playing field. Cultural theorists Stallybrass and White have critiqued carnival's tendency to displace abject status onto marginalized people, "women, ethnic and religious minorities, those who 'don't belong' " (19). Similarly, feminist critic Frances Gray notes that in Bakhtin's discussion of carnival, "Nowhere are sexual barriers, as opposed to class barriers, seen as being challenged" (31).

Gender plays a complex role in the Annoyance carnival. Through its permissive, licentious approach, the company manages to present some of the most objectifying, debasing, and even abusively misogynist images of women in Chicago theatre, while the troupe simultaneously earns a reputation for providing rare support and opportunity for women improvisers. Women who succeed at the Annoyance must be tough and aggressive, but to give the company its due, female players are appreciated for this toughness, not punished for it, as many have been in other troupes. The company's long-running musical *Co-ed Prison Sluts*, for example, was created through improvisation; and Susan Messing and Ellen Stoneking, the two women in its nine-member cast, were instrumental in creating each low-comedy joke and potentially degrading action they perform. Both women revel in portraying female grotesques, sexual aggressors, and laughing hags.

Napier says, "The powerful women I know give no credence to the concept that men are in any way, shape, or form involved in their process of learning and growth" (Pollack). Here again, Annoyance policy is based on individual relationships, willfully ignoring the broader social or political context. Yet, the Annoyance was also the first (so far the only) improv theatre in Chicago to offer a course for women designed expressly to help them overcome feelings of powerlessness on the improv-comedy stage.

Most contemporary Chicago improvisers agree that the Annoyance Theatre broke new ground— launching what I have defined as the third wave of Chicago improv-comedy. Many third-wave companies admire and consciously imitate the Annoyance. A few, such as the Free Associates, are more critical of the group's carnival attitude—seeing it as cultish, self-indulgent, and (still) sexist. Nevertheless, the company's exploration of its own generational identity—through both risky improvisations and postmodern parodies of familiar genres—captured the attention of Chicago audiences for more than a decade. Perhaps even more important, their carnivalesque approach helped revitalize Chicago improv in the late '80s, appealing to, and even creating, improv's next generation of audiences.

On a Saturday night in October 1996, an adventurous theatre-goer could attend any one of three shows at the Annoyance Theatre. At nine p.m. (the early show), the company offered its newest experimental show, *The Really Really Strange Couple*. At 10:31, as usual, the Annoyance presented its signature show and economic mainstay, *Co-ed Prison Sluts;* and at one in the morning, die-hard improv fans could see the company's uncensored and uninhibited improv set, *Screw Puppies*. While only one of these three presentations is fully improvised in performance, the Annoyance develops all of its shows through a very loose, improvisational process they believe is organic and unforced. As Napier told one reporter, the theatre's mission statement includes the mandate "to have all the shows be developed as freely as possible with no or as little bull as possible" ("Theatres Take It to Limit" 16).

The projects resulting from this process are usually short on plot and long on eccentric characters, pop culture references, and opportunistic, ribald humor. For the Annoyance, making sense has a very low priority, while having fun is paramount. Napier rejects any suggestion that the company is creating "art," although colleagues in the improv community have heard him compare the Annoyance philosophy to that of Tristan Tzara, who valued anarchy and "non-art art" (Gagné personal interview).[1]

The Really Really Strange Couple is a prime example of the Annoyance Theatre's willingness to suspend all judgments as to taste, credibility, or coherence. In this postmodern homage to Neil Simon's *The Odd Couple*, actor-director Napier portrays the sloppy roommate who virtually covers himself with food throughout the forty-five minute performance. As the audience groans in delighted dismay, Napier douses himself with milk, pours spaghetti sauce down his shirt, eats food off the floor, and smears large gobs of peanut butter on his head—all with carnivalesque abandon. As the show progresses, Napier and his neat roommate, Adolf Hitler, are joined by a squad of other characters, including a kindly postal worker, a madwoman, and two Cambodian refugee sisters—one played by an Asian American woman, and the other by a white man in haphazard drag. As a plot of sorts unfolds, each character reveals a desperate and immediate need for cash to pay for such things as rent, citizenship papers, and even a new kidney.

Hearing the rumor that their wealthy landlord likes anything "all-American," the motley group bands together to put on a production of *Our Town*, hoping the millionaire will like it and give them money. Their living-room performance of Thornton Wilder's play is, of course, a failure, and their potential benefactor storms away in disgust. The group then decides to murder the landlord—immediately retrieving not only his money, but his kidney for their ailing friend. So much for happy endings!

A brief analysis of *The Really Really Strange Couple* reveals certain themes (largely unacknowledged by the group) that recur in many Annoyance shows. Their productions almost always depend on the audience's collective memories of familiar narratives to give coherence to convoluted plots and to produce the double-coded pleasures of its skewed citation of remembered texts. In *The Really Really Strange Couple*, the neuroses of Simon's characters are taken to bizarre extremes, until the slob becomes a sexual deviant and the neatnik becomes the fascism of Hitler's ethnic cleansing. Napier also exploits the homoerotic potential of the "strange" pairing of men, a potential that Neil Simon merely flirts with in his play, by elevating innuendo into overt representations of homosexual desire.

When these characters are joined by other misfits who reflect the vast heterogeneity of modern American society, the play compounds its reference to conventional American culture by invoking Thornton Wilder's *Our Town*. The harder this group of gender benders, immigrants, and outcasts tries to reproduce a Norman Rockwell image of New England family life, the more absurd their efforts become. Characters are wildly miscast; lines are badly read and largely forgotten; props are broken and lost. The acting becomes more and more desperate. Finally, the little group's failure and frustration leads to violence—one act they can perform successfully.

Arts critic Sid Smith has commented on the Annoyance's "deliberately messy aesthetic" in which stage blood, animal parts, food, and water are often liberally splattered on both sides of the footlights ("Beyond the Fringe").[2] As the actors revel in them, various forms of glop and goo take on a sensual, sexual energy that seems both threatening and exciting to the squirming audience. Throughout *The Really Really Strange Couple,* the messiness, not only of Napier's slob character but of the plotting and production values, seems also to be a deliberate rebellion against the idea that contemporary Americans can ever fit neatly into the molds that mainstream cultural productions have taught us to expect. In a manner that again parallels Bakhtin's notions of the grotesque, "Annoyance people reject product, reject the very concept of 'finished' as a matter for faith and experience" (Adler, "In Your Face" 93). In its shows, the company cultivates an unpolished, amateurish quality that often works to create a unique rapport with the audience, drawing them into the playfulness on stage. At *The Really Really Strange Couple* performance that I attended, loyal Annoyance fans laughed and groaned appreciatively, but this play was more baffling than most and did not catch on with the wider public, as many of the troupe's earlier efforts have done.

Co-ed Prison Sluts, developed in much the same way as *The Really Really Strange Couple,* became the troupe's flagship show and most consistent moneymaker. Opened in 1989, the musical was still playing in 2000, and its ticket income paid the theatre's rent and funded other more experimental shows for years. In the company's cavernous theatre, every Saturday night at 10:31, the mostly college-age spectators sat on a miscellaneous assortment of furniture, freely passed bottles of beer and hard liquor, and thrilled to cheery musical portrayals of violence, masturbation, child pornography, and masochistic nymphomania.

Finally, for sleepless loyalists, the Screw Puppies took the stage. In this late, late show, Annoyance improvisers test their own boundaries—pushing the limits of acceptability far beyond the material in *Co-ed Prison Sluts.* Shows are raunchy, and fearlessness and realness are valued to the point where actors may perform drunk, spit or urinate on stage, and sometimes draw from extremely personal and intimate experiences for subject matter. *Screw Puppies* has an exciting intensity, and in some shows performers demonstrate a compelling vulnerability as they try to strip themselves of all protective masks. Other performances are simply a barrage of clever, X-rated comic bits with little regard for scenic values such as environment or character.

Throughout the 1990s, the Annoyance presented new improv-based shows, the longest-running musical in Chicago, and spontaneous improv each week. Yet in some ways its easy-going public face belied the artistic, financial, and personal struggles that have marked its history.

The history of the Annoyance Theatre can be seen as a contest between idealism and commercialism, process and product, anarchy and business, the desire for free play and the reality of no free lunch. The story begins with Mick Napier, and the development of the troupe's philosophy is intertwined with his personal artistic journey. In 1983, Napier was a college student at Indiana University, where he soon abandoned his studies in veterinary medicine to become a theatre major. But Napier recalls being bored by rehearsals and the traditions of Method acting taught at Indiana. None of it, he says, provided "freedom enough to have fun while I was doing it. I wanted to have fun. I wanted to enjoy it" (qtd. in Adler, "In Your Face" 93).

When Napier came upon *Something Wonderful Right Away*, Jeff Sweet's oral history of the Compass and Second City, he began to envision a solution to his fun shortage. Reading about the playful, uninhibited exploits of these early performers inspired Napier to try his hand at improvisational theatre. With little more to go on than the descriptions of games and beliefs in Sweet's book, Napier and his friend David MacNerland put together a group of actors and created an improv-comedy troupe called Dubbletaque. With their name, a fancy spelling of the low-comedy device (the double take), the troupe seemed to promise a self-conscious, even a double-coded, comic approach.

In their ignorance and exuberance, Dubbletaque created their own ad hoc performance style in response to a half-understood idea of the Compass. Their enterprise was so successful on the Indiana campus that Napier and many of his cast decided to try their luck in Chicago. By 1986, Napier was enrolled in Second City's training program and was simultaneously taking classes with Del Close at ImprovOlympic. Napier was greatly influenced by Close's work with long-form improv, and he saw the Harold as a big step closer to free-form improv than Second City's approach. Napier impressed the management of both groups immediately with his intensity and his instinctive understanding of improvisation. Within a short three-month period, he went from student to teacher at Second City's training center and had begun teaching at ImprovOlympic as well.

Although Napier was able to bypass some of the hierarchy at Second City and ImprovOlympic, he and many of his fellow improvisers felt restricted by those companies' established systems and structures. Second City had become an entrenched institution, with its training center organized into five levels of instruction. At ImprovOlympic, teams, teaching, and performance schedules were rigidly controlled by producer Charna Halpern. In both companies, improvisers were constantly aware of being judged as they competed with one another for stage time and membership in the elite troupes. The process of improv was strongly influenced by the need to create a successful comedy product. In 1987, Napier reunited with many of his original Dubbletaque friends, including MacNerland, Faith Soloway, Joe Bill, Eric Waddell, and, later, Mark Sutton, to create an alternative improv troupe that would embody their ideals of improv. Sutton, performer, director, and unofficial Annoyance historian and managing director explains, "If you work at Second City, you've got to do what Second City wants, and at ImprovOlympic you kind of have to do the Harold. So, we wanted a place where you could do anything. And anything was acceptable as long as it was a challenge . . . a place where you'd have the freedom to fail" (personal interview).

The Indiana alumni were joined by several players from Second City and ImprovOlympic, including Ellen Stoneking, David Razowsky, Gary Ruderman, and Richard Laible. The troupe was determined from the start to remain as unofficial and informal as possible. Sutton says, "It was all a collaborative thing. Mick was kind of the founder, and everybody just worked together. There was never any real hierarchy or official titles or anything like that" (personal interview). In an effort to maintain complete equality, the group eliminated obvious forms of structure and authority, although they did create a sense of family and belonging. Cofounder Ruderman mused, "Maybe it's like where the kids in *Lord of the Flies* try to set up this society without titles" (Adler, "In Your Face" 110). Yet, even without a title, the fearless Napier was unmistakably their leader. Troupe members worked to create an atmosphere of total, nonjudgmental support and to avoid the chilling effect of conventional measures of success such as money and mainstream approval.

This conglomeration of self-defined misfits began to perform weekly games-based shows in a room upstairs from Chicago's Cabaret Metro. Adapting the name of the space, they christened themselves "Metraform." Within a few months, the group moved to the CrossCurrents theatre, where they took the small upstairs theatre while ImprovOlympic occupied the larger ground-floor space. There, Metraform expanded beyond games and, after playing with long-form improv, developed their first full-length show— *Splatter Theatre*—an irreverent parody of teen horror movies. The sets were simple, and the humor was broad, bawdy, and frequently graphic. Each show began on a bare stage with four stark white walls. Then, as each clichéd teen character was murdered in turn, more than five gallons of stage blood were literally splattered from floor to ceiling, and animal entrails were strewn liberally about the floor. Although it was popular with young audiences, the show

As the sinister "Balloon Boy," Mark Sutton terrorizes the streetwise Cassie (Ellen Stoneking) and other patrons of a bar in the Annoyance musical *Your Butt*. This dark comedy, loosely based on Eugene O'Neill's *The Iceman Cometh*, was created by the Annoyance players with director Mick Napier and composer Faith Soloway—the team responsible for the success of *Co-ed Prison Sluts*. Photo: Courtesy Annoyance Theatre.

made very little money. But for the troupe, money was not the point. It was fun. *Splatter Theatre*, says Napier, was "one of the best experiences I ever had in my life" (Adler, "In Your Face" 92). Yet, as Metraform shows began to attract public attention and larger audiences, the group was forced to deal with mounting financial pressures.

The evils of commercialism came home to them most clearly in the failure of *Splatter II*. Eager to cash in on the energy and popularity of *Splatter Theatre*, independent producers approached the Metraform group, offering a partnership. Bigger sets, more costumes, paid advertisements, doubled casts, and doubled performances were designed to capitalize on *Splatter's* appeal. But the producers were overly ambitious, and the fledgling company couldn't manage their suddenly expanded financial commitment. Nor, in many ways, did Metraform want to buy into a more businesslike way of operating. Napier remembers *Splatter II* as a time when the troupe lost sight of its priorities:

"Creation in that show wasn't important. The product was important" (Adler, "In Your Face" 110).

Splatter II opened in the renamed and reconfigured space where *Splatter Theatre* had played. No longer CrossCurrents, the downstairs space now housed a blues bar called Cotton Chicago. But while audiences enjoyed *Splatter II*, Metraform was unable to recoup their outsized financial investment. At the end of the run, company members found themselves exhausted, disillusioned, and fifteen thousand dollars in debt. Most of the large double cast of *Splatter II* moved on to other projects. Only nine improvisers remained with Metraform, hoping to put on another show. According to Sutton, there was a certain freedom in knowing the group had nothing left to lose. Their desperate situation helped to reaffirm the original attitude of fearlessness and "fuck-it-ness" that had been the company's founding mandate (Adler, "In Your Face" 93). In the winter of 1989, in the spirit of one last fling, the Metraform faithful decided to create the first improvised musical in Chicago. They began the project with an arbitrary, but suggestive, title: *Co-ed Prison Sluts*. And the rest, says Sutton "is history" (personal interview).

As with virtually every play at the Annoyance, *Co-ed Prison Sluts* was developed through improvisation. Company member Susan Messing remembers the way the project began: "All Mick knew, for *Co-ed Prison Sluts*, is that he wanted a musical. He knew the people he wanted in it but he didn't tell them who they were [as characters]. He wanted a fight between a clown and a drag queen, because he thought it would amuse him. He wanted a hamster; he wanted his dog in it; he wanted tap dancing; and he wanted it to be called *Co-ed Prison Sluts*" (personal interview).

With these few "givens," a group of actors, handpicked for their commitment to the Metraform way of life and art, built the show that was to become the theatre's bread and butter for the next decade. Although its performances were not improvised in the strictest sense, the dialogue and actions were never set in stone but continued mutating and evolving—resisting the aesthetic closure that Bakhtin would call "the ready-made and the completed" (24). Anyone requesting a script of the show is told that the original text bears almost no resemblance to the performance they may have seen on stage.[3]

According to Sutton, the process of play development at the Annoyance follows a certain loose progression. Early rehearsals are devoted to improvisations centered on the creation of a variety of characters. The director and actors then experiment with these characters by combining them in scenes—sometimes imposing certain locations, situations, or tasks with which the

Ellen Stoneking as the proud but crazy Dame Toulouse and Susan Messing as sweetly masochistic Alice sing "A Love Song" in the Annoyance signature show, *Co-ed Prison Sluts*. Photo: Courtesy Annoyance Theatre

characters have to deal. Scenes that work—and sustain dramatic interest for the group—are sometimes re-improvised and developed further.

But the company avoids imposing or even acknowledging any kind of theme or meaning in its work—seeing analysis as akin to paralysis. Determined to keep the creative process open, Napier explains, "We just say fuck it and play, and take the best of what we do. I think that when people create material through improvisation, they spend a lot of time talking about it, and looking at it, and not a great deal of time improvising. The trickiest part of it for us is the left-brain process of putting it all together in a story—because we're not very plot-oriented. That's not an easy thing for me" (Helbig, "Mick's Bunch" 12). Nevertheless, a through-line of sorts eventually emerges from the troupe's improvisations, and additional dialogue or music may be specifically created to fill in the gaps or link scenes to one another.

Original songs became crucial elements in the construction of most Annoyance projects. In the case of *Co-ed Prison Sluts* and other Annoyance musicals, a composer would improvise right along with the troupe in rehearsals. In the Annoyance rehearsal process, composers look for key scenes in which songs can take the place of dialogue and for opportunities to create incidental music. Sometimes song lyrics have to be honed and crafted once the melody and basic premise have been created. Other times, the song springs fully formed from the improvisational moment. Faith Soloway composed the music for *Co-ed Prison Sluts* while maintaining a paid position as musical director for Second City Northwest.

In the final stages of this creative process, the play's scene order, climactic moments, and songs are fairly set, but the dialogue is rarely nailed down word for word, and actors continue to improvise throughout the run. Using this technique, a cast of six men and two women (along with Napier's dog, Kahlua) created *Co-ed Prison Sluts,* the show they credit with revitalizing the troupe both spiritually and financially.

As a logical outcome of the rehearsal process, this play brings an unlikely crew of eccentric characters together in a provocative location: a prison rec room. Susan Messing's character, Alice, evolved as *Co-ed Prison Sluts'* ingenue—a naive, "happy masochist" and incest victim, now in prison for killing her parents. As the new girl on the cell block, Alice became a convenient tool for evoking exposition about the unusual population of this surreal penitentiary. The prisoners included Dame Toulouse, an elegantly crazy actress (Stoneking); Slick, a sleazy pedophile (Ed Furman); and a twelve-year-old boy named Skeeter (played by adult actor Sutton), in jail through some unexplained bureaucratic snafu. Throughout the play the audience will also meet a cross-dressing prison psychiatrist (Tom Booker); a mysterious, murderous clown (John Harizal); a twisted hamster lover (Joe Bill); and Henry, a childlike, psychotic killer with cannibalistic tendencies (Bob Fisher). Henry becomes Alice's love interest, as his desire to hurt and her masochistic desire to be hurt mesh in surprisingly touching moments.

In most of *Co-ed Prison Sluts'* songs, the dissonance between the lyrics' ghastly subject matter and the bouncy, hummable tunes is reminiscent of Brecht-Weill musicals. In the rousing opening number, "Hey! We're in Prison," the cast sings with a smile, "Hey! We're in prison! / It's not a walk in the park / It's not a social schism / So don't drop your soap in the dark." Later, Messing's character tunefully tells her story of abuse: "My mother was a prostitute / Made me do coke / It was a hoot. . . / [I] had very little time to play / 'cause Daddy raped me every day."

Messing remembers the night the cast improvised the most popular and notorious song in *Co-ed Prison Sluts,* a ditty that *Chicago Tribune* columnist Sid Smith calls "the first completely unquotable song in musical theater history" ("Beyond the Fringe"). In rehearsal, actor Ed Furman, playing Slick, the charming child-molester, began teaching Alice the list of obscenities she would need to survive her time in stir. The song, says Messing, "is what I sang, based on what Eddie taught me and what Faith played" (personal interview). The number is a slew of slang words for genitalia and sexual insults. It became the high point of the performance, and indeed became crucial in setting the tone for entire show.[4]

Sutton recalls that preview audiences for *Co-ed Prison Sluts* were stunned by the crude subject matter and the light treatment of such issues as child abuse, rape, and murder in the play, and were unwilling to enter the grotesque, iconoclastic spirit of the proceedings. Overnight, director Napier rearranged key elements of the show to let the spectators in on its unique perspective. Napier moved Messing's cheerfully offensive song to the first scene and added an invitation to the audience to sing along. With that inoculation, audiences began to catch on sooner and allow themselves to enjoy the no-holds-barred action that followed.

When the show opened in the spring of 1989, audiences loved it, packing the seventy-five-seat space at Cotton Chicago every weekend. Many critics appreciated the new musical, especially its tunes, believing that "a quality of grace insulates and protects these songs from mere coarseness because they spring from the spontaneity of improvisation" (Adler, "In Your Face" 108). Other critics were not as forgiving. In an elaborate parody, *Windy City Times* critic Wayne Scott wrote a review of *Co-ed Prison Sluts* from the perspective of a "typical fan": "*Co-ed Prison Sluts* is hilarious because it makes fun of musicals, and everyone knows that musicals are for fairies anyway. . . . But that one song, 'Hey Little Girl,' took the fucking cake! What a perfect anthem of rebellion for these modern times, with all the lesbo-feminists whining about sexual abuse and calling every guy and his brother a date rapist. Jesus H. Christ! 'Hey Little Girl' is a totally touching song about a child molester singing to this little girl that he's interested in fondling. It was a really poignant moment in a night of hilarious fun. Take back the night, guys!" (Scott).

Scott skewers the kind of audience he imagines would relish *Co-ed Prison Sluts'* apparent misogyny and cruelty. Yet, while the show does appeal to stereotypical frat boys on one level, its double-coded social satire continues to be well received by a wide range of audiences—both men and women.

Even key troupe members have accused Napier of lacking respect for women, citing *Co-ed Prison Sluts* as an example of misogyny. But Messing and Stoneking, both cast members and co-creators of that musical, defend the play, insisting that the characters they improvised retain their own kind of integrity and strength in the face of degrading circumstances. Messing asserts, "I'm up there doing it, and if I felt that anything I did was demeaning to me as an individual, I wouldn't do it. I just wouldn't. It's make-believe.

You *can* do anything. You're not going to get hurt as an individual. It's a comment. If you make someone a *happy* masochist, people can watch it and laugh. If you make her an unhappy masochist—that's different. And at the end [Napier] makes Alice empowered by making her the one who shoots the evil clown. He does these things for a reason" (personal interview).

Messing's views resonate with those of a new breed of sex-positive feminists (including sex expert Susie Bright and performance artist Annie Sprinkle, both former porn stars) who believe that any form of sexual practice and pleasure, including masochism and prostitution, is compatible with feminism if it is powerfully chosen by the woman. From Messing's perspective, her portrayal of Alice is all the more feminist because it challenges repressive sexual mores—even those limitations motivated by feminist sensibilities.

Stoneking plays a more clearly powerful role in the play: Dame Toulouse, a crazy but commanding actress who remains aloof and sexually unavailable to the other prisoners. Throughout the play, this character proclaims absurdist lines in a classical style, then cries, "With that, I slap my ass at you," as she sweeps off the stage. Interestingly, Dame Toulouse's strength comes from her distance from most of the action and her non sequitur responses to the others. This tactic recalls Mina Kolb at Second City and other women comics who have used the device of "kookiness" to be at once funny and unthreatening. Stoneking, too, believes that her character wins at the end of the play. Both women subscribe to the company philosophy that personal fears and issues are the only obstacles to equal opportunity—at least on the Annoyance stage.

Co-ed Prison Sluts was a triumph for the Metraform nine. The show's convergence of unfettered process and popular response reaffirmed the ideals they seemed to have lost in the *Splatter II* debacle. Building on the hipness and popularity of *Splatter Theatre, Co-ed Prison Sluts* soon developed a core group of aficionados, mostly in their teens and early twenties. In particular, a group of young punkers—with spiked, dyed hair and pierced noses—began to attend almost every show, every week. Each night, while the theatre seats in Metraform's performance space were occupied by audiences in their twenties and thirties (with a few older spectators), the first several rows of floor-space seating would be crowded with these teenagers.

Over the years, the Annoyance has cultivated its status as a hip hangout where shows are enjoyed in repeated viewings and audiences can develop a sense of belonging and membership. As journalists would later note, the Annoyance attracted a "young, nontraditional theatre audience" with performances created for "a new generation" (S. Smith, "Beyond the Fringe").

In the early days, frequent attendance at *Co-ed Prison Sluts* was facilitated by the show's affordability. In keeping with Metraform's ambivalent attitude toward money, admission to *Co-ed* was free. Spectators were then asked to make a financial contribution as they left the theatre. The company was confident that its audiences would like the show so much that they would choose to give generously. When the time came to pay, however, most of the younger fans would donate fifty cents or a dollar, returning the next night to do the same. Economic realities later forced the company to change this admission policy to a fixed rate. But Metraform thrived on the energy and enthusiasm of their youthful following, who were short on cash but long on devotion. In the tiny theatre, the improvised dialogue and late-night informality closed much of the distance between audience and actors. Young fans even began to think of themselves as members of the group. In an article on the burgeoning youth appeal of "cult" shows at the Annoyance and other theatres that followed in its footsteps, Adler suggested, "The very shoddiness of the stage values is an attraction—it emphasizes the unmediated, breathing reality of the thing. To an audience born to television, raised on Calvin Klein ads, and brought to maturity in suburbs where the basic political unit is the mall, this is living. This is genuinely alive" ("Life of Brian" 16).

Annoyance shows like *Splatter Theatre* and *Co-ed Prison Sluts* derive directly from familiar media images. Young spectators took pleasure in recognizing the specific references to recent and classic films and television. They memorized the Annoyance show and, night after night, watched for every slight variation the improvisers made in the loosely structured performances. Fans were drawn not only by pop images, but, more viscerally, by the way the company linked familiar mediatized texts to a palpable experience of spontaneity and community.

What had been planned as a four-week run for *Co-ed Prison Sluts* soon stretched into several months. The company began to hope that income from the show would help dig them out of debt. One morning, however, shortly after celebrating the anniversary of their seventy-fifth performance, members of Metraform were shocked to discover that all of their sets, props, and costumes had been unceremoniously dumped on the street outside of Cotton Chicago. They later learned that the manager of the club, who had sublet the upstairs theatre to Metraform, had not been paying rent for either space to the building's owners. In evicting Cotton Chicago, the landlord had ousted Metraform as well, emptying the theatre space on a Sunday when no performances were scheduled.

An anecdote demonstrates the level of devotion this troupe had inspired in its young audiences. Recognizing the discarded sets and costumes, teenage fans who regularly hung out on the street near the theatre kept a vigil over the pile of Metraform belongings throughout the night. Original *Co-ed* cast member Joe Bill remembers, "We like couldn't believe it; we come up and there's all these little punkers guarding our shit!" (personal interview). With the (fondly meant) term "little punkers," Bill demonstrates the generational distance he feels from the rising Annoyance fan base. The company had found a style that appealed not only to its own late boomer–post-boomer contemporaries, but to a significantly younger group as well.

Seeking their own subcultural identity, these teens in green hair and tattoos latched onto the Annoyance in much the same way that young fans followed *The Rocky Horror Picture Show* from the late '70s on. This next generation was potentially more at home with the Annoyance postmodern vision than the original company members themselves.

Meanwhile, devastated by the loss of their theatre, and thus their income, the members of Metraform scoured Chicago to find an alternative space. As weeks passed, cast members regularly volunteered to go down to Cotton Chicago to meet disappointed devotees and assure them that *Co-ed* would soon resurface. Finally, marshaling every financial resource the company could muster—from credit card advances to loans from relatives—the homeless company put a ten thousand dollar deposit down on a former drag club on Chicago's Broadway. Troupe members spent countless hours of unpaid labor to modify the club into a theatre. In February of 1990, four months after they had found their sets on the sidewalk, with the renovations half finished, the company reopened *Co-ed Prison Sluts*.

Mark Sutton remembers the night the group made its collective decision to give their new home its own name: "So one night—we'd been working for weeks, tearing stuff down and swinging sledge hammers, and then—we just got a bunch of beer and we sat down on the floor upstairs in this room and decided to name the place. And everybody just started throwing out names and I started writing them down. And then we read them off and started crossing them out until we finally—it could have almost been 'Le Ping Pong.' That was one of the finalists" (personal interview).

After rejecting such titles as "Unlucky Pets" and "The Very Affected Theatre," the gang settled on "The Annoyance," and the name stuck. For a while, the company still announced its projects as "Metraform presents *Co-ed Prison Sluts* at the Annoyance Theatre," but the moniker they chose for their building was quickly conflated in the press and the public with the troupe itself, and the company didn't object.

Napier had negotiated six months of free rent in the three-story building, after which time the rent would begin at one thousand dollars a month and steadily escalate to a maximum of four thousand a month. For the first time, the troupe took full responsibility for the rent, renovations, and maintenance of their own building—a move that both solidified and altered the company's identity in the Chicago improv community by providing expanded opportunities and unforeseen pressures. The theatre, with its multiple rooms, gave the troupe a playground where more of them could turn ideas into full productions. The building soon became a clubhouse for the company and reinforced the feelings of family and solidarity among its members. The core group even spent Christmas together in the as-yet-unheated building, drinking and playing games and struggling to find the money just to get the heat on (Sutton interview). Realizing that the Annoyance couldn't pay its bills based on a single show, Napier called composer Faith Soloway, recruited additional improvisers through his contacts at Second City, and began work on a new musical called *That Darned Antichrist!* With this project, the Annoyance launched into a period of ever-increasing production and never-decreasing financial obligation.

Created through improv in much the same way that *Co-ed Prison Sluts* had been, *That Darned Antichrist!* mimicked a television situation comedy. According to Sutton, the actors began with the simple idea of "the worst possible premise for a sitcom, where you could resolve everything and be happy at the end and you have a wacky neighbor and all that" (personal interview). In other words, the play would employ both the plot structure and the stock characters of the familiar sitcom format, exploding a variety of recognizable cultural references for shock value and comic effect. For *That Darned Antichrist!* the troupe improvised the story of a single mother and her three kids who lived on a houseboat. The only trouble in paradise was that the youngest son had been turned into the Antichrist by an evil nun and a local scoutmaster. Predictably, a number of comic adventures ensued.

With *That Darned Antichrist!* the Annoyance continued its practice of using well-known genres as a framework for their willfully disorganized process. By alluding to classic popular culture genres, Annoyance actors were free to improvise bizarre characters and unlikely scenes with the confidence that the audience would make the intertextual leap—using their own knowledge of sitcom conventions, for example, to fill gaps in the narrative and logic of the Annoyance version.

On the surface, the company's improvised stories took the customary characters and situations to absurd lengths, and spectators laughed at the disparity between these representations and the way they knew a sitcom or other convention "should be." At a deeper level, these ridiculous rewrites also critiqued the societal assumptions on which these classic conventions are based. In *That Darned Antichrist!* for example, the mother was played by a male actor (Benjamin Zook) in drag as "a cross between Ethel Merman and Ernest Borgnine"

In Annoyance hit *That Darned Antichrist!* beleaguered lesbian Grace (Susan Messing) sings "I'm a Butterfly"—a plea for tolerance directed toward her lover, socialite Judith Wentworth (Ben Zook) and her family. Pictured (clockwise from bottom left): Tom Booker, Ed Furman, Ellen Stoneking, Mark Sutton, Zook, Messing. Photo: Courtesy Annoyance Theatre

(Walls 17). This performance choice scores an easy laugh, but it also points to the equally unrealistic performance of femininity presented by the classic sitcom homemaker, as she cooked, cleaned house, and smiled in heels and pearls.

The zany next-door neighbor, played by Susan Messing, turns out to be a lesbian with a crush on the mother. Messing's character is continually wounded and maimed throughout the plot—appearing in each succeeding scene with new bruises, bandages, and finally on crutches. At a key point, the two sing a sunny duet entitled "It's Okay to Be Gay." The incongruity of the lesbian in the sitcom kitchen points out the invisibility of gays and lesbians—even in '90s television—and the intense repression (and pain) of gay and lesbian lives in the decades of *Father Knows Best* and *Leave It to Beaver*—and still today. Throughout the play, a narrator (Gary Ruderman), seated in a centrally located armchair, makes comments (e.g., "This is a moment of irony") and shares knowing winks with the audience. This figure seems to blend Brechtian distancing with postmodern cynicism as he joins us in the guilty pleasure of talking back to the "TV."

Despite its satanic overtones, the content of *That Darned Antichrist!* was rather mild compared to *Co-ed Prison Sluts*. The sitcom premise kept vulgar language to a minimum, and the show was irreverent in a light, upbeat way, while still maintaining the anarchic sensibility associated with the Annoyance. Opening at Easter time (no accident), *That Darned Antichrist!* proved to be a very popular early show, running at 8 P.M. on weekends while *Co-ed* continued to draw crowds at 10:31. The company maintained its informal "Brechtian smoker's theatre" atmosphere. As one reviewer noted, "Drinking and smoking in the theatre is encouraged, in fact, it is almost necessary" (Walls 17).

The troupe was steadily climbing out of debt, but it seemed that solvency was always just out of reach. The graduated rent agreement for the building caused the group's expenses to rise each month, so that, despite the popularity of the shows, the troupe could never catch up with its bills. Regular admission charges were now a matter of course, and company members supported themselves with day jobs—sometimes even chipping in for rent from their own outside incomes. These financial pressures were a continual test of their commitment always to perform for fun and never for money.

In 1990, the Annoyance added two more shows, *Manson, the Musical* and *The Real Live Brady Bunch*. While *Manson* continued the troupe's taboo-breaking habits, putting cheerful tunes to horrid tales of fanaticism and multiple murder, *The Brady Bunch* project, a recreation of a television rerun, was very much a departure for the company.[5] Ironically, this show would bring the Annoyance national attention and financial security, while at the same time threatening to destroy the company's unity, stability, and soul.

The first *Real Live Brady Bunch* performances at the Annoyance Theatre began as a lark, according to Sutton. Faith Soloway, a longtime member of the company, and her sister Jill came up with the idea one night while laughing at their friend Becky Thyre's uncanny imitation of the oldest Brady sister, Marcia. Soloway approached Napier with the proposal of recreating a favorite *Brady Bunch* episode as a fun, off-night performance event. Napier agreed and even took on the role of youngest brother, Bobby. To make a full evening, the *Brady Bunch* episode was paired with *The Real Live Game Show,* a similarly campy tribute to television conceived by Annoyance member Eric Waddell the same week. The new show was announced for a Tuesday night. With the exception of a handful of flyers, no special publicity was created for the *Brady Bunch* event. It was simply included in onstage announcements preceding *Co-ed Prison Sluts* and *That Darned Antichrist!*

When that Tuesday in June 1990 arrived, however, the theatre was packed to capacity, and the following week a line of eager spectators formed at the box office, spilled out of the theatre, and extended all the way down the block. Annoyance actors were bewildered when the opening night crowd gave the

Characters from several successful Annoyance shows from the company's golden age surround artistic director Mick Napier. From left to right: Becky Thyre as Marcia Brady, Ed Furman as Slick in *Co-ed Prison Sluts*, Jim Carrane from *I'm 27, I Still Live at Home, and I Sell Office Supplies*, Mark Sutton as Skeeter from *Co-ed Prison Sluts*, Tony Stavish from *Viva Las Elvis, Elvis, Elvis*, Napier, Ben Zook as Charles Manson in *Manson, The Musical*, Ellen Stoneking as Cassie from *Your Butt*, Tom Booker as Balloon Boy in *Your Butt*. Photo: Courtesy Annoyance Theatre

show a standing ovation. Napier reflected, "What was interesting to me was that we don't have a set, we get costumes from thrift stores and we maybe spent six hours rehearsing it. And just by pure association it made those people stand and applaud" (Helbig, "Mick's Bunch" 12). Responding to audience demand, the company began to present a new *Brady Bunch* episode every other week. Says Sutton, "It ran for fourteen months—never had an empty seat. And I can't remember a night when we did not turn people away. It was insane" (personal interview). The extra income generated by the *Brady Bunch* shows was hard to pass up, as the theatre's rent continued to squeeze the company's resources. But no one at the Annoyance was prepared for the immense popularity of their *Brady Bunch* recreations, nor for the pressures and decisions it would soon force upon the young theatre group.

The pleasure for a generation of *Brady Bunch* watchers in seeing *The Real Live Brady Bunch* rested in the actors' faithful, if slightly exaggerated, representation of every remembered moment of the original programs. As Napier told *NewCity* in 1990, the performers presented each episode "word for word, line for line. Faith Soloway does all the incidental music exactly the same. We even try to move the same way. . . . And we have a laugh track, and the laughs come up at exactly the same places" (Helbig, "Mick's Bunch" 12).

The Annoyance mission, however, was to create new, iconoclastic works through improvisation—spoofs of older genres, perhaps, but not re-creations. Napier mused:

> One of my goals for theatre is to bring in young people. I have this feeling the way things are with MTV and television, that it takes a lot more than *Three Sisters* to get a kid twenty years old to come out and see a show. I don't know if people my age—in their twenties and early thirties—I don't know if we are appreciating the quality of work on the stage anymore. Or the production quality as much. [Getting the standing ovation] I was sad and I was happy. I was Bobby Brady, so I was getting a standing ovation. At the same time I was sad because it was [the *Brady Bunch*] getting a standing ovation. (Helbig 12)

At first, despite Napier's reservations, *The Real Live Brady Bunch* benefited the company, helping to stave off debt and worry. It attracted national media attention and brought thousands of new audience members to the theatre, many of whom returned to try the other Annoyance offerings. But Napier, Sutton, and others were uneasy at the thought of their theatre's national reputation being based on a show they considered a fluke—and not at all indicative of their company's artistic ethos.

For Napier, *The Real Live Brady Bunch* represented the antithesis of his ideal for improvisation. For all his arguably postmodern embrace of low-culture forms and his refusal of individual authorship through collaboration, Napier was still invested in the originality of Annoyance productions. While he publicly disdains the idea that Annoyance productions constitute "art," Napier clearly holds certain modernist notions of artistry—including its originality. Improvisation is ephemeral, process based, and ultimately unreproduceable. *The Real Live Brady Bunch,* on the other hand, was a copy of a copy of a copy. Napier believes that television is the "greatest example of a product-oriented medium in entertainment," where creativity is a commodity—without even the illusion of a gap between process and product, a gap that improvisation tries to preserve (personal interview). In his unhappiness over *The Real Live Brady Bunch,* Napier, it seems, was seized with a certain postmodern panic—wanting to distinguish one level of simulation as more authentic than another.[6] Like most improvisers, even while Napier rejects the notion of meaning in his work, he is creating provisional truths that seem to matter—at least in the moment.

Ironically, the Annoyance made its reputation by commenting on the con-

ventions of mass culture by using their own "liveness," attitudes, and spontaneity to reinvent classic genres. *The Real Live Brady Bunch* could be seen as
the logical extension of this practice. One critic wrote, "On paper, the show
sounds like mere camp. Live, it's a mystical reunion with creatures from the
silly putty psyche of an entire generation" (Davis).

While claims of mysticism may be exaggerated, there was something elec-
trifying about these live *Brady Bunch* episodes for audiences of a certain age,
addressing a desire in the new generation of theatre-goers to have its own
memories and experience dramatized. Writing a year later, a critic for the
Village Voice analyzed the popularity of the *Brady Bunch* stage show:

> Every generation reaches out for childhood as it approaches middle age. The return
> of the Bradys is one more sign that the twenty-somethings have come into their own.
> . . . Is anyone surprised that the new generation would define itself by a sitcom? . . .
> One "Brady theory" cites the show's innocence. . . . But finally the appeal is that this is
> theater, not TV. These actors and these production values would seem just a pale imita-
> tion on the tube. Live, the audience's rabid enthusiasm becomes part of the show. It's a
> return to childhood with your adult friends, more slumber party than a play. There's a
> camaraderie in the shared guilt of having been shaped by the Bradys. (Massa 100)

Most *Real Live Brady Bunch* fans came from the rerun generation, adults
in their twenties who were in grade school or junior high in the mid-to late
'70s. They had watched this fictional family not in first-run episodes, but in
afternoon repeats that played five afternoons a week, just as they got home
from school. It was a daily ritual, a childhood mainstay.[7] Live performances
made that private ritual public, a communal affirmation of childhood fantasies. Co-creator Jill Soloway explained the phenomenon this way: "Those of
us who never got to protest, and weren't part of the MTV generation, are left
with the *Brady Bunch* and *Saturday Night Fever*." Faith Soloway added, "As
embarrassing as it is, it's something that people celebrate. It's ours, and we
can laugh at it" (qtd. in Davis).

At the same time, the live performance made the *Brady Bunch* world more
tangible and more ridiculous. On television, the Brady's petty concerns and
inane platitudes were an accepted part of their sitcom universe. Out of the
box, each line and gesture became more obviously excessive through the simple fact of its material embodiment. The audience laughed in affectionate
recognition of the beloved *Brady Bunch* characters, but it also laughed at itself
for once believing in them—for wanting *to be* them. The obvious mimicry of
an earlier style and the disparity of age between actors and characters invited

a new critical distance—a reassessment of the norms and expectations that the *Brady Bunch* had foisted on its impressionable young audience.

In one interview, Jill Soloway reevaluated the character of Alice, the maid, from a '90s perspective: "There's a lot to Alice that we of this age are starting to figure out. She was the dark side of the Bunch. She represents what'll happen to you if you're not a member of the Bradys: You'll be old and unmarried and have to run around, chasing after other people's kids, slipping on Chinese checkers" (Davis). In a gesture to Alice and another side of '70s experience, each *Real Live Brady Bunch* show included an epilogue in which a recorded version of the drug anthem "Go Ask Alice" played as the Brady kids passed a marijuana joint. Susan Messing, who played youngest sister Cindy in blonde pigtails, notes, "It's also sort of mind-blowing that . . . the Vietnam war and 'The Brady Bunch' shared an era" ("Here's a Story").

Throughout the 1990–91 season, biweekly episodes encouraged repeat attendance, expanding the Annoyance cult following. At its high point, this low-budget theatre event evoked the kind of energy and enthusiasm usually reserved for rock concerts. The company had been nervous about obtaining and affording the rights to the original show. But in October 1990, *Brady Bunch* (and *Gilligan's Island*) producer Sherwood Schwartz came to check out this stage version of his creation. Audiences recited the words along with the episode, in *Rocky Horror* fashion, then erupted in cheers when the venerable creator was introduced, chanting "Sher-wood! Sher-wood!" The seventy-three-year-old Schwartz told the *Chicago Tribune*, "It was the most incredible experience I've ever had. . . . I felt like a rock star—at my age" (qtd. in Caro). Schwartz was so pleased with what he perceived as the affection and respect the actors showed his work that he intervened with Paramount Television to make the Annoyance performances legit, arranging for a token royalty that satisfied the studio's legal department. [8]

Sutton calls the 1990–91 season a renaissance year for the Annoyance, which at one point had four successful weekend shows running at once and several experimental projects or short runs playing midweek. Core members of the company were free to develop projects whenever inspiration struck. In addition to *Co-ed Prison Sluts*, *That Darned Antichrist! Manson, the Musical*, and *The Real Live Brady Bunch*, the season included *Sex Boy*; *Pup Tent Theatre*; *Your Butt*; *Ayn Rand Gives Me a Boner*; *Viva Las Elvis, Elvis, Elvis*; and *Tippi: Portrait of a Virgin—An Afterschool Special Gone Bad*. Virtually all of these were based on recognizable genres, such as a Vegas club act or an afterschool special, and tended to include ever more outrageous and scatological material.

From her position as a relative outsider, Jill Soloway felt that women at

Well-meaning parents simply don't understand teen angst in the Annoyance musical parody
Tippi, Portrait of a Virgin: An Afterschool Special Gone Bad. Pictured: Bob Morand and Susan
Messing as Mom and Dad, Dave Summers as brother Terence, and Melanie Hutsell as the
aggressively virginal Tippi. Photo: Courtesy Annoyance Theatre.

the Annoyance spent too much stage time "decorating the male action" or
"attending male needs" (personal interview). Faith Soloway was more attuned
to the Annoyance way of life and art where "no one is spared." She advised,
"The only way to make a change, or to make your mark was to *do* something"
(personal interview). The Soloways were feeling confident and even powerful
given the enormous success of their *Brady Bunch* idea. They invited all the
Annoyance women to join them in creating an original show representing a
female point of view. Six signed on (including Susan Messing). The group
began to explore, to discover what happened "when women are together
without worrying about men" and to find their own comic sensibility (J.
Soloway interview). Jill recalls the rehearsal process as a "freeing experience
for all of us. We would turn off all the lights, put on music loud, take our
shirts off, and dance around. It was a beautiful, trusting thing. We laughed
and improvised and came up with *The Miss Vagina Pageant*" (personal interview).

The Miss Vagina Pageant was a feminist parody of the sexist beauty industry, using the contest to comment on body-image issues and the objectifica-

tion of women. Audiences and critics raved about the show, and the group was offered a Los Angeles tour. *Saturday Night Live* producer Lorne Michaels later cast two of the "contestants," Beth Cahill and Melanie Hutsell, after seeing them in the *Pageant*. The success of *The Real Live Brady Bunch* made her proud, Jill says, but the *Pageant* "was our hearts" (personal interview).

At its peak in 1991, the Annoyance had grown to encompass more than forty actors, many of whom played in several shows each week, often two or more shows in a night, with late shows and late-late shows on weekends. To manage this schedule, the Annoyance was forced to break with its own traditions of amateurism to pay a part-time administrator. Mark Sutton took the job. Yet, Napier and many of the core members of Annoyance were ambivalent about their financial success. By company agreement, the actors still played for nothing more than a free dinner between shows. The troupe could ill afford to pay all of the performers now participating in its many productions. On a philosophical level, Napier was convinced that money was the root of Second City's and ImprovOlympic's fall from grace. "I know what happens when the dollar enters the picture. I've seen it too much," he told one journalist. "It can mess up what happens on stage. It can mess up the freedom. People start working against each other. If I had a million dollars in the bank, betcha I'd pay actors. But I'd probably figure out some socialist or communist way of doing it" (Spitznagel 32).

Burned by past experience, Napier strove to keep three months' rent in the bank at all times. But the troupe was "concerned about not making artistic decisions based on money"(S. Smith, "Beyond the Fringe" 25). After six months, they closed the still-lucrative *Manson* because they felt it was time. And Napier informed the press, "[W]e might close the 'Brady Bunch' this summer if we feel it has run its course" (25).

The only moneymaker the company did not close was *Co-ed Prison Sluts*, because, said Napier, the show was created from the "ashes" of their commercial and artistic failure with *Splatter II*, and "it means a lot to us" (S. Smith, "Beyond the Fringe" 25). *Co-ed Prison Sluts* represented the work of hardcore Annoyance loyalists who had demonstrated their commitment to process. Its artistic and philosophical integrity could not be questioned. As such, *Co-ed* could be permitted commercial success—it could even be exploited as an ongoing financial crutch for other ventures. *The Real Live Brady Bunch*, however, had become such a commercial commodity that it forced the Annoyance to an unpleasant realization of their overall dependence on ticket sales to support their process.

But the national notoriety of the *Brady Bunch* concept offered financial reward and career opportunities beyond Chicago and the Annoyance Theatre.

At first, the Soloway sisters resisted the possibility of taking the show further. In 1990, Jill Soloway told the *Chicago Tribune* that moving the show would ruin its appeal: "I think that the charm would be lost if it were a big money making venture. . . . Faith and I make not a dollar off of it. The money goes into the theater so they can perform 'legitimate' shows" (Caro 5). Yet, in the fall of 1991, when New York producers offered to sponsor the show at the Village Gate, the Soloways accepted. They took the Bradys—and more than half the Annoyance troupe—to New York, creating a schism that wracked the company, shaking beliefs and straining friendships.

At first, the trip was billed as an Annoyance touring company and had the troupe's cautious support. But the departure of so many key actors jeopardized the home team's survival. Some Annoyance members saw the New York offer as a moment to declare their personal priorities and to choose between improvisation as an art form and rote performance as a springboard to careers in entertainment. Sutton recalls, "Everybody had the option, either go or stay. I chose to stay because I couldn't see myself growing as a performer by doing the *Brady Bunch* eight times a week in New York—no matter how much money" (personal interview).

But for the Soloway sisters the choice was "not an integrity call, but a life choice call" (F. Soloway interview). In their mid-late twenties, the Soloways were ready to progress from the playground to the adult world of professionalism. Faith enjoyed her collaborative composing with the troupe and respected Napier's artistic vision for the Annoyance: "It's a family, a community, a philosophy, and a way to keep creating." She especially appreciated the way Napier empowered actors "to be the best they can be" (personal interview). But she did not belong to the subculture or social scene of the Annoyance the way many of the actors did, and did not want or need the same things many of them got from it. Jill saw the New York move as a painful power struggle between Napier's ideas of selfless commitment and her desire to take care of the actors by getting them paying gigs. She never thought of the venture as "selling out" but as "getting to work as a professional" (personal interview). With some replacements (including Andy Richter stepping in for Mark Sutton), the casts of *The Real Live Brady Bunch* and *The Real Live Game* show headed for the Big Apple.

The remaining Annoyance loyalists struggled to sustain the eleven weekly performances on the theatre's schedule. Many, including Sutton, found themselves in every show, working virtually seven nights a week. At the same time, *The Real Live Brady Bunch* packed audiences into the Village Gate, garnering feature coverage in the *Village Voice* and *Newsweek* and on television talk shows.

Journalist Adler attended a 1991 Annoyance company meeting where players in touch with the New York contingent reported that the *Brady* cast was bored and missed "the fun of playing the Annoyance way, where nothing is ever finished" ("In Your Face"). The group also discussed a request from *Brady* performer Tom Booker, who hoped to reproduce Annoyance hits at a New York branch to be called "Annoyance East."

Sutton threw the proposition open to the group, and Napier led the discussion. Yet, his inquiry did not focus on finances or franchise fees: "Napier's questions are directed at issues of aesthetic and communal integrity: How are we going to protect our process? How are we going to maintain our family? How are we going to keep it fun? In short, he's very deliberately critiquing the proposal on the basis of its essential fuck-it-ness" (Adler, "In Your Face" 91).

As Adler notes, the group seemed uncomfortable talking about legalities and finances at all. They finally agreed to allow Booker to bill productions as "originated at the Annoyance." Like many efforts to remount classic Annoyance shows using scripts and legitimate actors instead of improvisers, Booker's project inevitably failed. In the same year, an independent, Annoyance-sanctioned production of *Co-ed Prison Sluts* had a well-reviewed but very short life off-off-Broadway.

Meanwhile, *The Real Live Brady Bunch* flourished. The Annoyance's involvement in the project now was rarely even mentioned by the press. But the real break between the Chicago faithful and the New York troupe came when the Soloways signed an independent contract with their new producers and entered negotiations for a Los Angeles engagement without acknowledging the Annoyance as a co-owner or producer. The Annoyance had mounted the original show from its inception, just as it did with any of its original shows, providing the space, publicity, and labor, and paying for the thrift-store costumes and minimal sets. For their parts, the Soloways had conceived the idea of the live performances, transcribed the television shows, and recreated the music, laugh track, and acting style. No contracts were ever drawn, and no promises of payment were ever made to the performers or directors. The Annoyance had always operated on the understanding that everyone worked together for the sake of the work itself and the ongoing financial health of the company.

Thus, when the Soloways hired a lawyer to determine their rights to *The Real Live Brady Bunch* concept, it seemed to many at the Annoyance to be an affront to their entire value system. Moreover, it forced the Annoyance to confront issues of property that the troupe had studiously avoided. Ambivalent about ownership, the company had always assumed collective ownership and collective authorship of its improvised work. Angry and hurt, Napier and crew did little to fight the Soloways' claims. In the absence of a legal agreement, the Soloways began sending the Annoyance a check for $250 each week of the *Brady Bunch*'s run, although they were careful to call the payment a gift rather than a royalty.

The Soloways' rift with the Annoyance was interpreted differently by the various parties involved. As Napier would later allegorize it, the Soloways had succumbed to the joyless proselytes of money and commercial success who wanted nothing more than to destroy the carnival, the utopia that was the Annoyance. But to some outsiders (and former insiders), the Annoyance had begun to resemble a cult that exploited its talented performers by paying them with feel-good philosophy instead of fair wages for their labor. Jill Soloway "didn't want to be part of the Mick cult anymore" (personal interview).

The Soloways were grateful for the opportunity to mount *The Real Live Brady Bunch*, but they knew the project was only a "bastard child" at the Annoyance. Napier and company "didn't want to own it, didn't want to run it on weekends" (F. Soloway interview). The sisters reasoned that fourteen months of income from the show was enough payback for the theatre's original investment. If they and the performers could ride the *Brady Bunch* to wage-earning careers in entertainment, they deserved that chance.

For Napier, Sutton, and many others at the time, the *Brady* defection seemed the height of betrayal. Of all the players who left for New York, very few returned to Chicago or to the Annoyance, though a handful did go on to make careers in show business.[9] In cooler hindsight, Sutton and Napier say they understand the actors' need to pursue career opportunities, adding that they wouldn't want to stand in anyone's way. But they clearly see this episode in their history as another example of the evils of money and product over process. Now a respected folksinger/composer in Boston, Faith says she looks at the Annoyance and the *Brady* show as "a huge learning experience that I still draw on today" (personal interview). Jill, a television comedy writer in Los Angeles, still struggles to reconcile supporting herself and saying what she wants to say. She believes that Napier "is the new Del Close—a revolutionary in theatre. He'll keep training young people in his brilliant way" (personal interview).

Despite the company's conflicting emotions about the place of *The Real Live Brady Bunch* in the Annoyance mission, however, this project struck a chord with the same young audiences that enjoyed the pop-culture send-ups in other Annoyance productions. In fact, the company went on to produce popular live performances of the animated television favorites *The Grinch*

Who Stole Christmas and *A Charlie Brown Christmas* as holiday audience pleasers.

At the same time, the touring *Real Live Brady Bunch* garnered even more national attention, and the ensuing Bradymania proved a powerful catalyst for many other television-based theatre and film projects, including two *Brady Bunch* movies directed by Second City alumna Betty Thomas. Sutton notes with chagrin that no one involved with the films acknowledged Annoyance's part in setting this trend.

Over the next few years the theatre regrouped and continued to generate improv-based shows that consistently derived much of their humor from re-combinations of pop-culture references and idiosyncratic characters. The company often refused to articulate any philosophy beyond that of "having fun," but a more complex and cynical Annoyance ideology emerged, clearly colored by their *Brady* experience. Late in 1992, the Annoyance suffered yet another financial setback—again based in part on the willful carelessness they practiced in economic matters. An unexpected tax bill suddenly put the company fifteen thousand dollars in the hole. Staggering under this new debt, the Annoyance muddled through the next two seasons, looking for a new, more affordable space and for fresh sources of income. In 1994, the Annoyance found a new home on Clark Street, mere blocks from Wrigley Field and the club spaces where ImprovOlympic performed.

For the Annoyance, as for most working improv theatres, classes and workshops offered by senior members of the company were an important source of income. By 1993, an increasing number of up-and-coming improvisers were taking classes in several places at once, supplementing the regimented Second City training with the alternative techniques they could learn at ImprovOlympic, the Annoyance, and other growing theatres. By this time, it was commonly known that taking classes with the Annoyance was one of the few means of working one's way into the company. Annoyance directors never held auditions, pointing out that there were no parts to cast since actors created their own roles through the improvisational rehearsal process. Instead of auditioning, performers were invited to participate in individual projects, perhaps because the director had seen and liked their work, or perhaps because they had been hanging around long enough—attending shows, helping clean up or build sets, or taking classes.

Anyone with enough persistence and the ability to live the Annoyance credo might even wind up with a personal key to the theatre building. For example, one fan, a middle-aged film booker for DisneyCorp, Ken Manthey, saw *Co-ed Prison Sluts* more than one hundred times before taking a class with the Annoyance. Within a few months he was playing the prison warden in *Co-ed* on stage and running the Annoyance box office.

In classes, the Annoyance regulars feel free to explore their battered carnival ideals. Napier says, "I feel purest and safest and most empowered in my classroom because that really sticks to getting on stage and doing scenes—just really pulling it out of the air. And that's just the purest form of it, and that's where I feel the most clarity" (personal interview).

After teaching and directing for some time, Napier realized that it had been several years since he had actually performed improv. Admitting his own fears of being judged by students and colleagues, Napier leapt back into the fray, if only so he wouldn't have to "wake up a hypocrite" each morning. Indeed, Napier's main lesson to students is to "fight the fear" in themselves (personal interview). He coaches them to make powerful choices and stick to them, and tells students that strong commitment to their own idea (rather than immediate support for someone else's) *does* support the scene. He teaches them to break the conventional rules of improv, focusing on character behavior instead of abstract structures. Much as in any other school of improv, he valorizes the instinctive over the intellectual, believing that improvisation is akin to a force of nature:

It's a visceral philosophy, believe me, but I truly believe that an improv scene—I believe that anything that's worth anything in the world is an extension or microcosm of fucking or of sex. And I believe that that's why [improv is] like two people together, coming together to create life. That's what sex is, that's why we enjoy it, and that's why we are here, to propagate our species; and an improv scene can be an experience that rises in its action as much as that. The metaphor is intact for me because what I've noticed in a really good improv scene is lack of judgment, a spirituality about it. My body issues disappear, my self-judgment and judgment of my partner disappear and all we're doing is going, going, going—doing more of what we're doing, doing more of what we're doing—whatever it is—and we both climax, scene transforms, lights out, have a beer. You know what I mean? (personal interview)

Napier's linkage of improvisation and sex elicits once again the analogy between the Annoyance version of improv and Bakhtin's description of carnival. According to cultural critic Frances Gray's analysis, however, this very connection proves a gender disparity underlying Bakhtin's idea: "The carnival world is one of material pleasures, of food and drink, song and dance and sport, and, inevitably, sexuality. But for the last three and a half thousand years sexuality has meant male sexuality. Women's right to pleasure has certainly been from time to time envisaged. But I can't help wondering what it

was like for a lone woman to walk the streets at carnival, and whether in this
free communion she had the right to say no; and who looked after the subsequent babies if she didn't" (31–32).

In the theatrical world of improv-comedy, the consequences of heterosexual white male dominance are far less material than those Gray describes.
While improvisers might represent violence or sexual aggression, they do not
actually carry it through. Nevertheless, as I have demonstrated in earlier chapters, the "right to say no" is a contested issue within the field of improv play,
where laws of *agreement* are paramount. Improv is a fantasy world, to be sure,
where both the carnival and the sex act are metaphors of performance. Yet
these parallels are powerful, affecting interpersonal dynamics on and off the
stage and thus shaping both the process and the representations in each improvised scene.

Yet, according to Napier, "It's not really men that place women in subordinate roles, it's men exhibiting *x* amount of power onstage, and women, because they're in the minority or because everything they've experienced in
their lives dictates that they do so, find themselves in reaction to men" (qtd.
in Pollack B22). To address this problem, in Annoyance terms, women need
to commit themselves all the more thoroughly to the improv process, although not necessarily to such rules of improv as perpetual agreement. Stoneking asserts, "The Annoyance gives you permission to say 'no' and
permission to be strong. 'No' can be a gift—because drama is conflict" (personal interview).

At the Annoyance carnival, each member is expected to play as an individual, responding to the impulses, desires, and inspirations of the character, the
scene, and the moment without regard for larger constructs of power and
identity. Napier insists, "It's very difficult for me to go up on stage and improvise if I'm in reaction to a social phenomenon or in reaction to a gender. It
puts me in a very powerless position" (personal interview). By focusing on
the individual, Napier, Stoneking, Messing, and other Annoyance regulars
genuinely believe that their improv utopia can escape worldly restrictions.

By the late '80s, and increasing with the third wave of improv, more
women started to participate in Chicago improv, and many of them began to
object to exploitation and manipulation throughout the improv community.
Many who had endured first- and second-wave misogyny had now matured
to become role models for those who followed. Women in the third wave
began to develop and share strategies for survival. Many searched for ways to
assert their own power without destroying the free-flowing qualities they still
valued in the improv process.

In 1993, Napier sponsored a course designed to address the issue of woman bashing in Chicago improv. He supported the project, he says, only because he was "tired of hearing women whine about unfairness" (personal interview). His tough talk is in line with the Annoyance credo that individuals are responsible for their own baggage, but Napier's actions consistently show him to be receptive to women's issues. Annoyance rhetoric notwithstanding, the classes, taught by company members Susan Messing and Jodi Lennon, were crowded with women players, from beginners to members of Second City's mainstage cast. The focus of the course—get tough and stop complaining. Although Lennon left for New York shortly after the first workshops ended, women improvisers have urged Messing to continue offering similar classes each year.

Messing's third-wave philosophies regarding women in improv were formulated from her long and often embattled experience in second-wave troupes. A theatre major at Northwestern University in 1987, she discovered improv at ImprovOlympic, where she began taking classes with Charna Halpern. Messing persevered at ImprovOlympic through sheer stubbornness, or what she calls "masochism," while many other women dropped out, discouraged by the competition and Halpern's unrelenting criticism. Halpern, Messing recalls, was particularly harsh with the few women in her classes and almost never supportive. Messing next found herself "the girl" on the breakout team Blue Velveeta. With this gonzo group, Messing earned the reputation of being able to take, and run with, anything that was thrown at her—and the material was often raunchy, physical, and sexually explicit. Through Blue Velveeta, Messing became known as "one of the best woman improvisers in Chicago," though she rejects the qualifier "woman," questioning what "having a vagina and breasts and the ability to bear children" has to do with being a great improviser (personal interview).

Messing also flung herself into what some call the improv lifestyle—which almost always included heavy drinking, pot smoking, and other drugs. While Messing herself is not a big drinker, she describes the alcoholic impulse in her fellow improvisers as an insatiable need to find alternative realities, as they do in improv: "Improv is constant escape. For some people it's exploration, and for other people it's escape" (personal interview). Messing has whiskey-soaked memories of one Blue Velveeta tour, sponsored by Southern Comfort distillers, in which she and five men visited army barracks across the United States. The most common suggestion from the audience, Messing remembers, was "Show us your tits!" (personal interview). She prides herself on staying focused and committed to the improvisational moment through every challenge. Nevertheless, it became clear to Messing that men on both sides of the footlights used the suggestibility of improvisation to push her into conventionally objectified positions.

Partly because women were scarce in improv circles, Messing also found herself with a very active social life. But male improvisers, she says, are often dysfunctional in real-life relationships. Repeating a charge expressed by many women on the improv circuit, Messing says of some of her partners, "It's hysterical that onstage they can have the permission to say anything they've ever wanted, to be whoever they want to be—goals and yearnings and expressions of love and fear and tears. And then they get offstage and it's like [short raspberry]—nothing" (personal interview). Though Messing does not comment further, this disparity may help explain the attraction of improv for many people who need permission to express themselves.

After Blue Velveeta broke up, Messing became a devoted member of the Annoyance, helping to create *Co-ed Prison Sluts* and performing in that show almost every Saturday night for over seven years. While Second City would normally have tried to recruit a woman with Messing's talent, Second City director-administrator Anne Libera believes that some directors found Messing too intense and unpredictable for that institution, where they preferred their women younger and more "trainable" (personal interview).[10]

At the Annoyance, however, Messing's toughness and aggressiveness was valued, as it meshed with the group's philosophy of personal empowerment. While she performed with many groups throughout the city, the Annoyance remained Messing's home base because she felt accepted and free to create her own projects there. She earned her living doing commercials, industrials, and voice-overs in Chicago, and frequently tithed her own income to the Annoyance to help pay expenses. To women who would call the company sexist, Messing answers that men and women are treated completely equally at the Annoyance—with respect but no mercy. According to Messing, a woman just has to be strong enough to take whatever is dished out and give as good as she gets.

In the women's workshops, Messing allowed her students some time to vent frustrations and experiences but resisted allowing the class to become an encounter group. Instead, she taught assertiveness and self-permission, saying, "If you make a choice for yourself, a very powerful one, right off the bat, then they won't make your choice for you, number one" (personal interview). And if someone does make a character choice for her, Messing adds, it becomes her job to turn it into a powerful one. Instead of resenting being defined as a whore, she says, embrace the opportunity to make that whore a unique character with a key role in the scene. Messing advises, "[A lot of women] feel very manipulated. And this is an art that *you* have to manipulate.

You have to manipulate yourself through space, and so if you are led through the space, you might be angry about it. I am not angry about it. I never am. I have been given choices, choices have been made for me that I have not cared for, and I have to swallow it, swallow the judgment, and make it work . . . as time and tide and perspective come around, you realize you can play with anything" (personal interview).

In her workshops, Messing teaches that most women's trouble centers on their belief that they must obey the rules of agreement while they watch men break those rules. Yet she insists that this should never be an excuse for weak playing. Messing gives her students permission to break the rules themselves. Better still, she says, maintain agreement but practice *defenses and escapes*. If a scene partner ignores you, make the scene about a relationship in which the man ignores the woman. If he denies your reality, become a character who is confused about the facts of the situation, and make it work for you. Messing gives the example of a scene in which she established a beach location in Barbados. An insensitive scene partner denied her reality, placing the scene in Las Vegas. Messing accordingly built her whole character around the notion that she had constant fantasies of being in Barbados.

Is it unfair that women have to work through defenses and escapes more than men do? Why must women be on guard, proactive, and aggressive when men can afford to experiment with passive roles? How can women fight their own socialization and the larger systemic rules that become naturalized as archetypes and truths? Messing dismisses these questions by saying, "Don't fight. Just do it. 'Cause that's what improv is about—doing it. It's not getting off the stage and saying this system is askew—we're all aware that this system is askew. I'll be the first one to tell you, through watching and action, that this is not an equally balanced system. Comedy in general is a man's sport. . . . But as a strong, funny woman, I show that women can do it" (personal interview).

Despite her assertion that the "system is askew" and her many experiences of sexism in improv, Messing believes, with Napier, and most players, that good improv is (or should be preserved as) a neutral space untainted by politics or ideology. She concurs with many improvisers that conscious resistance to society's status quo comprises a political agenda and that any agenda (particularly a feminist one) interferes with committed improv. Many believe that actors with something specific to say tend to force a scene instead of allowing it to unfold. Refusing to take a demeaning suggestion can also cause players to be stiff and self-conscious on stage. Napier says that a conscious politics simply doesn't work improvisationally: "I've been there with that. I've been there with my homosexuality, I've been there with the way I think things are in the world. I've been there in a lot of ways. . . . Susan's been there. But it's not because I want to go out there and speak and defend homosexuality. I can't improvise that way" (personal interview). But Messing, Napier, and many other players seem willing to ignore the underlying ideology of the status quo and the so-called neutral spaces—no less political for being un-marked and naturalized as "the way things are." At the same time, Napier insists, no one should ever improvise anything contrary to his or her own values. In other words, he believes the power is in the process—not in a preconceived idea but in the emergent interaction and specific instance. He is confident that genuine free play will always challenge oppressive limitations—taboos, prejudice, hypocrisy—but in an organic way. At the Annoyance carni-val, according to the company, there are no politics—only relationships. At one level, Messing recognizes that those personal interactions *are* political. She pursues her own feminist agenda moment by moment, tactically and opportunistically, as a good improviser knows how.

While several women have found a supportive home at the company, oth-ers are uncomfortable with the carnival atmosphere at the Annoyance and the aggressive intensity it requires. Some, like the women of Free Associates, sought a safer environment and a more organized approach to improv.

Since the move to their third home in 1994, the Annoyance maintained its position in Chicago as an important alternative theatre, improv school, and youth hangout. Recognized as the spiritual link between Del Close's Harold at ImprovOlympic and serious long-form troupes such as Jazz Freddy and Ed, the Annoyance was also widely acknowledged for paving the way for a new generation of pop-culture theatres. The Factory Theatre and the Torso Theatre, for example, deliberately emulated the postmodern parodic style of *Co-ed Prison Sluts* to create their long-running shows, including *Cannibal Cheerleaders on Crack* and *Shannen Doherty Shoots a Porno*.

The Annoyance continued to produce improv-based shows, including *Brainwarp the Baby Eater*, *The Idiotic Death of Two Fools*, *Modern Problems in Science*, *Poo Poo Le Arse*, *Ladies on the Couch*, *Carpet Full of Pain*, *Pigs is Pigs*, and *Donkey Improv* (featuring live donkeys). While none of these attained the cult status of *Co-ed Prison Sluts*, several Annoyance projects went on to na-tional or international acclaim. *So I Killed a Few People . . .* , created in 1997 by Gary Ruderman and David Summers, played successfully in San Francisco, New York, and London. According to the *Village Voice*, this brutally funny one-man show about a serial killer is "terrifying and oddly moving . . . a chilling impersonation within killing distance" (Russo).

In 1998, Messing adapted and directed *What Every Girl Should Know—An*

Ode to Judy Blume, based on Blume's popular books for adolescent girls. The show garnered capacity crowds of mostly female audiences—and a call from Blume's lawyer. As with Schwartz and the *Brady Bunch*, Blume withdrew her objections after seeing the show and the audience's passionate response.[11]

Co-ed Prison Sluts continued, throughout the 1990s, as the longest-running musical in Chicago history—becoming a virtual rite of passage for local college students. Sutton even considered launching an ad campaign capitalizing on the phenomenon: "*Co-ed Prison Sluts*—if you haven't seen it, you must be a freshman" (personal interview).

Through classes and other programming, company members actively encouraged new blood and fresh ideas by involving younger actors in their work. While a growing number of women participated in classes and shows, the hangout factor so important to Annoyance membership remained largely a male phenomenon, perhaps, in part, because the aggressive Annoyance ethos takes more effort for many women to sustain. Although grateful for the enthusiasm and energy of these new players, Sutton was also concerned that improv's next generation was increasingly disconnected from the life experiences that are the crucial material of improv: "They don't know anything but improv. I don't want to be insulting, but read a book; go see a play that's not an improv show" (personal interview).

The Annoyance branched into other media with Napier's film project, *Fatty Drives the Bus*, an independent feature that took two years and eighty thousand dollars of hard-earned money to produce (finally released in 1999).

Susan Messing's *Ode to Judy Blume* featured (left to right) Julia Wolov as Deenie, Christina Gausas as Catherine from *Forever* and Dana Goodman as Margaret from *Are You There, God? It's Me, Margaret*. Photo: Aaron Gang.

Napier also directed *Exit 57,* a limited-run television series for Comedy Central. In 1999, the company established Annoyance Productions to pursue additional television and film projects and set up a small production studio at the theatre.

With official Annoyance blessing, mainstay members began exploring outside opportunities as a guard against burnout. In a move that seems to bring the waves of Chicago improv full circle, Napier directed several important mainstage shows for Second City.[12] He was almost immediately credited with revitalizing that company's flagging energy. His 1996 venture, *Citizen Gates,* was reviewed by the *Chicago Reader* as "one of the keenest mainstage revues yet" (Bommer). The show was praised for its use of long-form–inspired innovations such as running sketches and surreal scenic elements, but was also lauded for its "refreshing absence of TV-generated humor" and its sharp political satire (Bommer). Perhaps even more important, Napier cast the first gender-balanced troupe—three women and three men—to create a show for Second City's mainstage and gave unusual focus and comedy opportunity to the women players.[13] For Napier, this simple shift freed the women from being purely functional in male scenes and opened fresh opportunities for him as a director. He was also aware that each Second City TourCo worked from the archives of mainstage scripts, saying, "I'm happy that now they'll be able to find a relationship scene for two women" (personal interview). Again, Napier acts like a feminist even while he denies it.

Napier brought a third-wave attitude and second-wave long-form structure to this first-wave institution. But he was also able and willing to focus the material on Second City's mainstay—social and political satire—which required far more conscious scripting than the Annoyance usually prefers. Napier directed several more critically acclaimed shows for Second City, maintaining a gender-balanced cast. With *Paradigm Lost* (1997), the director shared his creative process with fans and fellow improvisers over the internet, posting regular entries of his *Paradigm Lost Journal* on the Annoyance web site. In his next two outings, Napier replaced departing Second City players with core members of the Annoyance family, casting Susan Messing in *The Psychopath Not Taken* (1998) and Ed Furman in the fortieth anniversary show, *Second City 4.0* (1999).

For years, Messing had been considered too much of a loose cannon to work at Second City. To preempt any criticism, Napier gave his colleague a long list of rules designed to contain her behavior in rehearsal, and Messing took them to heart—so much so that she felt her improv became tentative and self-censoring. While Messing admits that a male improviser (Furman, for example) would probably not have been so strictly instructed, she harbors

Susan Messing as a fierce housewife and Rich Talarico as a hapless burglar in a scene from *The Psychopath Not Taken*, directed by Mick Napier for Second City. Photo: Michael Brosilow

no resentment: "My power is about acquiescing. Maybe my power isn't 'fuck you and your rules'; maybe it's 'how can I use those rules to get better?' " (personal interview). Most Second City players say it takes a year to feel confident on the mainstage, and Messing was no exception. Once she had proven she had good "table manners" in the rehearsal process, Messing was able to express herself more freely. Looking back on her career, she reflects, "Had I gone through the Second City path first, I might not be as powerful now" (personal interview).[14]

Their increasing involvement with Second City gave Annoyance directors and performers more prestige in the rapidly growing national improv community. By the mid-nineties, the company was recognized as one of a triumvirate of important Chicago training centers, along with Second City and ImprovOlympic. But as core members split their focus between the company and other opportunities, some began to feel a loss of energy and vitality in Annoyance productions. By 1999, Napier had gone four years without devising a new show for the Annoyance. Even *Co-ed Prison Sluts* was beginning to show signs of wear.

The following year, Napier did return to create *Madcap*, an original Brechtian-style musical featuring a number of Annoyance veterans and with a score, written in faithful homage to Kurt Weill, by Lisa McQueen (composer of

Tippi: Portrait of a Virgin). But even as rehearsals began, the owner of the troupe's Clark Street home announced he had sold the building to developers who planned to tear it down to create parking for patrons of Wrigley Field.

Fans and students of the theatre company were devastated by the news. Napier was undaunted. After thirteen years and ninety-two original stage productions, he admitted, "[Y]ou want to try something else. The prospect of doing something innovative and groundbreaking is very exciting for me" (qtd. in Kim). With Sutton and the other Annoyance leadership, Napier seized the opportunity to reinvent the Annoyance mission. An avid navigator of cyberspace, he recognized that developments in digital technology were creating new markets, new audiences, new modes of production, and new forms of entertainment. As Sutton noted, "There are two types of people in the market right now: those that have the technology and are looking for content and those that have the content but don't know how the technology works. We want to fuse the two together, a one-of-a-kind place that houses both the technology and the art" (qtd. in Moe).

Napier and Sutton announced a final two weeks of performances, after which the Annoyance would close its doors. Even *Co-ed Prison Sluts*, at eleven years Chicago's longest-running musical, would close "forever." The company, they promised, would reemerge in a new form after funding, finding, and designing a "new media production site with a state-of-the-art digital production studio, a smaller live venue; and a continuation of its training arm, where improv and acting classes are offered" (qtd. in Obejas 3).

The Annoyance orchestrated farewell reprise productions of several of its classic shows, including *That Darned Antichrist! Tippi: Portrait of a Virgin*, and *So I Killed a Few People . . .* , along with several special showings of *Co-ed*. From this overview of original material, the Annoyance approach to gender, sexuality, and race on its stage could be clearly seen. Annoyance women had had ample opportunity to play bimbos and sexual objects over the years, but they had also created a wide range of female characters—from the lesbian couple in *Antichrist* and the unsinkable Tippi to *Co-ed*'s Dame Toulouse— who were powerful and desiring subjects.

As the parade of characters and situations passed in review, the company's lack of diversity was also apparent. The only player of color to appear in the last weeks, Marz Timms stepped into a role in *Tippi* originally improvised by a white actor. As Rocky Brewster, illegitimate son of the tyrannical Waldo Brewster of Brewster Falls, Timms improvised several new lines to play up his African American identity and its implications for the plot. Timms also took a turn as Skeeter in *Co-ed*. Annoyance policy had always been to welcome any individual who wanted to play and to adapt or create material accordingly.

Sutton once cast Timms as Rudolph the Red-Nosed Reindeer in a Christmas spoof to make a sly reference to racism when Rudolph is excluded from the "reindeer games." But the intense carnival atmosphere at the theatre could appear intimidating and inaccessible to outsiders, and the Annoyance had not had the resources actively to undertake diversity programming as Second City had in recent years.

Several of the Annoyance revivals spoofed the homophobia so often prevalent in improv and comedy circles. In *Tippi*, for example, a pair of football heroes suddenly find themselves in several intimate situations. The first two times it seems they might kiss, these macho men catch themselves, recoil, and back away in horror. The audience laughs at the familiar fear-based joke. But the third time "Rocky" and "Clark" are thrown together, they toss caution to the wind, embrace one another, and sing a sweet love song ("You're My Favorite Tight End"). Through the rest of the play, they are a happy, unstereotypical, and unapologetic couple.[15] And the audience goes along, sometimes despite themselves. Overall, Annoyance shows depict a spectrum of desire—female and male, heterosexual, gay, lesbian, transvestite, transsexual, and beyond. Each embodiment of that desire is shown to be equally grotesque, equally life-giving—and equally, joyfully comic.

For their final night in the old space, the Annoyance planned a gala performance of *Co-ed Prison Sluts* to feature most of the original 1989 cast. Second City granted Messing and Furman the night off to reprise Alice and Slick, while Bob Fisher flew in from New York City to play sweet, sadistic Henry. The reunion was also an occasion for healing old wounds. Composer-pianist Faith Soloway traveled from Boston and actor Tom Booker (Dr. Bello) took time from his theatre company in California to participate in the alumni production. It was the first time since the *Brady Bunch* rift years earlier that either had returned to the Annoyance, but all sides were eager to repair the relationships. Napier explained, "We were young, we had opinions; I had an opinion. What we found was that creative ventures are difficult and we found—more importantly—that we liked the people we were fighting with more than being right about the discrepancy" (qtd. in Obejas 3).

Bearing cases of beer and souvenir programs, the four hundred fans fortunate enough to score a ticket thronged into the theatre to say good-bye to a show that had become important to many. One couple in their late twenties or early thirties confessed they had seen *Co-ed* seventeen times over the past seven years. "It was our first date," said Michelle, "and we always bring someone new. I feel sorry for all the people who will never get to see it" (personal interview). Backstage, emotions were running high, with many of the actors fighting tears. "I'm glad *Co-ed* is closing, although it's heart-wrenching," admitted Stoneking, who had almost never missed a performance of the musical in eleven years. "I've felt for a year that the time had come to close the show" (personal interview).

The crowd cheered as Napier walked onstage to introduce the final performance. The director made the usual announcements, welcoming spectators to smoke and drink, pointing to the rest rooms behind the spray-painted proclamation "Theatre Sucks." Napier then spoke with pride about Annoyance accomplishments, "No one's ever been censored here. . . . We created material uncensored and unfettered."

The audience sang along with every song, echoed or anticipated every line, laughed and cheered each favorite joke or newly improvised moment, and finally rose to their feet as the final number ended. Napier reemerged, introduced and praised each cast member, then invited anyone from the Annoyance family who had ever taken part in *Co-ed* to join the group on stage. More than forty "sluts" past and present soon filled the space, embracing, weeping, and congratulating one another. Napier reminded the crowd that the Annoyance was not dead but "on sabbatical"—improv classes would continue, exciting plans were in the works, and the latest news could always be found at the Annoyance web site. Then, in true carnivalesque style, Annoyance family, friends, and fans partied through the night.

Founded with all the idealism of a new wave, the Annoyance Theatre battled fearlessly to maintain its ideals of openness, equality, and freedom. Although they were not able to fully realize their hopes for diversity, particularly with regard to race, the Annoyance nonetheless blazed a trail for other independent improv-based theatres to follow—demonstrating that the very rules of play were subject to change. As new third-wave troupes emerged in the '90s, some women and people of color began to construct their own improv communities and their own relationships to the rules. Although this movement has the potential to ghettoize minority concerns in improv, for many it seemed the only way to create a space for their own carnival of spontaneity.

CHAPTER 5

The Free Associates: the rules of the game

The Free Associates specializes in highly structured long-form improvisation and first made a modest name for itself on the Chicago improv scene with parodies of Tennessee Williams plays—billed as *Cast on a Hot Tin Roof*. The company was founded in 1991 by a gay man, Mark Gagné, with early support from two straight women, Liz Cloud and Lynda Shadrake. From the beginning, they produced, directed, and cast their projects with an eye toward creating more opportunities for women improvisers and a less sexist and less heterosexist working environment than they had found in the second-wave improv companies of ComedySportz and ImprovOlympic.

Perhaps not coincidentally, the group is also more concerned with quality than with carnival in their improvisational work. Both Cloud and Shadrake were married, with children to raise—they were not looking for the kind of surrogate family that the Annoyance offered many of its members. For them, as for Gagné, the Free Associates represented a real chance to develop their craft. Different from the Annoyance credo, here the product is paramount. While they are committed to improvisation, they see it primarily as a means of group script-writing. Bored with the "stream of consciousness" techniques popular at ImprovOlympic and the Annoyance, Free Associates founders "wanted to create theatre. We wanted depth" (Gagné interview).

In a theatre community that often typecasts or excludes women and gay men, the Free Associates create their own opportunities. As Shadrake said, "We're all tired of the male-dominated improv world" (personal interview). For many years the Free Associates was the only independent improv company in Chicago to feature a predominantly female troupe. For his part, Gagné explained, "I begin with who I am. The token gay male in improv in Chicago" (Ciesla 4). From his position on the margins, Gagné led the Free Associates on a very different path toward improv utopia than the one followed by Napier and the Annoyance.

As artistic director of the company, Gagné exerted a great deal of control over the framework of each project. He believes that only within structure and rules is there real freedom to create. Gagné's performers consider themselves actors who create specific characters within an established literary form, using carefully chosen audience suggestions to create an element of indeterminacy. The highly circumscribed nature of the Free Associates' work, they believe, protects their players from the abuses of sexist, heterosexist, or racist players. In contrast to the competitive atmosphere at ImprovOlympic, which Gagné calls "Improv Darwinism," any performer found railroading other players at the Free Associates is likely to be fired and replaced.

Some in the improv community have hinted that performances at the Free Associates are too structured to be genuine improv, as style, character, and content are created within such strict parameters. A number of men, and even some women, have found the Free Associates limited in scope, neither as financially rewarding as Second City nor as potentially transcendent as ImprovOlympic. Dee Ryan, for example, left the Free Associates to work at the Annoyance, which she found anarchic and exhilarating, and Second City, which she found lucrative if frustrating. Like Susan Messing, Ryan believes the pure art form requires a certain amount of risk and toughness. But many other players, particularly a number of women who worked with Second City, ComedySportz, and ImprovOlympic, feel they were finally able to blossom in the safer atmosphere of the Free Associates.

Although they retain certain elements of free play, the Free Associates' skillful send-ups of literature are perhaps more camp than carnivalesque. The term "camp" has been variously defined, yet most critics agree that it is a style that derives from a gay sensibility and manifests itself through irony, aestheticism, theatricality, and humor (see e.g., Babuscio). Although Gagné and his troupe would define themselves as theatrical rather than camp performers, much of their work can be best understood in this context. After a few early productions, in which the company featured gay male drag performers, most of the female impersonation they present has been done by women. Although some feminists critique camp as a male appropriation of women's representations, the women of the Free Associates enjoy parodying the exaggerated types in Tennessee Williams and other genres and thereby being able to comment on the constructedness of femininity.

Other theatre groups have found Williams' work inspiring as a base for deconstructing gender. Lesbian-feminist theatre group, Split Britches, collaborated with Bloolips, a pair of gay British performance artists, to create *Belle Reprieve,* a campy parody of *A Streetcar Named Desire* in which Stanley is portrayed by Split Britches' Peggy Shaw while Blanche is depicted by drag queen Bette of Bloolips. Feminist critic Lynda Hart describes a multilayered encounter between the characters/actors, who alternately play and contest the reality of the Williams dialogue. For example, in an exchange between actors, Bette challenges Shaw for not being "a real man" enough to play a scene "straight." In reply, Shaw reminds him of the dangers of playing a woman, pointing out that "the woman in this play gets raped and goes crazy." Her warning about women's frequent fate in the realistic theatre gives Bette pause—he thought all it took to play a female character was putting on "a nice frock" (Hart 4–5).

In his essay "Strategic Camp," David Bergman points out that camp has much in common with Bakhtin's theories of the grotesque and the carnival spirit, including punning, masquerade, the questioning of norms, inverted hierarchies, and sexual humor—all key features of improv-comedy at Annoyance and Free Associates. Like carnival, camp provokes ambivalent laughter, in which mockery is directed as much at the self as at the other.

Bergman is careful, however, to acknowledge significant distinctions between camp and the carnivalesque, saying, "The carnivalesque is always visible, an open provocation of the dominant culture; while camp frequently separates gay culture from straight culture" (100). Carnival celebrates the grotesque "becoming" of reproduction, transformation, and nature. Camp performers, on the other hand, see much of this version of the grotesque as the province of conventional heterosexual culture because of its focus on coupling, pregnancy, and childbirth as examples of the natural processes that defeat fixity. "It is in its critique of 'the natural'," Bergman writes, "that the camp grotesque may be said to offer a more radical posture of opposition than the carnivalesque" by using art and artifice to question and denaturalize social categories (100).

Players at the Annoyance valorize their version of the natural, believing that unself-conscious improvisation in a spirit of carnival can create freedom and belonging for its group of misfits. The Free Associates, on the other hand, employ a more "self-conscious questioning of categories" associated with camp (Bergman 101). Gagné and company maintain control over their humor and representations through the imposition of aesthetic shaping that places a significant emphasis on style. They are aware of the resistant potential in their excessive citations of gender through the Williams model (and other parodies) but they rarely take their performances to the level of overt political commentary.

On a tiny stage in the basement of the Ivanhoe Theatre in Chicago, three men and three women stand in their underwear. It is October 15, 1994, and the Free Associates are celebrating opening night at their new theatre space at the Ivanhoe with a benefit performance of their signature show, *Cast on a Hot Tin Roof.* As usual, the show begins with the actors, clad in elegant slips or old-fashioned T-shirts and boxer shorts, as neutral figures who are ready to be dressed with audience suggestions. Founding members Cloud and Gagné elicit ideas from the audience—variables that the company will then work into a "completely improvised play *not* by Tennessee Williams."

At each performance of *Cast*, the performers begin by asking for a year, fixing the historical time within the span—between 1930 and 1965—during which Williams set his actual plays. The group instituted this parameter after months of dodging too frequent suggestions based on contemporary pop culture. With the time element set, players can respectfully refuse such offers as "Madonna" or "MTV," which they believe force them into a cheaper brand of humor. Free Associates actors also enjoy working in period styles and strive to bring in the appropriate historical references, fashions, and attitudes. Gagné and his mostly female troupe also find a rich vein of dramatic tension by setting their plays in a time frame when the codes of behavior for women and gay men were more overtly constrained. At this performance, the suggestion is 1959.

The actors then take audience recommendations for a family relationship between two people and typical southern names for each. The crowd comes up with two cousins, named Ashley and Annabelle. Then, the actors ask for a third family member, inviting the audience to concoct a name that would be unusual in the south. Ashley's daddy, Rudolph, is the resulting creation. "Now because this is Tennessee Williams," says Gagné, "one of these three characters, Ashley, Annabelle or Rudolph, is a repressed homosexual. Choose one." Laughing, the audience chooses Rudolph. To further the Williams motif, the spectators must then invent a terrible, dark secret for Ashley (he has an original Barbie doll at home) and a desperate dream for Annabelle (she yearns to own a car wash). The audience may then choose a character from any of Williams' actual full-length plays to add into the mix. A list of plays and significant characters is helpfully provided in the show program, as is the statement, "Something to keep in mind: Stella is not Blanche. Blanche is not Stella."[1]

For this performance, a patron shouts "Maggie the Cat," and Gagné provides a short synopsis of this character from *Cat on a Hot Tin Roof* for anyone in the house who might not be fully Williams literate. With a picture of the original Maggie in mind, the audience is asked to come up with an occupation that Williams would never have assigned this character. Someone calls out "nuclear engineer!" to general acclaim. To wrap up the audience participation segment, Cloud asks for a gerund, an unrelated noun, and a real southern state. The result is the location for the action, "Dripping Teapot, Georgia." After recapping all of the suggested elements, Cloud asks the audience to come up with a title for "their new play." Once again, the program provides the titles of all of Williams' own full-length plays and another list showing some of the past productions created by Free Associates' audiences, including such titles as *Blanket Full of Anger; Talk to Me like a Log, and I Will Listen; I'm a Drunken, Gay Southerner;* and *A Breadtruck Named Wayne.* Another voice from the nuclear-engineering contingent offers "Containment Building of Love," and Cloud writes it down with a nod of approval, "Oh, very, *very* Williams."

Though the show has barely begun, there is now a short intermission, during which the cast retires backstage to apportion roles, don costumes, and find appropriate props. The break is about ten minutes long, not enough time to plan any of the plot or surprises that will later emerge. In fact, the players hold it as a point of honor that everything in the play to follow is freshly minted on the stage. When the actors return, they are in character, dressed in period suits and dresses from the fairly extensive costume collection the Free Associates keep backstage. They reprise the suggestions—this time with each character introducing him or herself. For example, Gagné shyly murmurs, "My name is Ashley, I have a cousin Annabelle, and Rudolph's my daddy. My dark, festering secret is that I have an original Barbie doll at home. Oh, I'm so ashamed." The fifth and occasionally sixth actor also introduces him or herself as the extra character, who will float through the play portraying any additional roles the plot requires—from an important lover to a convenient delivery boy.

With the final sonorous announcement of the title, *Containment Building of Love,* the play begins. In the first few scenes, the performers work to present embedded exposition, dropping hints related to their respective secrets and dreams. As in any other long-form improvisation, skillful play consists of listening, remembering, and reincorporating elements that have been improvised by other players, until the final scene seems to emerge as the inevitable result of the action that preceded it. Layered over this basic format, the Free Associates present a very specific style of performance. Through acting, voice, and gesture, they strive to replicate the character types, mannerisms, emotional outbursts, poetic language, and southern atmosphere reminiscent of Tennessee Williams. The troupe has done its homework. Each actor must be thoroughly familiar with Williams' canon and has been assigned to watch the classic films made from Williams' plays. Often, the style choices on stage will reflect performances by Vivien Leigh, Marlon Brando, or Elizabeth Taylor as much as anything inherent in Williams' texts.

As *Containment Building of Love* unfolds, the odd jumble of types and characters throws stereotypes of gender and sexuality into comic relief. Daddy Rudolph emerges as a character very much akin to Big Daddy in Williams' *Cat on a Hot Tin Roof*. Bluff and blustering, Rudolph finds many occasions to accuse his family of "mendacity." Yet this forceful father figure is the repressed homosexual, while his spineless son is a (presumably heterosexual) Barbie fetishist. Portrayed by Mary Fahey, Maggie, the nuclear engineer, appears in a hard hat and a tight-fitting gown. Maggie's barely controlled sexual energy takes on atomic proportions as she tries to construct a power plant on land where the shy and nervous Annabelle (played by Cloud) is equally determined to build the car wash of her dreams. Fahey next turns her smoldering desire toward Ashley, but no amount of seductive posturing will attract the attention of the Barbie-obsessed cretin. "Look at me!" Maggie expostulates, bosom heaving. "Ah am a *real* woman!" Fahey's skillful "female impersonation" suggests a certain amount of social and political consciousness. The Barbie image provides Fahey with a particularly rich opportunity to comment on the utter *unreality* of Williams' women and the impossibility of contemporary expectations for female achievement: nuclear engineer, sexpot, *and* a twenty-three-inch waist?

Unlike an ImprovOlympic long-form improvisation (or Harold), each completely original play *not* by Tennessee Williams progresses scene by scene, with two or three players at a time working to evolve a complex narrative. At the back of the house, a technician operates the critically important sound and lighting cues. In each scene, as the actors reach a climactic moment, they will hold a dramatic pose as lights fade and music swells—soap opera style. Often these tableaux are extremely comical, as the audience recognizes the incongruity between the familiar stricken gaze out the window and the source of the character's angst, such as the discovery of a tiny pink high heel in the bottom of a bourbon glass.

These snapshots also crystallize much of the camp style and attitude in Gagné's direction and the players' performances. The frozen moments at the end of each scene halt the improvisational process for a few seconds of aesthetic framing in light, sound, and stylized gesture. Spaced intermittently through each long-form improvised play, these pauses invite the irony and distance of a camp sensibility to shape the emergent material. In the Free Associates context of Williams' repressed homosexuals and frustrated females, the freeze-frame very often captures a crisis in gender performance that mocks theatre and film representations of gender and sexuality as well.

On most weekends, patrons of the Free Associates can see an early show and a late show each Friday and Saturday night; other performances are avail-

Artistic director Mark Gagné and founding member Lynda Shadrake parody a torrid Tennessee Williams love scene in the Free Associates signature show, *Cast on a Hot Tin Roof*. Photo: Courtesy Free Associates

able midweek. *Cast on a Hot Tin Roof* has been followed by a Brontë sisters parody, called *Blithering Heights,* and a medical center television drama, *BS* In each show, audience suggestions are used to set the parameters of the plot, and stylized gestures, movement, and language are the focal points of the performance. In *Blithering Heights,* each scene's final tableau is framed as a single character in a spotlight, to create what Gagné calls "a portrait in the style" (personal interview). In *BS*, the actors have been directed to play to imaginary television cameras throughout the performance, and each scene ends with a familiar *close-up shot,* or stop-action moment. Throughout *BS*, performers have been instructed to make random busy crosses through the action on stage to simulate the harried visual style of television shows like *ER* and *Chicago Hope*. Gagné is very precise with the actors on each project, making sure the elements of style and structure are clear, but leaving performers free to create the content within those limits.

The Free Associates, like the Annoyance Theatre, was born out of dissatisfaction with the prevailing second-wave improv rhetoric and practice. Yet

With *BS,* a take-off of the medical drama *ER,* the Free Associates broadened their repertoire to include parodies of popular culture as well as of drama and literature. Pictured (from left to right): Joe Reilly, Tasha James, Jenni Lamb, Andrew Glasgow, Kecia Cooper, Todd Guill. Photo: Jennifer Girard.

Gagné and founding members Cloud and Shadrake took a path very different from that of the Annoyance rebels.

Like many of the Annoyance group, Gagné had been a college student in the early '80s, when ideas about Chicago-style improv had percolated into theatre departments and extracurricular activities throughout the United States. He took workshops at Northeastern University with a member of Boston's Second City–inspired improv company, the Proposition (now disbanded), and other acting classes where the instructors taught "with Spolin's book in one hand" (personal interview). By 1987, the twenty-four-year-old had started his own troupe, the Angry Tuxedos, which successfully drew audiences from the Boston community.

Because improv privileges spontaneity and groupmind, performers can often resist artistic direction and criticism. Thus, although Gagné was interested in exploring the surreal and experimental potential of improvisation, most of his players insisted on creating commercial comedy sketches. After a little more than a year, internal tensions caused Gagné to abandon the group.

In his later work with the Free Associates, Gagné would be much more careful about casting and would make it crystal clear to all players that his was the prevailing vision for the company.

In 1988, Gagné joined the new ComedySportz franchise just starting in Boston. Although he resisted their techniques at first, Gagné learned a great deal from his ComedySportz experience. Particularly valuable, he says, was his eventual recognition of the creative freedom produced by structural constraints. A strict framework, Gagné believes, allows the improviser to relax and "empty out," free from the intimidating vastness of infinite possibility. At ComedySportz, the challenge of completing an entire scene within four minutes, and using additional, assigned restrictions, forced Gagné to let go of self-consciousness and second-guessing. Gagné feels strongly that structures help to stave off the kind of self-indulgence and "mental masturbation" that can result from the free-flowing approaches touted by ImprovOlympic, Annoyance, and others. According to Gagné, "If an improviser is willing to go in and find the freedom within the structure, you're going to do your best work" (personal interview).

But in rehearsals and note sessions Boston ComedySportz director Jay Patrick fostered a competitive, misogynist atmosphere that made Gagné and several other players uncomfortable. Moreover, Patrick was often late or missing from practice sessions—leaving his mostly inexperienced actors at a loss. As Patrick's absenteeism became serious, disgruntled players turned to Gagné for guidance.

Eventually, Dick Chudnow exercised his control as head of the Comedy-Sportz conglomerate. Sending Patrick to the showers, Chudnow officially assigned Gagné to direct the company. Under Gagné's strong leadership, Boston ComedySportz had a successful and far more woman-friendly season. But even as he assumed the director's responsibilities, the ambitious Gagné had already set his sights on Chicago.

Through the ComedySportz network, Gagné was immediately cast as a member of Chicago's franchise when he hit town in 1990. But Chicago attitudes proved a real culture shock. Despite Patrick's prejudices, nothing at Boston ComedySportz had prepared Gagné for the sexism and heterosexism he encountered on the Chicago team. Unlike most gay men in Chicago improv, Gagné made no secret of his identity—a risky choice at the time. He recalls a number of improvisers who would meet him for drinks and reveal their own status as gays undercover, insisting, "Don't tell anyone I'm gay" (personal interview).

Perhaps because he was not "one of them," Gagné felt his work suffering in the competitive setting of Chicago ComedySportz through the lack of support from fellow players. Gagné was used to getting laughs in improv, and even to being a star of sorts. But in Chicago, he says, "I was shy, I was doing horrible work. I was really tentative because I wasn't getting any reinforcement" (personal interview). One night, he was even physically pushed off the stage in the middle of a scene. Furious, Gagné confronted the veteran player who had manhandled him. The actor replied, "I did it because you weren't ready, you didn't want it, and you weren't making a decision one way or the other. You didn't leave the scene; I pushed you off the stage. I don't see anything wrong with that" (Gagné interview). This experience gave Gagné even more empathy for the conditions many women faced in Chicago improv-comedy and reinforced his desire to change things.

After a brief leave of absence, Gagné returned to ComedySportz, determined to be confident, aggressive, and "ballsy" on stage. He soon achieved the status of workshop teacher and featured player. Nevertheless, his greatest allies were the women on the team. He created a mutual support network with Joanie Cloonan, Lynda Shadrake, Liz Cloud, and others, most of whom would eventually work with him as Free Associates. Gagné remembers Cloud in ComedySportz as a dedicated performer and producer who was treated "like a dog" by the troupe. Gagné recounts the way the director of the team, Dave Gaudet, would critique Cloud's offbeat characters and gentle, eccentric style by saying, "Liz, I want to see you do pretty characters" (personal interview). Cloud and other women were often bullied off the stage, much the way Gagné had been. Cloud bowed out of the company a few months after Gagné arrived.

Shadrake and Gagné hit it off immediately, helping one another over the hurdles of ComedySportz competition. Shadrake had trained at Second City and had extensive improv experience at ImprovInstitute, an independent company whose best-known show, *Flanagan's Wake*, was in the interactive environmental mold of *Tony 'n' Tina's Wedding*.[2] Shadrake was a bit older than the other players and was often able to rise above the fray at "the boys' club," as she called the Chicago team (Shadrake interview). Gagné believed that Shadrake was one of the best improvisers in Chicago, her solid acting skills underappreciated at ComedySportz.

In 1991, while still teaching and performing with ComedySportz, Gagné began looking for a venue to produce a script he had written called *The Dog and Pony Show*. He found the Celebrity Club, a "strange patchouly-smelling [*sic*] massage-parlor-health-food-juice-bar with strange hours," where the managers offered him free use of their stage if, in return, Gagné would produce three months of improv-comedy entertainment for them (qtd. in Ciesla 4). After his experiences in Boston, Gagné was not enthusiastic about starting another troupe. But he gathered a group for some ad hoc improvs to fulfill his contract. Different from most Chicago improv-comedy companies, the troupe included three women (Cloud, Shadrake, and Virginia Montgomery) and three gay men (Gagné, Mark Francoeur, and Vince Kracht). Although Gagné was tempted to call this group the Misfits, he settled instead on the name the Free Associates.

To fill their commitment to the Celebrity Club, this crew presented an evening of popular improv games. In one gimmick game called Styles, an MC collects suggestions from the audience for a variety of familiar film styles or theatre genres, ranging widely from film noir to Shakespeare to soap opera. The actors must establish a scene, quickly switching acting styles as the MC calls out each suggestion. The Free Associates modified this format, sustaining each scene and style for longer periods of time until they began to present entire playlets in the modes of well-known authors such as Mamet, Pinter, and Tennessee Williams.

Williams' melodramatic situations, lush language, and flamboyant characters proved a gold mine for these performers, many of whom were trained in legitimate acting techniques. The women felt particularly empowered, as character, detail, and emotion became more important than aggressive wit or pop-culture references. For the gay men in the company, Williams' excessiveness and "repressed homosexual" characters provided the opportunity to perform in a camp style largely frowned on in mainstream Chicago improv. Actors and audiences alike enjoyed the Williams parodies so much that the company found itself doing entire evenings devoted to that specific genre.

In August 1991, the Celebrity Club changed hands and names, becoming the Bop Shop. The new owner offered Gagné continued free use of the stage if the Free Associates could come up with a marketable concept for an ongoing show. A few days later Gagné was inspired with an idea and a title: *Cast on a Hot Tin Roof. Cast* would recall some of the earliest kinds of long-form improv performed by the Compass Players. In 1991, long form was practiced primarily at ImprovOlympic (as the Harold) or at the Annoyance Theatre. Gagné says, "We sort of stake our claim—this is quite a claim—to starting the resurgence of the long-form movement. Because when we first did *Cast*, and our first long-form stuff, it was only 1991, no one was doing it—no one" (personal interview).

Like ImprovOlympic, the Free Associates would weave one long improvised performance from initial audience suggestions, rather than perform a number of short, comic scenes. Like the Compass, they would use a *commedia*-inspired format in which stock characters could be recombined in a variety of classic situations, although they did not use preconceived scenarios.

Instead, the actors studied Williams' work to find the basis of most of the dramatic conflicts that drive his plots. These include *the burning secret, the unrealized dream,* and *the misguided representation or identity,* although this last was soon modified to the simpler idea of a character's repressed homosexuality.

To reproduce the details of Williams' characters and style, the first cast of *Cast* gathered in study groups to discuss Williams' biography, watch every classic film made from his plays, and pore over each of the playwright's works, familiarizing themselves with all of his major characters. As a high school English teacher who loved literature, Shadrake particularly enjoyed their rehearsal process, and she describes their start-up work as "one of the best months I've ever spent. . . . It was a very heady time" (personal interview). The actors became such experts in Williams' details that Shadrake was concerned that the general public would not have the cultural competence to appreciate the thoroughness of the company's parodies.

But when *Cast* opened, it was an immediate success. In the influential *Chicago Reader,* Jack Helbig named *Cast on a Hot Tin Roof* a "Critic's Choice," writing, "Ever since David Shepherd began experimenting with commedia dell-arte scenarios at the Compass in the late 50s, long-form improvisation, in which plays are spontaneously created before the audience, has been the Holy Grail of improv. A few local companies—most notably Mick Napier's Pup Tent Theatre—have recently realized aspects of Shepherd's dream. But none have come as close to creating consistently funny, literate and well-crafted fully improvised plays as the Free Associates do in *Cast on a Hot Tin Roof.*" As a result of this positive press, the show quickly found a supportive audience willing to venture into the grungy, out-of-the-way Bop Shop, where the Free Associates shared space with a variety of musical groups.

As time went on, the company kept *Cast* running, while they experimented with other improv-based and semi-scripted shows. In their first year, Free Associates' output was strongly influenced by the talents of its gay men. In 1991, the group presented *Cherry Pie! What a Slice!* a campy sitcom constructed to showcase the drag-queen character Cherry Pie created by Francoeur. *Cherry Pie!* featured a new script every two weeks. In one episode, Cherry Pie was joined by troupe member Theresa Mulligan, who impersonated JoAnne Worley—a comedian best known for her appearances on the '60s television show *Laugh-In.* This character inspired the group to create *The JoAnne Worley Family Christmas Seance* for the 1991 Christmas season and *The Hollywood Squares, Not,* a campy game-show spoof, in 1992.

While the Free Associates promoted its gay performers with these projects, Gagné was also supportive of the women in his company. An ardent feminist, Virginia Montgomery urged the artistic director to produce an improv-based show with, by, and about women. Gagné was intrigued by the idea of featuring women's unsung improv talents. In 1992, with *Cast* still going strong at the Bop Shop, the Free Associates cast seven women improvisers to create and perform a revue called *Hear Me Roar* under Gagné's direction.[3] *Hear Me Roar* attracted a great deal of attention from the Chicago-area press as one of the first improv projects to address the issue of women in improvisation.

In one feature article, Shadrake asserted, "Working with all women, we ended up being freer with our ideas. . . . I don't think we judged ourselves quite as quickly. And we weren't trying to be funny, which I think is a trap you get into" (qtd. in Enna D3). With a female cast, Shadrake and company felt free to allow their own brand of humor to emerge.

Shadrake gave Gagné a great deal of credit for making the project happen: "We all feel—in Chicago, especially—that the comedy business is really dominated by men. [But] I don't think we would have done it without Mark. He's really the backbone for the group" (qtd. in Enna D3). For his part, Gagné explained, "I personally feel the work that women do in improvisation is more interesting and less predictable [than mainstream improv]" (qtd. in Enna D3).

The show forged comedy from such topics as feminine hygiene products and mother-daughter relationships and also created parodies of male roles and genres. In at least one sketch the women created their own opportunity to perform in drag, making camp-carnivalesque commentary on gender roles.

The scene was titled "She Ain't Bluffin' " and followed a traditional Wild West gunfighter scenario—including ornery card sharps, the peacemaking barkeep, the town drunk, and the tough, no-nonsense sheriff, played by Shadrake. According to one critic, "The fact that these roles are all played by women, *as* women, adds an automatic spin on the goings-on, particularly when the citified and helpless little lady wanders in with parasol and hanky" (Enna D8). In the macho context of the Western, these women's performances highlighted the constructed nature of both masculinity and citified, helpless femininity.

By this point in 1992, the Free Associates were scattered and stretched across several locations and multiple artistic goals. They had reached the point where they could either disperse or reorganize. A core group, including Gagné, Shadrake, and Cloud, decided to forge ahead. Yet, at this crucial point, the Free Associates made choices that were vastly different from the survival tactics the Annoyance brought to bear at similar times of crisis. In the first place, the Free Associates incorporated their company and applied for nonprofit status—acts of officialdom that Annoyance had long rejected. To qualify as a worthy nonprofit, the Free Associates cited the educational value of their literary parodies.

In keeping with this instructional bent, the troupe applied for and received a Community Art Assistance Grant, which they used to create an educational touring children's show called *Stages through the Ages*. Gagné recruited a board of directors for the company. As he told one journalist, "I think that's when we said, we are a group. We are here. We're doing literary improv. No more crazy stuff. Our main focus is doing educational improv, improv based on literature. And it's theatre" (qtd. in Ciesla 4). Ironically, as they worked to refine improv, they also continued the stereotype of high culture as the province of women and gay men.

For Gagné, Shadrake, and Cloud, calling their improv work "theatre" gave it legitimacy and set their productions apart from the throngs of short-form improv-comedy troupes struggling for recognition in the Chicago improv community. For many women in the company, this distinction between theatre and comedy had a significant impact on their confidence as performers. In a 1995 interview, Susan Gaspar, a longtime member of the company, suggested that early improv was closer to ensemble theatre work, but that the genre had since shifted:

> It got more closely associated with stand-up comedy, which is a very male-dominated business. Comedy has always been a stigma for women. Unless you're ugly or fat or bitter, you're not funny. [But] true improvisation's a theatrical form . . . where women have always been allowed to be strong. But not in comedy. And I think that because the Free Associates are so theatrically-based . . . women have a chance to show that strength without being afraid and labeled as a bitch or any of those things they've been labeled over the years . . . without being a dizzy blonde, or somebody's girlfriend, or something like that. (qtd. in Ciesla 4)

As the troupe refocused, its membership grew and shifted. The drag performers moved on, and a few straight males joined the group. But perhaps more significant for the direction of the company, the troupe continued to attract large numbers of women. In fact, the Free Associates soon became the only Chicago improv company to feature more women than men in its regular performances. Unlike the Annoyance Theatre, the Free Associates did hold auditions for specific roles in shows. If an actor clicked with the group, he or she could be invited to become a full-fledged member of the company. Gagné cast some of the genuine misfits of Chicago improv—women who were not conventionally attractive. As Gagné explains, this policy became the Free Associates' greatest strength: "My ensemble is full of what casting agents would call difficult types—who are very talented. No one wants them because they don't look this way or that way, but I let them play whatever they want. I think we have some of the best improvisers in the city—and I don't say that as a boast. I feel blessed. And I want women. I keep trying to even the ratio out, because you can obviously do more if you have an equal number of men and women, but I work well with women" (personal interview).

Some might argue that Gagné works well with women because they are more likely to support rather than challenge his directorial authority. But the women Gagné welcomed into the Free Associates also shared many of his attitudes about improvisation. Unlike Messing or Ellen Stoneking of the Annoyance, they did not see toughness as an essential quality of good improv. Like Cloud and Shadrake, many had been burned by experiences at Improv-Olympic or ComedySportz and felt out of place at the Annoyance.

Mary Fahey, who joined the Free Associates in 1994, believed that Improv-Olympic and the Annoyance were both "dangerous" places where peer pressure and the attitude that "anything goes" can encourage alcoholism and serious drug use. While she admits this is a "gross generalization," Fahey also feels that both groups enforce very specific codes of behavior, and "as much as they say they foster the individual, 'you can do anything here,' it's under these very rigid guidelines that are unspoken, and the bigger freak you are the better you'll do" (personal interview).

Fahey's naturalistic, emotional style of play was not welcome at Improv-Olympic or the Annoyance. Her improvisations were slow to unfold, too nuanced and detailed for the aggressive comic mode in most companies. But her approach was a perfect fit for the Free Associates and their Williams work. Even as Free Associates' comedy depends on their campy, exaggerated approach to Williams' already excessive characters, the actors also seek to create a poignant humor by infusing their creations with real feeling. Gagné had some allegiance to the Stanislavsky's Method approach—a system that has always operated in a tension between artifice and nature. Tired of the supposed apathy of his generation's cultural output, Gagné wanted audiences to feel for the characters on stage. To be convincingly "natural," his actors relied on training and technique, not the spontaneity of raw improvisation.

At the Annoyance Theatre, by contrast, a lack of formal theatre training is a badge of honor. Yet the company's raw improvisations often lead to bizarre, unnatural characters and situations. Critics and Napier himself have compared Annoyance productions to the Brechtian smoker's cabaret where, although audiences may be caught up in the carnival, they are emotionally distant from the characters. The lack of boundaries between spectator and performer encourages fans to feel more of a connection to the troupe itself than to their representations on stage.

At the Free Associates, a clear line has been drawn at the proscenium's edge. Although the company interacts with spectators, it also maintains a "fourth wall" of aesthetic distance and (heightened) realism—even with its camp elements. As in Brecht's description of "culinary theatre," this separation invites the audience to enjoy a greater emotional involvement in the representational action but also makes them less likely to question its foundations. Thus, while many of the actors believe they are resisting repressive gender norms through excessive portrayals of femininity and masculinity in Free Associates' shows, their acting quality may undermine their critique. Audiences are often tempted to take their exquisitely rendered Williams characters at face value—missing the intended ironies in these double-coded camp performances.

Gagné created a number of structures, both artistic and managerial, designed to maintain what he considers the proper working environment at the Free Associates. Actors are cast not only for their talent, but for their willingness to share the attitudes and values of the company. The Free Associates have had something of a challenge keeping heterosexual men in the company, as many straight male improvisers feel they are more free to "have fun" in another group. Gagné recalls one example of an actor who persisted in making racist and anti-gay jokes that company members did not believe were simply a feature of the characters he was portraying. After several talks, during which the performer accused Gagné of trying to censor his free improvisations, Gagné fired him.

The troupe strove to create a safe, supportive, even nurturing atmosphere. According to other schools of improv thought, this safety might be seen as antithetical to the risk and utter freedom that improv should offer. In distinct contrast to the Annoyance rehearsal style, Gagné directs with a strong hand, making it clear who has the last word. Ensemble work is stressed and each show is thoroughly researched and carefully structured. Performers improvise within a specific literary style, according to a set of variables created through audience suggestion, and framed by light and music cues as well as other directorial devices. For many Free Associates, these structures undergird an intensely satisfying improv experience.

By 1993, the Free Associates recognized a need to branch beyond their dependence on *Cast on a Hot Tin Roof* for a sustained, income-producing product, and to appeal to audiences unfamiliar with Williams' work. Even as they searched for a new home for the company, the troupe opened *Pick-a-Dick: The Completely Improvised Select-a-Detective Play*. In the opening sequence, audiences were given a choice of detectives from popular mystery novels. Selections most often included Miss Marple, Nancy Drew, the Hardy Boys, Philip Marlowe, Hercule Poirot, and Chicagoan V. I. Warshawski. Using a number of other specifics gathered from the audience—including victim, motives, secrets, and relationships—the cast would weave a murder mystery plot. Once again, the emphasis was on style and detail, with actors recreating the hard-boiled machismo of Raymond Chandler, the wholesome can-do attitude of Nancy Drew, or the British elegance of Agatha Christie. The show drew respectable crowds on a consistent basis.

In 1994, the company moved into their new home in the Ivanhoe Theatre's basement, which featured a rustic decor of exposed beams and stone walls. With the volunteer labor of actors and board members, the troupe transformed the place into a proscenium theatre, with a small stage, backstage area, light booth, and fifty seats in raked rows. But many board members and core company members resisted the move, concerned that the monthly rental obligation would crush the infant enterprise.

As it had been for the Annoyance, the acquisition of a home was a mixed blessing for the Free Associates, making increased creative output both possible and economically necessary. The troupe put two new literary improv shows into development: *As We Like It: Shakespeare in Your Face* and *Blithering Heights*, drawn from the gothic romances of the Brontë sisters. They created limited-run shows, such as *A Dysfunctional Dixie Christmas* (*Cast* with a seasonal spin), and mounted several performance fund-raisers, such as *Stanley 'n' Stella's Wedding* (*Cast* with an interactive *Tony 'n' Tina* spin). The company was constantly on the lookout for touring opportunities and also hired out for custom-written interactive murder mysteries at parties and special events. In addition, the Free Associates began to offer a series of classes in improv—both as an important source of income and as a means of training potential members.

Also in 1994, the Free Associates were invited to bring *Cast on a Hot Tin Roof* to the eighth annual gathering of the prestigious Tennessee Williams/ New Orleans Literary Festival. The show was a huge hit with the New Orleans audiences, who knew their Williams but had never watched improv performers at work before. Festival organizers were so impressed they immediately booked the group for a return engagement the following year.

In the 1995–96 season, the group stepped outside of their literary format to present *B.S.* and *Divamatic,* a cabaret parody designed to showcase the improvisational singing talents of several women in the company. 1996 also marked the theatre's increased commitment to producing original scripted plays in its regular season. They began with *Chicago on the Rocks*, written by

Cast on a Hot Tin Roof: A Dysfunctional Dixie Christmas, a special holiday version of the successful Williams parody, was for years an important fundraising event for the Free Associates. Pictured (from left to right):Matt Tiegler, Susan Gaspar, Mary Fahey, Mark Gagné, and Lynda Shadrake. Photo: Courtesy Free Associates

Chicago Reader reporter and then company member Neal Pollack. *Rocks* was a series of monologues based on eccentric real-life personalities Pollack had interviewed for the paper. The play gave several of the theatre-trained Free Associates a chance to enjoy the detailed character work so often curtailed even in long-form improvisation. Gagné made plans to include more scripted work in the theatre's repertoire.

Because *Chicago on the Rocks* called for a black actor, the company recruited its first African American troupe member. Bill Underwood was an actor and improviser who had worked with Second City's Minority Outreach Program and the all-black improv troupe Oui Be Negroes. He appeared in *Rocks* and the contemporary improv shows such as *B.S.* and *Pick-a-Dick* (but not in the period pieces).

The group soon learned not to make assumptions about the marketability of literature. While their Shakespeare show was quite successful, *Blithering Heights* struggled to find an audience and was soon put on hiatus. In 1997, the theatre also developed a new genre piece, entitled *Scryptogram*, based on David Mamet's plays. By branching beyond Williams, and even beyond strictly literary genres, the troupe was able to attract more of the conventional improv-going audience—young people who enjoyed comic references to popular culture.

Structure and organization were key elements of the Free Associates' business plan as well as its artistic approach. Gagné and company were determined not to be a passing fancy, like so many of the short-lived improv troupes that came and went in Chicago through the '80s and '90s.

As with most struggling arts organizations, the Free Associates did not have adequate income to hire a general manager or other staff to do publicity, house management, tour booking, accounting, fund-raising, and other management tasks. But the company created an organized system for sharing day-to-day administrative duties. In contrast to the Annoyance Theatre, where official documents are anathema, at the Free Associates incoming players are offered a contract detailing their rights and responsibilities as company members. According to the contract, each actor must perform at least four tasks per month, in areas including audience development, house management, physical maintenance, and the organization of Free Associates' classes.

Determined to be professional, the Free Associates also insists on paying its members, distinguishing the company from most Chicago troupes. Player contracts provide that ensemble members earn points for each scheduled performance and additional points for touring shows and murder mysteries—although the contract allows management to require up to three unpaid promotional or benefit shows every six months. Members also earn points for each hour spent pursuing their monthly duties. Monthly, the Free Associates distribute a percentage of their net income to the players, with each member receiving money based on their total points for that month. This payment fluctuates with the company's fortunes, keeping the troupe solvent and motivating the actors to help increase ticket sales. "We've had fifty cent months," says Gagné ruefully. "But we've also had months where actors took home checks for more than two hundred dollars" (personal interview).

For the most part, women have been more willing to take on the added administrative work and are more dedicated to the Free Associates than the male players, staying with the company for years instead of months. From the beginning, Cloud and Shadrake shared responsibility with Gagné, helping to run the business, teach classes, and raise money, from the yearly tag sale to writing grant applications. By 1996, after two years at the Ivanhoe, the troupe had increased production and income sevenfold. Even with the point system, it was increasingly difficult for the Free Associates to manage performance schedules, administrative tasks, and the regular day-jobs most performers maintained in order to pay their rent. After celebrating their fifth anniversary, tensions were high, and Gagné, Cloud, and Shadrake were nearing burnout.

For *Blithering Heights,* Free Associates actors studied the works of Charlotte, Emily and Anne Brontë, and created a smoldering, gothic style of acting worthy of Cathy, Heathcliff and Jane Eyre. Pictured: Liz Cloud, Mark Gagné, Adrienne Smith. Photo: Courtesy Free Associates.

The Free Associates attacked their problem in typically strategic fashion. At a retreat in October of 1996, the company planned a highly structured reorganization. Cloud and Shadrake ceded many of their responsibilities to a new team of managers, including performers Susan Gaspar and Mary Fahey. All of the core members who stepped into positions of leadership at this point were women, with the single exception of a male performer recruited to work on audience development, who would resign from the company a few months after the retreat.

Gagné discussed a redistribution of duties that would allow him to focus more on artistic supervision. Former board president Valerie Dunbar stepped down from the board to become general manager. She outlined short-term and long-term goals for reorganization, worked with core members of the group to create a new mission statement, and facilitated a debate as to the relative value of the nurturing, family model that had so long informed the company's internal relations as opposed to a business-based model. The family approach had helped to forge the improv ensemble and to create the safe environment they wanted, but it was often an exhausting effort for the three leaders.

Many voices now called for aggressive self-promotion, hard-line standards, and increased discipline for players. Some members urged colleagues to maintain a balance of family feeling and business; others insisted that the Free Associates needed to be more demanding and less self-effacing in its internal and external relations. In a striking comment on the gendered nature of the company, Dunbar suggested that the Free Associates' low self-esteem and self-imposed limitations were "symptomatic of a feminine process of self-criticism." The troupe, Dunbar said, had emerged with an admirable " 'feminine' energy of the nurturing company." However, in order to succeed, she continued, they now needed "a burst of 'masculine' energy to push us across the breach." A confident attitude and careful planning, Dunbar added, would allow the company to professionalize and "still serve the goddess and feel all right about it" (Retreat transcript).

At several points, the planners explicitly cited the Annoyance Theatre as a counterexample, suggesting that Napier and company's refusal to plan ahead has had a negative impact on both performance and business decisions. Many Free Associates felt that the Annoyance was a cult of personality, where controlling hierarchies are present but unspoken and willfully unexamined.

At the same time, the Free Associates has never captured the excitement of the Annoyance free-for-all. Free Associates' loyal patrons are for the most part older, more sedate, and less involved than Annoyance fans, and the Free Associates has never had audiences lined up down the block to see a show for the fifteenth time. In many ways they have willingly exchanged this carnival intensity for a safer product—consistent and high quality, if rarely thrilling.

On the business side, Dunbar said, the Annoyance is an "unconscious company," where "everybody's operating out of self-assigned roles, [doing what] they perceive they need to do" (Retreat transcript). Eschewing the idea of a cult or even a family model for their group, the Free Associates determined that it would be a "conscious" company—both administratively and artistically. They would create an organizational flowchart and a five-year business plan. They would be politically conscious even in their improvisations. They even coined the slogan "Conscious Comedy" for use in publicity releases.

In 1997, the Free Associates put *Cast on a Hot Tin Roof* on indefinite hiatus. Since 1995, the Williams parody's audience had dwindled. At the same time, many of the company's newer literary shows opened to critical acclaim but suffered a swift drop in attendance once the fans of a particular genre had seen them. Their television takeoffs, however, were gaining in popularity. *Back in the Shadows Again*, Gagné's new spoof of the '70s vampire soap opera *Dark Shadows*, was a hit. Its success helped reenergize Gagné and encourage many in the troupe.

For some early stalwarts, such as Shadrake and Fahey, however, it seemed that Gagné had all but abandoned the most important and distinctive aspects of the Free Associates. Fahey felt the new television parodies were less valuable forms of theatre and did not fit her particular acting style or talents the way the literary genres had done. Moreover, she and several others felt that the new businesslike attitude fostered by Dunbar was not conducive to the supportive, family atmosphere they had treasured at the Free Associates. Amidst bitter recriminations, and charges of ingratitude on both sides, Shadrake and Fahey retired from the company in 1997—ironically only a few months before Dunbar left to return to law school. Once grateful for the controlled atmosphere at the Free Associates, some former members had come to believe that the balance of rules and free play was now off-kilter.

Despite these growing pains, the Free Associates weathered the seven-year anniversary that few small theatre companies survive. They increased their income, recruited eager new improvisers, and continued to receive excellent reviews for their performances. A young marketing assistant even came up with a campaign to sell the Brontë piece to those put off by its literary qualities: "*Blithering Heights*—No Reading Required!" New shows included *Chancing at Lunacy* (Brian Friel parody), *Long Play's Journey into One Act* (Eugene O'Neill), and several scripted plays. Women still comprised more than half the company. Kecia Cooper, a founding member of Oui Be Negroes, shifted her allegiance to the Free Associates because she believed the troupe was better organized and presented more acting opportunities. The troupe even managed to retain a heterosexual man or two, including Joe Reilly, who performed and worked as technical director.

In 1999, the Free Associates were invited to participate in the prestigious

ArtsBridge business incubator program designed to help small companies move to a higher level. The same year, Gagné decided to resign as artistic director to pursue other professional opportunities, saying, "I want to be an artist again instead of a businessman" (personal interview). He agreed to shepherd the company through the 1999–2000 season and to make sure the ArtsBridge grant was not jeopardized, but he also believed the company could and should survive without him. At a company meeting, he explained, "What we've created is a groupmind thing. No one person is essential" (personal interview). Although Gagné's personal energy had long been the driving force of the troupe, the organization was clearly structured enough to sustain a transfer of power. Artistic associates Gaspar and Cooper agreed to take on leadership responsibilities.

The Annoyance Theatre and the Free Associates have approached their status as misfits in diametrically different ways—one valorizing fearlessness and anarchy, the other emphasizing safety and rules. Each has created an alternative culture of improv that supports their ideals and values. But many improvisers, especially those from already marginalized groups, still do not believe they can or should "fit in." While carnival or improvisation may seem to create a free space by their very forms, it is only when the pattern of play allows for a real play of difference that improvisers can negotiate the tension between free expression and belonging.

The next chapter centers on the different tactics employed by two African American women as each has struggled to make a place for herself and for other women and people of color in Chicago improv-comedy.

improv in black
and white

African American influence on mainstream popular culture has been undeniable—and increasing—for more than a century. In practical terms, by the late '80s and '90s, African American expression, such as rap music, had been popularized through the medium of MTV, packaged, and sold to a global market. As an improvisation-based form, rap was not subsumed and appropriated by white performers the way much rock 'n' roll had been.[1] At the same time, comedy programming on network television and comedy films began to feature more black performers. It is in this context that Second City began to question its viability as an all-white institution, and that Oui Be Negroes was conceived.

This period also saw a significant shift in many improvisers' attitudes about their own marginalization. While Aaron Freeman took personal responsibility for his improv struggles a decade earlier, third-wave players of color began to confront the political, structural, and institutional sources of the many unacknowledged barriers to their success in improv-comedy. One young woman decided to attack the problem head-on. Frances Callier was a sixteen-year-old high school student in 1987, when Freeman was on the Second City mainstage. She first discovered Second City when a high school teacher suggested the talented young actor take a class there: "It wasn't a place my family frequented—and if you look at the demographics of [Second City] audiences now, we don't have many African Americans or many minorities or many from the lower strata of the economic sphere. You know, Cabrini-Green's right across the street and you don't have anybody coming over to the theatre" (personal interview). Second City had long reflected Chicago's history as a racially divided city. But Callier crossed the line, took a basic improv class at the training center, and she was hooked.

Throughout her Second City apprenticeship, Callier found that she was usually the only person of color in classes and workshops, with the rare exception of one or two Latino students. Despite her passion for improv, she began to be seriously disillusioned about the way improv's ideals of groupmind and agreement were practiced:

> My humor has modified. . . . You can almost say that at times I have whitewashed my humor. If we go to play together—to support me you have to know the references that I'm making. . . . And so if you don't find [my ideas] funny, then I'm gonna pull back on my own personal humor or humor from my culture. And that's what happens . . . you just play generalities. And very rarely is it a specific woman, an African American single mother in the projects; very rarely is it an African American lawyer dealing with employment problems at her firm; very rarely does it become anything specific (personal interview).

Troubled by the resistance, and sometimes even the hostility, that she encountered in the touring company, Callier did a great deal of soul-searching about race and gender in improv. She knows the specific page in Jeffrey Sweet's *Something Wonderful Right Away* where the late Roger Bowen opines that minority actors are too unsophisticated to contribute to Second City's cosmopolitan satirical comedy and believes that some white players at the company would still agree. But there is a long tradition of improvisation in African American life and art independent of (and influential to) Second City's brand of improv. As psychologist James M. Jones writes, "Improvisation is a historical legacy of black culture following in part from a present-oriented cultural style, in part from a context of oppression in which the future was unreliable, unpredictable and not guaranteed to occur at all. . . . Thus an improvisational style for black people is both preferred (by many) and demanded as a consequence of survival" (283).

In 1989, when producer Bernie Sahlins was asked why so few blacks had ever appeared with Second City, he replied, "Blacks didn't present themselves. When they did, we hired them. It would be arrogant on our part to go looking for black actors" (qtd. in Sachs 6). But according to Andrew Alexander, the limitations of Second City's all-white troupes became painfully obvious the day of the 1991 Los Angeles riots. Alexander remembers, "I came into the theater that night, and saw our company, which was very talented, grappling with how to treat satirically what was going on" (qtd. in Johnson 12). Alexander felt that the improvisers had no base of personal experience or knowledge from which to address the riots in any way that could be both funny and tasteful. Finally recognizing the need for some kind of minority voice in the company, Alexander admitted, "[W]e've got to change" (12).

In 1992, Alexander asked Aaron Freeman to work with a diverse group of Second City performers, students, and touring company members in workshops "designed to address voice, perspective, and experience" for minority improvisers (Callier interview). But Callier believed strongly that a more assertive outreach program was needed before players of color could really feel welcomed and supported by Second City. She approached the producer and found him very receptive to her idea. The result was the establishment of Second City's Minority Outreach Program, with the twenty-five-year-old Callier as its director.[2] The program aggressively recruited talented minority performers and offered them a week-long accelerated summer session at no cost. Second City hoped then to mainstream them into the conservatory program and eventually into touring companies or the e.t.c. troupe. A few black comedians were insulted by the notion that they needed "special education," but Callier explained her reasoning:

> It doesn't matter what group you come from, if you're one, one woman, one African American, one gay person, you don't have a chance to explore your voice. You don't have an opportunity when you are learning improvisation to learn what your voice is or bring your voice out. And what you tend to do is assimilate. Women assimilate to men. African Americans assimilate to the whole "normal" culture, which is white culture. And references come from that basis. So you don't bring up as many feminine references, you don't bring up as many African American references, and so on. So what I wanted to do was provide an opportunity for people to become strong in their voice. (personal interview)

For a number of years, Callier directed and taught two sessions of the Minority Outreach Program in the summer and performed as a member of one of Second City's touring companies during the rest of the year—though she was never cast for a mainstage company.

But minority improvisers remained difficult to recruit. The cry of "They don't audition" or "I can't find anyone" has been a time-honored excuse for most white improv troupes' lack of color. Minority performers' reluctance may be attributed to the way groupmind often marginalizes women and people of color in improv practice. But there is also a more pragmatic explanation for improv's whiteness: money. While some white, middle-class players hope to use improv as a springboard to comedy careers, many more play merely for the personal, artistic, and social benefits of participation. But many minority actors do not have the luxury of paying to play. African American improviser Shaun Landry explains, "For many blacks, success is very important, and success means money. And there is very little money to be made in improv" (qtd. in Horwitz). In fact, Second City is the only theatre where improvisers can consistently make a living wage. Yet most minority performers cannot afford the time and money involved in Second City's extensive training.

Jerry Minor, an African American comedian brought into Second City's e.t.c. company in 1996, was originally recruited in Detroit. Like many minority performers, he had been largely unaware of Chicago-style improv-comedy as a separate genre and was making his way as a stand-up comedian. Second City was determined to have a racially integrated company in the Motor City, partly because they were beginning without a built-in audience and hoped to attract Detroit's large African American population to their theatre.

Because the Detroit company had no tradition of its own, Minor was cast without the long training period that most players go through before they make it to the mainstage. Had he lived in Chicago, Minor says, he's not sure he would have ever made the leap: "I probably would have taken classes, or whatever, but there's so much time that they have to take without making money, whereas the other venues, especially in the minority community, are hot. You can do really well in stand-up right now, if you are successful" (personal interview).

Chicago, on the other hand, drew a mostly white, suburban, and tourist-based crowd that did not support change in the company's approach to casting or comedy. Chicago also had historic traditions of apprenticeship that informed their casting policies. Nevertheless, Callier and Second City staffers worked hard in the first few years of the program to identify and reach out to black, Latino, and other performers of color in Chicago. The minority program had little immediate impact on Second City's resident companies, but there was eventually some progress with the touring companies. It was also at the Minority Outreach Program in the summer of 1994 that four black improvisers first met and decided to create Oui Be Negroes.

On October 28, 1994, the following blurb appeared in the *Chicago Reader:* "Oui Be Negroes. The Underground Theatre Conspiracy's comedy revue seeks to offer an alternative to what spokeswoman Shaun Landry calls the 'real white and real guy orientated' nature of Chicago improv" (27).

Oui Be Negroes was the brainchild of Shaun Landry and her husband, Hans Summers, a white man. Both were experienced improvisers who had taken classes at a number of Chicago improv schools, including ImprovOlympic, ImprovInstitute, and Second City, where Landry often found herself the only person of color in the room. Her interest in starting an African American troupe began in the '80s, but that was a decade, says Landry, when "it was incredibly difficult to find black improvisers. . . . Literally, me and John Hildreth, and Frances Callier . . . were the only three people in town who were black and doing improv" (qtd. in Neet). Until the third wave, challenges to the "white guy" domination of Chicago improv-comedy were rare and primarily limited to the isolated struggles of a few individuals.

Landry's experience technically made her over-qualified for the outreach program. She had performed for two years with Geese Theatre Company, taking interventionist, interactive theatre into prisons. She was also a founding member of Summers' Underground Theatre Conspiracy in the late '80s. Nevertheless, Landry enrolled, she says, "to hone my skills and to find other black improvisers for my own company" (personal interview). Of the fifteen or so participants in the program that summer, thirteen African Americans and two Latinos, she chose to approach Kecia Cooper, Bill Underwood, and Dante Richardson, inviting them to join the nascent Oui Be Negroes. Summers would remain as the lone white performer. "He's our Jim Carrey," jokes Landry, referring to the white actor on the black comedy show *In Living Color* (personal interview).

According to Landry, the project's name is a play on "black English," with a bilingual pun (we/oui) as an homage to black jazz singer and comedian Josephine Baker, who delighted Parisian audiences in the 1920s. The title also refers to the novelty and scarcity of black performers in improv-comedy. Landry enjoys audience discomfort with the company's humor: "We're very un-PC and it makes the poor white liberal head spin. . . . They lower their voices and say, 'Are we *supposed* to call you Negroes?' They don't quite understand that we're about parody and homage" (qtd. in Horwitz 26).

While Landry acknowledges that on one level the idea of an all-black troupe is a good publicity gimmick (almost necessary for third-wave companies), she has more important reasons for wanting to work with other black improvisers: "We wanted to develop our own comic voice. We've always had the feeling that improv was based on the urban and suburban white male experience with lots of white male bonding. Improvisation came to be known as a 'white thing' " (Horwitz 26).

Landry and Summers first presented *Oui Be Negroes* as the latest production from the Underground Theatre Conspiracy. The show, which premiered at the Café Voltaire in the fall of 1994, received an encouraging review from the *Chicago Reader*. Taking note of the overwhelming whiteness of Chicago improv, the critic welcomed Oui Be Negroes' fresh perspective (Langer). The following year, adopting the name of their first show for the new company itself, Oui Be Negroes presented its second original project, *Can We Dance with Yo' Dates?* at Sheffield's, a small nightclub theatre.[3]

On the night I attended *Can We Dance with Yo' Dates?* the fifty-seat space was populated largely with white improv fans, although there were a number of African American spectators enjoying their first improv-comedy performance. The show featured a number of sketches drawn specifically from African American experience. Landry and new cast member Crystal Marie Smith created the "Weave Girls," who compared the various hair products and makeup

Chicago critics praised Oui Be Negroes' ability to satirize racial stereotypes in the company's second venture, *Can We Dance with Yo' Dates*. Pictured (clockwise) Hans Summers, Crystal Marie Smith, Shaun Landry, Dante Richardson. Photo: Courtesy Oui Be Negroes

they used to minimize their black features. As black feminist critic Patricia Hill Collins explains, black women are often judged by white standards of beauty. High values placed on straight hair and light skin negatively affect "Black women's self-images, our relationships with one another, and our relationships with Black men" (80). As the Weave Girls, Landry and Smith produced comic commentary on an issue that had many layers of meaning for them as black women on display.

Later in the evening, Landry portrayed African American lesbian feminist poet Shamika, who would nightly improvise an angry, radical poem on any topic the audience chose. Behind her, Dante Richardson performed a hilarious interpretive dance that corresponded to her imagery. In a game-show sketch called "Who Do You Blame?" contestants were asked to guess the culprit responsible for a variety of crimes from purse snatching to the Iran-contra affair. The correct criminal was always shown to be a black man in a stocking cap. This scene took on added significance as it played during the O. J. Simpson trial. Landry notes, "Black audiences know when to laugh, and they'll talk back to the performers. [White audiences] often don't know how to react" (qtd. in Horwitz 26).

By localizing their creative power, the members of Oui Be Negroes are free to create humor based on their own perspectives and culture. In contrast to Callier's early experience at Second City, these actors mutually reinforce, rather than work to minimize, the African American frame of reference in their comedy. Landry explained that she was tired of being the only black actor at every improv audition and in every improv company. By founding her own group of African American improvisers, she explicitly avoided the mind-set that undermined Freeman—the notion that she is responsible for representing "blackness" in a white troupe. Cooper echoed the sentiments of the others in the group when she expanded on this idea: "If you are the only black there in a group, whether they admit to 'you're our token black person' or not, you end up getting a lot of the same stuff. You're expected to play certain stereotypes, and even if you don't, there's a lot of pressure on you because you're the only one. And certain things can't be fed; certain things can't be done. It's limited in that way. . . . You get into a group, and they kinda just want you to do what they want you to do" (personal interview).

Like Landry, Cooper and Underwood come from middle-class backgrounds. Each has trained for and pursued a career in legitimate stage acting, only to be stymied at every turn. Cooper, a beautiful actor with an elegant, sophisticated style, has often been told by directors that she is not "black" enough for a role—meaning not her skin color, but her dialect and mannerisms. But she was also not "white" enough to be considered for other roles.

Underwood has encountered the same expectations and notes, "You go to an audition and you run into that. 'Can you do more dems, dats, and dose for us?' Hell, I'm doing Greek tragedy next" (personal interview). Both of these actors were fairly new to classic improvisation when they decided to participate in Second City's Minority Outreach Program. They saw improv as a valuable skill in their actor's arsenal, hoping it would make them more marketable in the improv-influenced Chicago theatre scene.

On the other hand, Richardson, a gay actor from a working-class background, had evolved his own particular brand of improvisation before he was even aware of Second City. "I was always improvising," he says. "I just didn't know to call it that" (personal interview). Landry is more attuned to the connection between improv-comedy techniques and her African American cultural heritage: "I think African Americans . . . do so incredibly well at it because we're so used to riffing and using those beats and working like that" (personal interview).

For its actors, Oui Be Negroes provides what cultural critic John Fiske defines as a "locale," a time and space that gives them some measure of control over their own performances and their own representations. The troupe's work becomes a temporary yet fulfilling escape from the prescribed roles for blacks available in the legitimate theatre, in their own lives, and even through improvisation at Second City—which in many ways operates as a "station" or controlling institution. Oui Be Negroes creates its performances collectively, and although Landry is the director, every actor participates in creating their "as if" world, "where the imagination is materialized by being given spatial and temporal dimensions, and thus turned into experience" (Fiske 138). Improv creates a local space of cultural activity, enabling these players imaginatively to redefine their identities and relationships (for a time).

Oui Be Negroes often trades in some of the very stereotypes that disturb its members when they are portrayed in other media—roles they might even refuse to play in another venue. Cultural-political critic Michael Omi suggests that "situation context" is crucial for determining the meaning of specific stereotypes and images. Using the example of racist jokes, Omi writes that "Jokes about blacks where the teller and audience are black constitute a form of self-awareness; they allow blacks to cope and 'take the edge off' of oppressive aspects of the social order which they commonly confront" (121). The same joke told across the color line, says Omi, may only serve to reinforce stereotypes. As Oui Be Negroes actor Underwood says, "For me it's control. If I'm doing a black stereotype, and *I* decide to do it, I have license. But if someone else or [a white director] goes, 'Why don't you do an Uncle Tom?' I say *no*" (personal interview).

Oui Be Negroes' locale extends to their mode of rehearsing, the lack of hierarchy within the group, the absence of male dominance, and their own interpretation of such concepts as agreement and the surrender of individuality to the groupmind. Theorist Collins argues that Afrocentric culture values the unique individual within the community, pointing to "the polyrhythms in African-American music, in which no one main beat subordinates the others"(215).

Landry, Cooper, and the others resist the power of groupmind in mostly white troupes. They state flatly that while they can trust their fellow *Negroes,* in an integrated company they would refuse to *agree* to be *endowed* by a white player with any demeaning racial or gender stereotype. They would sooner break the rules against denial than honor an unacceptable initiation. Neither Cooper nor Landry has much sympathy for the large number of white women who say they feel bashed by the white men who dominate improv-comedy and who believe that the rules of agreement are often deliberately manipulated to disempower women and other minorities. Cooper found the complaints pathetic, saying, "I have spent my whole life not being that. I'm not one of *those* kind of women, I would say" (personal interview). And Landry proclaimed, "Oh, you can break the rules, and still say 'YES*and*—.' It's easy as all get-out. If you're good, it's easy. Trust me on this. I've been breaking the rules—I've been saying 'YES*and*—fuck you' " (personal interview).

Both women are very clear in their priorities—there are roles they will not play, lines they will not say, and things they will not do. Their predetermination goes against the teachings of Second City's style of classic improv, where complete openness is valued and preconceptions are called *blocks* that must be overcome. Responding to the suggestion that she was being more self-conscious than the rules of classic improv indicate, Cooper replied, "Well, you have to. It's part of being black in America" (personal interview). [4]

As black women, Landry and Cooper have little reason to rely on the official rules to support or protect them, whether in an improv scene or in society in general. Already precluded from enjoying any privilege associated with white womanhood, they do not have the investment that many white women have in the idea of a fair or just system. As African American women, they have learned to make, break, or ignore rules as they deem necessary. Nor do they have the motivation to struggle against the role of the "good girl," a part they have never been asked to play. In "Outing Whiteness," feminist critic Kate Davy writes, "As the work of many critical theorists of African American womanhood suggest, a presumptive good-girl status has not been a prerogative for African American women in dominant culture. White women and black women share the last 300 years but from crucially different sociohistorical spaces" (194). Davy maintains that "the array of meanings which adhere in 'middle-classness' are virtually laminated with the array of meanings that constitute an institutionalized whiteness," effectively explaining why Cooper has been accused of not being black enough (198 n. 29).

Davy also points out that "Representational strategies built around performing alternative notions of sexuality *excessively* are not necessarily strategies that black women would employ to enact counter-hegemonic disruptions; the histories inscribed on the bodies of African American women ensure a circulation of meanings quite different from those assigned the bodies of other women of color as well as white women" (199). The mere fact of a white girl as masochistic prostitute in *Co-ed Prison Sluts* is shockingly funny to audiences at the Annoyance. For Susan Messing, the improviser, this fantasy role is an amusing liberation. But for a black woman, there is no similar need to shed constraining images or assumptions about sexuality, nor do audiences laugh automatically at the all too frequent stereotype of a black woman as oversexed or masochistic.

Given the pretty one–funny one dichotomy that has pigeonholed white women in Chicago improv, black women are even more limited by mainstream assumptions. Collins delineates four distinct types that society uses to control and categorize black women: the mammy, the matriarch, the welfare mother, and the "Jezebel." According to Collins, whites posit the mammy, who loves her white bosses (and their children), as the good black mother. The stereotypical matriarch represents the bad black mother, constructed as the too-powerful female head of household responsible for emasculating black men. The welfare mother represents a "failed mammy," and the sexually aggressive Jezebel exists to justify white male control and exploitation of black women's sexuality (Collins 77). These images give African American women no place to stand, attacking them for aggression and passivity, strength and weakness, sexuality and asexuality.

When Angela Shelton was cast in the first Detroit Second City company in 1993, she was well aware of her status as the second black woman ever to appear on any Second City mainstage. In Shelton's experience, the roles for all women are severely limited by type and are often determined by a woman's weight—producing larger women as "funny" and thin women as "pretty." Shelton says, "You're either Nell Carter or you're Halle Berry. There's not a lot in between—for white women either. You're either Roseanne or you're Michelle Pfeiffer. So women in general get screwed. And that's the other point—the simple fact is that the quotients are made up before you get there" (personal interview).

Shelton believes that at Second City, as in much of the entertainment industry, fitting into the slot is more important than actual talent. The Chicago Second City troupe traditionally featured two slots for women, but none designated for a black woman, making it difficult for her to move from Detroit to the Chicago cast as her colleague Jerry Minor managed to do—albeit in the alternative e.t.c. company.

Landry takes the independent attitude that black women must and do compete with men on their own terms—louder, faster, funnier, and more aggressive—in order to win equal time on stage. A large, imposing young woman, she is even willing to risk being typed as a matriarch in order to be heard. It is clear from her own words, and from the others' admiring stories about her, that Landry can take care of herself on stage.

One story from their work in the Minority Outreach Program is particularly telling. It begins with a game of Freeze Tag, where players must stop the action of an ongoing improv scene, then go onto the stage, assume the exact physical position of one of the previous players, and, replacing that person, begin a new scene that justifies that pose. Landry entered a scene to play opposite a particularly aggressive and disrespectful African American man: "I had my hand on my face—I took someone out and she had her hand on her face—so I said, 'Why did you hit me?' And I said 'Why did you hit me' because I knew what he was going to say—because he was so predictable. And he goes, 'I hit you, bitch, because I love you.' I hit you, bitch, because I love you! And I knew he would say that, and so I felt Kecia burning from the back of the line—I felt her eyes searing in the back of my head. So I said, 'You hit me because you love me?' He goes, 'Yes.' So I turned around and cold-cocked him. I said, 'I love you too' " (personal interview).

The improvised exchange Landry describes—"Why did you hit me?" "Because I love you"—would be extremely unusual among white improvisers. Here, the black male player drew on a stereotypical image of black male violence against black women without (according to Landry) seeming to critique that image. Rather, he appeared to use it as an expression of power in the scene. Landry clearly holds the actor responsible for his misogynist choice, linking his fictional improvisation to his general attitude toward her and the other women in the troupe. Her reply, too, crossed the line between a character response and her own personal reaction. Her answer was a sharp critique of the scene's premise, and of the man himself. Here was the "YES*and*—fuck you" moment. Landry "agreed" that violence expressed love—then she punched the actor ("cold-cocked him") while proclaiming her affection.

Power plays like these and the desire to manipulate her own image as a black woman were important elements in Landry's decision to create her own African American troupe, where she might not need the belligerent postscript to her "YES*and*—" interactions.

Callier smiles at Landry's intolerance of women who do not fight more aggressively for their rights. She notes that Landry has not really worked the mainstream system, to infiltrate and integrate it from within, and does not fully understand how that game must still be played. In Callier's world, there are more compromises, but there is also a different, perhaps a more spiritual, kind of idealism. While she recognizes its misuse, Callier believes wholeheartedly in the power of "YES*and*—." True improvisers, whom she distinguishes from journeymen who simply work at improv, are men and women who live the principles of improvisation in their daily lives. In sophisticated improv, there is a positive way to say "YES*and*—" while neither denying yourself nor your partner's perspective.

An advocate of dangerous, unsafe improv that really speaks to social issues, Callier says, "I would love to get on stage and have somebody call me a nigger. Yes, go there" (personal interview). She believes that only by confronting these conflicts, and by responding to them by saying "YES*and*—" to the scene, while saying "No" to the character's views within that scene, can you create exciting theatre and meaningful social and political commentary.

Callier has operated within the Second City system for quite a number of years. Although she has worked for the establishment, she has drawn her own personal boundaries, resisting complete assimilation. She warns, "What tends to happen is that you're a wonderful rough stone when you come into Second City, and they smooth you down and smooth you down and smooth you down, 'til you just play with all the rest of the pebbles. You used to be a rock, you know, with wonderful jagged edges and something that was dangerous" (personal interview).

Callier instigated and directed the Minority Outreach Program, yet, at first, she saw the gender inequities throughout the Chicago improv community as a far greater problem: "You can't solve this race issue until you solve the gender issue. I think about it this way—minorities at Second City are even a smaller population than women. If the improv play is not correct and right for *half* the population, it's not going to be correct and right for anybody else" (personal interview).

From her tenuous early position as a touring company performer, and her summer job coordinating the Outreach Program, Callier had fought to learn how to beat the system without abandoning one of improv's only paying jobs. In the early '90s, she often found herself the only person of color, not only in the troupe, but in many towns on their tour: "I would turn around to the people in the back [of the bus] and say, 'I'm not getting out.' But I did. . . . It made me think that there is no place on this earth where I do not have the right to be" (qtd. in Hogarth). She occasionally encountered blatant racism on the road, such as an audience suggestion that she play a slave, but Callier found an even greater challenge trying to be heard in her own troupe's creative process.

Callier began work with her Second City TourCo, trusting that good, committed, and spontaneous improvisation would bring her visibility and give her a voice in the material developed for performance. She finally realized that the most successful (male) performers in the company brought ideas, outlines, and even fully scripted sketches or songs into the rehearsal process. Women were often forced to vie with one another to form contacts and alliances with the men who produced the material. Callier says, concerning Second City,

They don't invite the women to write. Women don't write. And if you do write, you write a woman scene or you may be allowed to put a character into someone else's scene and that's about as far as you're gonna get. If you are a woman and you can create—a woman who writes is a dangerous thing, because if she has the power of the pen, she does not have to soak off the tit of another man, another person. It's like being on welfare, you know? It's a welfare system almost. We are dependent upon you for our livelihood, and though we are able and capable people, I do not venture out to create anything or make success for myself . . . because I know that I will be safe [and] that I will be in a scene if you select me. So therefore I must be funny; I must be pretty; I must be this; I must be that to you. (personal interview)

The compelling image of "comedy welfare" is one that a white woman is unlikely to have used, though it describes a situation that a number of white female improvisers have experienced. As a black woman, perhaps Callier has a clearer view of the relationship between the marginalized individual and the system. Women's dependency in improv, as in the welfare system, is not based on any innate inability to succeed, but on larger controlling structures that foster passivity and undermine self-esteem. For Callier, recognizing this problem was the first step in doing something about it.

Touring companies develop very little original material, compiling "Best of Second City" shows from archived sketches written for a standard cast of four white men and two white women. Callier, who did not want to be on comedy welfare, worked hard to find alternative tactics for making her voice heard within the system. She formed alliances with other actors and made time to improvise original scenes, insisting on support from the director of her Second City TourCo. Second City's mainstage performers had far greater opportunity to collaborate in creating their material. But to move up, Callier needed to find her own comic voice.[5]

Callier realizes that humor from an African American perspective can make the mainstream Second City audience uncomfortable, as they wonder, "Should we laugh? Is it safe for us to laugh at this? . . . What do we say about ourselves by what we laugh at?" (personal interview). She believes you have to train an audience, just as you have to train actors and directors, to understand and accept diverse viewpoints in comedy.

Complex tensions from the intersection of minority and gender concerns can affect the creative process. Dee Ryan and John Hildreth were both members of Second City's e.t.c. troupe in 1994. In the early improvisational workshop phase for one show, Ryan proposed a premise for a scene based on her own frightening experiences of being alone at night in a large parking garage. Developing the scene with Hildreth, and re-improvising it several times in the late-night sets after the scripted revue, Ryan was at first interested in exploring her fear at encountering a stranger in the garage. But the young woman paused. Ryan says, "I actually asked, 'Okay, I'm afraid of you because you're a black man. Do we want to go there?' " (personal interview).

Considering the cultural predispositions of their white, middle-class audiences, Ryan decided it would be far more detrimental for Hildreth to embody the black stereotype of a criminal than it was for her to pursue the validity of a white woman's vulnerability to violence. Accordingly, the two actors improvised a scene in which Ryan played a clueless, hysterical suburban matron who was unreasoningly terrified of an utterly innocent black parking lot attendant (played by Hildreth). Ryan deliberately sacrificed her own perspective on the white woman–black man tension to prevent what she considered the greater injustice of supporting racist assumptions. But the context of their need to create comedy, the director's lack of finesse, and the (perhaps unfair) assumptions of their audience's intolerance prevented these talented actors from finding subtler, more balanced humor in the rich mine of their characters' brief encounter.

Many racial and gendered presumptions go unmarked in Second City scenes derived from improvisation, though some underlying conventions may be foregrounded by cast changes. In one e.t.c. show, Frances Callier understudied the role of a social worker originally created by white improviser Jenna Jolovitz. Watching Callier's performance, I wondered why the scene

In this sketch from Second City e.t.c.'s *One Nation, Under Fraud*, an innocent African American parking garage attendant (John Hildreth) becomes a violent savage in the overheated imagination of a suburban matron (Dee Ryan). Photo: Roger Lewin/Jennifer Girard Studio

didn't seem funny. I later learned that Jolovitz had originated the character as cavalier and uncaring, oblivious to the pain of the family she was supposed to be helping—creating a kind of outrageous comic scenario. While Callier had spoken most of the same lines, she had seemed to be weary and worn down, yet far from uncaring. These changes can, of course, be traced to each individual actor's persona and my own assumptions about a black woman social worker. But Callier clearly had a very different take on social workers and struggling families than her white counterpart. Bottom line, the scenario as scripted by whites didn't work (as comedy) with Callier playing it. She needed the chance to create her own material.

In 1995, Callier mounted an independent project using her Second City contacts to recruit experienced players. Ironically, while Landry's shows replicate Second City's sketch format, Callier's was a long-form, improv-based exploration of a serious theme. The show, *Ike and Tina's Wedding* (a title that consciously parodies the popular environmental improv show *Tony 'n' Tina's Wedding*), explored the musical career and personal life of Tina Turner.

The production featured Second City actor Hildreth as a narrator-preacher figure. In this guise, Hildreth was able to use the modes of ecstatic rhetoric and call-and-response familiar to many black church-goers to improvise from the pulpit whenever the action demanded. Tina Turner was played by a black gay man in drag, a device that foregrounded the constructedness of Tina's femininity but also threatened to remove a key female voice from the improvisation process. Three women portrayed the "Ikettes," often expressing a variety of responses to Ike's abuse of Tina. In her production notes for the show, Callier wrote,

This piece was an ensemble effort. The material was developed through character monologues and long-form improvisations that were taped, transcribed and worked into a script. Once finished, Ike & Tina's Wedding will be a show about domestic violence that uses performing in an African-American rock and roll revue as a backdrop.

The beats are scripted, but the actors are improvisors (Watch out!). At any time they are free to go off script or start a song to surprise themselves, their partners, and the audience.

The experience of working with an all African-American cast of improvisors was a first for all of us. This project was a success by attaining that mere fact.

—Frances Callier (*Ike and Tina's Wedding* program)

Ike and Tina's Wedding was loosely structured and seemed to follow a musical model of improvisation, with several set themes that were expressed through solo riffs, duets, backup vocals, and group jams. The show had a very limited run, but it seemed to demonstrate a distinctly African American style of improv and to deal with issues important to the African American community. Perhaps more important, Callier finally had the opportunity to work with other improvisers who understood her perspective: "You could make a reference to the Isely Brothers and not only know that it would be understood, but that your partner would respond by singing a song or telling you where they were when they first made out to it" (Callier qtd. in Hogarth). Although Callier is seriously committed to integrated improv, she found it necessary to move toward separatism, much as Landry had done, in order to improvise in an African American voice.

A year after *Ike and Tina* closed, Second City offered Callier an opportunity to helm a project that gave minority performers a chance to write, but also continued the company's practice of "separate but almost equal" (B. Johnson interview). In 1996, Second City opened a small studio theatre on the third floor of the Wells Street building. The hundred-seat SkyBox (later named "Donny's SkyBox" to honor Second City's late revered director and teacher Don DePollo) was allocated for experimental projects, once thought to be the province of the e.t.c. company.

Callier would direct the inaugural SkyBox production, a "minority show" that she would call *Soul Front*. Second City producer Kelly Leonard explained, "Look, everyone knows that in the standard Second City cast, you've got your big white guy, your thin white guy, your ethnic-looking female and your blond female. [But in *Soul Front*] when you have a multitude of black performers or Hispanic or whatever, you are then able to deal with something more than the black guy's problem with white society. Instead, you can look at the black community through their eyes, and problems that are intrinsic to their world" (qtd. in Johnson 12). Producers Alexander and Leonard worked far more actively than their predecessors to create casting opportunities for women and minorities at Second City.

Soul Front's cast was drawn from the Minority Outreach Program and several Second City touring companies. It consisted of four African Americans (two male, two female), two whites (one male, one female), and one Latino (male). The group developed its own material under Callier's direction, improvising in workshops, much the way any Second City revue is created. Some of the actors saw this process as an important opportunity to express their frustrations with American race relations. African American player David Pompeii explained, "I've felt like I've had some things I wanted to say, and I don't know that I necessarily wanted to say them to individual white people that I know" (qtd. in Johnson 12). *Soul Front*, Pompeii believed, would give him that chance.

The group developed standard format comedy sketches that included a parody of the black cable show *Def Comedy Jam*; a high-energy spoof of Telemundo, the Spanish-speaking television station; and satirical sketches about the O. J. Simpson trial, Texaco's racist corporate executives, and other material. *Soul Front* received mixed reviews, the influential *Chicago Reader* calling it unsubtle and unfunny. The *Daily Journal*, on the other hand, praised the show for "confronting racism in society, but without self-congratulation or self-righteousness" (Zeff). Whatever the project's quality, it did not seem to find its audience. Attendees were mostly white, with "more African-Americans onstage than in the crowd" on opening night (Johnson 12). The show closed after its four-week run. Ironically, the only member of *Soul Front* to be tapped for a mainstage spot was Rachel Hamilton, the one white woman.

Another identity-based troupe then took its turn in the SkyBox. Ed Garza, former administrator of the Second City Training Center, secured producer Alexander's support for several workshops aimed at gay and lesbian students on the model of the Minority Outreach Program. In mainstream improv, gay-themed humor rarely moved beyond stereotypes, presenting homosexuality from the perspective of straight fear. But, given the opportunity to explore their own issues and experience, Garza's players were able to create original comedy from a gay perspective. Their first show, *Whitney Houston, We Have a Problem*, was directed by Jeff Richmond. The critically acclaimed revue played to capacity crowds for twenty-four weeks, encouraging the players to form an independent company. In 1999, the troupe (dubbed GayCo) presented *Everyone's Coming Out Rosie!* and *Don't Ask, Don't Teletubby* in the SkyBox and planned tours around the United States and to the Gay Games festival in Amsterdam.

Second City supported a diversity of improvisers through its training center, Outreach Program, and SkyBox productions while the mainstage company remained mainstream. In some ways, this special-interest approach empowered marginalized performers to find their own comic voices. In other ways, it seemed to perpetuate their marginalization.

A few months after *Soul Front* closed, Oui Be Negroes opened a new show called *One Drop Is All It Takes* at the TurnAround Theatre. The title, cryptic for many theatre-goers, refers to the nineteenth-century notion of the "tragic mulatto"—considered black if he or she had as little as "one drop of black blood." *One Drop* featured new troupe members Marvin Howard and Merle Dandridge, along with Summers, Landry, and Richardson. It presented fresh material along with a number of Oui Be Negroes' favorite bits, including Summers and Landry as an elderly mixed-race couple reminiscing about their trials and triumphs and Landry's impromptus as an angry feminist poet who

GayCo Productions was founded with the mission to "create intelligent and thought-provoking sketch comedy based on gay and lesbian themes that will either entertain, educate, and/or enlighten our audience." Company members pictured (left to right): Ed Garza (founding artistic director), Judy Fajance, John Bonny, Richard Morrisey, Andy Eninger, Butch Jernic, Mary Beth Burns, Jennifer Shepard. Photo: Al Bonny

"when asked to improvise on the Cabrini-Green shoot-out conjured a lyric of astonishing power and sincerity" (Barnidge).⁶ One new sketch skewered black slackers who use antiracist rhetoric as an excuse for their own irresponsibility. According to Landry, African American audiences steadily increased throughout *One Drop*'s Chicago run, with black spectators outnumbering whites at some performances (personal interview).

The *Chicago Reader* gave *One Drop* a rave review, comparing it to *Soul Front*: "Second City's recent, much ballyhooed *Soul Front* purported to break with the urban-white-liberal bias endemic in improv comedy, but Landry and Summers have been doing precisely that for nearly a decade. They be professionals" (Barnidge). To be fair, it should be noted that *Soul Front* was cast with young improvisers recruited to fill minority positions in a large institution and brought together for a single show (albeit with Callier's inspiring leadership). The smaller, independent Oui Be Negroes used sketches polished over several revues and had more experience as an ensemble. Both endeavors served, at the very least, to provoke citywide discussion of the question of race and representation in Chicago improv. Oui Be Negroes toured

One Drop to Boston, where it attracted the attention of a college-circuit booking agent. Once on the agent's roster, the troupe found an eager market of university programs looking for comedy with multicultural appeal (particularly during Black History Month).

Following Oui Be Negroes' lead, other independent, identity-based troupes emerged throughout the decade. Stir-Friday Night, a group of Asian American actors and improvisers, produced their first show in 1995: *To Hop Sing, Thanks for Everything! Connie Chung.* Like Oui Be Negroes, the troupe found many of its early gigs through university student groups whose members were hungry for humor that reflected their own experience. One collegiate reviewer wrote, "Of the very few Asian performers in the entertainment industry, most play serious, Asian-oriented stereotypical roles. . . . However, Stir-Friday Night proved to the audience that Asian comedy can be funny. . . . The comedy troupe itself is composed of Asian actors of various descents. . . . The actors do not appear removed, but more familiar, like the John Kim down the street. . . . I understood the humor as an extension of my background and my history" (Ko). ¡Salsation! a Latino troupe, began performing in 1998 with a very similar mission—to provide opportunities for minority performers and to debunk stereotypes. Their performances assert, "We can do improv, too!"[7]

At the same time, Second City made concerted efforts to increase minority presence throughout its ranks. The number of black and Latino players in the touring companies rose slightly, and several of the troupes moved to a cast of three men and three women. This simple change in gender balance had an enormous effect on each Second City TourCo. In their recreations of classic Second City scenes from the past, the third woman often found herself playing larger and more interesting roles previously played by men. In fact, the female dichotomy of *pretty one* and *funny one* was forcefully interrupted by this wild-card third term, and all three women in each troupe found themselves freer to shift among a number of identities and more supported when initiating scenes in the improv sets.

In 1996, Alexander, Leonard, and director Mick Napier were instrumental in creating the first gender-balanced troupe on the Second City mainstage. But they also cast a white actor to fill an open slot that veteran improviser Hildreth thought had been promised to him. Exasperated with the glass ceiling that kept him at e.t.c when fellow (white) cast members were moving up, Hildreth quit the troupe. He directed several shows for Detroit's Second City, then returned to Chicago to pursue independent directing and performing. But Hildreth left an important legacy. Brandon Johnson, who understudied for him, asserts, "Without John Hildreth, I wouldn't have gotten hired. Once he created the need for black improvisers, they were much keener on hiring

Stir-Friday Night attacks Asian stereotypes with improv and sketch comedy in such shows as *The Return of the Yellow Menace!* and *Asians Who Can't Do Math*. Company members pictured (top to bottom): Quincy Wong, Wayne Eji, Ron Mok, Joe Yau, Ken Hamada, Daisy Castro, Jen Banzon, Jennifer Liu, Seema Sueko. Photo: Jack Yau

us. When you're in the touring company, you can pull from the archives scenes that you need to use. I always look for Hildreth's work because they are very black-specific and always gave a very good message" (personal interview).[8]

Brought in to replace Hildreth, Jerry Minor was very aware of his part in maintaining the minority-male spot at e.t.c. He focused on creating at least one "unmistakably ethnic" role in every show, partly to contribute to the "Best of" archives, and partly because, he says, "it allows other people to understudy me, and they can get work, and they can show what they can do" (personal interview). In the next e.t.c. revue, *40 Ounces and a Mule*, director Norm Holly boldly cast a second minority male, Chilean-born Horatio Sanz.[9] Sanz, who had also performed with several ImprovOlympic teams, was the

In their critically-acclaimed show, *Touched by an Anglo*, ¡Salsation! "creates comedy with a Latin flavor." Company members pictured (clockwise from top): Paul Vato, Aamer Arboleda, Ramon Charriez, Jr., Joseph A. Nuñez, Sandra Chavez, Eva Rios, Dianne Herrera. Photo: Pilsen Photo Studio.

first Minority Outreach participant to be cast in a resident company. For Minor, the presence of another person of color made a significant difference in the material he was able to write and improvise. Minor later moved on, leaving Sanz the sole minority performer in the following revue. In 1998, when Sanz became the first Latino ever cast by *Saturday Night Live*, e.t.c. dropped its minority-male position for a time. (Minor, too, later joined *SNL*.)

The twentieth e.t.c. revue, *The Revelation Will Not Be Televised*, represented a significant paradigm shift. In a deliberate move toward multiculturalism, director Richmond and producers Leonard and Alexander hired a cast of unprecedented diversity. Included in the ensemble were Angela Shelton, who had paid her Second City dues in Detroit, Toronto, and a TourCo and had rigorously dieted for this opportunity; David Pompeii, an Outreach graduate and performer in *Soul Front*; Martin Garcia, a gay Latino from Austin ComedySportz and *Soul Front*; Iranian-born Ali Farahnakian, a veteran of ImprovOlympic's the Family; Sue Maxman, a founding member of Jane; and Craig Cackowski, the lone white guy.[10]

Although Shelton had dreamed of playing on the more prestigious mainstage, she preferred being in a diverse cast to being the only black person or the only woman "because it's hard to write material" (personal interview). In the rehearsal process for *Revelation,* and for the revue that followed (*History Repaints Itself*), Shelton felt free to play with a variety of identities—even "white" characters. At the same time, like Hildreth and Minor before her, Shelton was determined to "create enough black scenes that they will feel compelled to hire minority talent" (personal interview).[11] Critics praised both shows, the *Chicago Tribune* noting that "the diverse cast manages to reflect multiple cultures without fear of offense or a self-congratulatory tone. And because Second City was white and male for most of its 40 years, this is no mean feat" (C. Jones).

On another front, in 1998, Callier was named executive director of the entire Second City Training Center, where she continued to make diversity a priority, often giving talented minority performers outright scholarships to Second City's conservatory program. In the meantime, she developed two important projects that would enable her to "give something back to the art form" (personal interview). The first was the Chicago Improv Festival (discussed in the next chapter). The other was Black Comedy Underground (BCU), a troupe of black Second City performers and alumni organized outside of the Second City stronghold. The players, including Callier, Shelton, Hildreth, Pompeii, and, from *Soul Front,* Thomas Greene V and Claudia Wallace, first gathered for a Second City benefit performance directed by Aaron Freeman, using classic Second City scripts. Callier recalls, "It was like putting a black face on white material" (qtd. in Hayford 5). The group decided to develop their own material, where they could finally express their own words in their own voices.

The BCU's first fully developed show was *Kill Whitey,* performed in Donny's SkyBox in 1999. Its aggressive title was meant, Callier said, to indicate a new mode of self-reliance: "It's about letting go of the mentality that you need someone in the power structure to validate your worthiness" (qtd. in Bannon 4). The sketches, developed through improvisation, centered on five "talentless" African American screenwriters. According to one reviewer, the production's characters bordered "on offensive stereotypes: the alcoholic welfare mother with 800 children, the self-righteous Muslim finding racist conspiracies under every rock, the homeless crack addict, the college-educated feminist out to persuade herself she's white" (Hayford 5). Yet several critics praised the talented and experienced troupe for bringing humanity, dimension, and depth to these provocative figures. Callier's work, focused on the theme of independence, was nonetheless made possible by support from Second City and Callier's own work developing African American talent there.

Landry's troupe also reaped the benefits of Second City's outreach (and

Frances Callier served as producer and ensemble member for Black Comedy Underground, the nation's first *all*-African American improv-based troupe, featuring an elite corps of Second City-trained improvisers. Company members pictured (left to right, standing): Thomas Greene, Claudia Wallace, John Hildreth, Frances Callier, Angela Shelton, (seated) David Pompeii and Brandon Johnson. Photo: Courtesy Black Comedy Underground.

the visibility of black improviser Wayne Brady on *Whose Line Is It Anyway?*). In 1994, Landry had struggled to find enough black improvisers to form a troupe. By 1998, she could choose from a much larger number of black men, although black women were still difficult to cast. The next group of *Negroes* included players who had studied acting in college and improv at the Second City conservatory. Each new member had a specific reason for wanting to join the company. Ronald Ray liked his Second City class, but says, "I definitely had to hold back. Every time I tried to initiate a scene, they'd take it somewhere else . . . so I'm trying to match them, trying to be where they are instead of where my angle was at. . . . I felt like Tootie from *Facts of Life*" (personal interview).

Nicole Tinnin wanted to learn improv in a supportive environment. Khristian Leslie was put off by the expense, and by the cliques, of ImprovOlympic: "I wouldn't walk into IO. If you look at that place and you don't know what's going on, that's damn intimidating" (personal interview). One of the few blacks who did play at ImprovOlympic, Cordell Pace continued with his team, Mourning in Denver, while studying at Second City, performing with Oui Be Negroes, and pursuing independent projects. Pace believed the identity-based group was important because "an audience will know that we are out there doing improv, too—from an African American point of view. . . . It was an opportunity to get together to see what would happen when you are performing with your own people" (personal interview).

Oui Be Negroes developed several new shows, including *All Coons Look Alike to Me* and *Absolute Negritude*. They also created improv structures that drew more directly from African American cultural forms. One new piece was based on the "shabooya," a rhyming chant first used by children jumping rope and later picked up by black fraternities and sororities. In a structure they call Negro Café, players improvise songs and poems in jazz rhythms while the rest of the company creates a jazz backbeat behind them. As Callier did with *Ike and Tina's Wedding*, the troupe also works with their own long-form structure based on a Baptist Revival meeting and the "patterns of verbal and artistic invention identified as call and response . . . in the rhetorical improvisations of ministers in the black pulpit" (Dyson xxi).

As Landry and Callier rang in the new millennium, each could note with pride the miles traveled toward equal opportunity in improv, while acknowledging that the journey was far from complete. At Second City, Callier's goals

Hans Summers, Nicole Tinnin and Shaun Landry perform Oui Be Negroes' jazz-based improv format, Negro Café, in their 1999 revue, *Absolute Negritude*. Photo: Fuzzy Gerdes

for true diversity had evolved with time. Though she once pushed for a general outreach to the minority community, Callier was no longer satisfied simply with increased visibility for these marginalized improvisers. What she and Second City had begun to realize was that "even though we put minorities in a room together, you still can experience ghettoizing, or the ghettoization of people, because all these minorities are not the same . . . these are really different voices" (Callier interview). Callier was committed to providing performers with the opportunity to develop "voice"—a sense of their own creative contribution—as a precursor to integrated groupmind improvisation.

With Second City's support, Callier organized Improvising New Voices, a series of workshops and performances for African American, Asian American, gay, Latino, lesbian, and transgender actors. What made New Voices different from earlier outreach programs was that Second City workshop leaders were partnered with guest ensembles such as Black Comedy Underground, GayCo Productions, ¡Salsation! and Stir-Friday Night. Participants could thus benefit both from classic training and from the experience of players who had worked in specific minority or integrated contexts.

Despite these improvements, Callier and Alexander recognized the limitations of this kind of outreach. Chicago's history of racial tension and segregation, Alexander reasoned, might well make minority performers feel intimidated or unwilling to investigate the opportunities on North Wells Street. Yet the producer had come to feel that Second City had both the resources and the responsibility to help increase diversity in the improv community (Alexander interview).

On behalf of Second City, Callier applied for federal funding to build an African American improv theatre in Chicago's inner city. The company received a million dollar empowerment-zone grant to renovate a space on Forty-seventh Street and King Drive, as part of the Bronsville Blues District Restoration Project. While Second City management planned to help establish a training center and performance space there, Alexander was "quite prepared to be a minority partner in this venture," ceding artistic control to community-based teachers. The benefit for Second City would be that "there is finally a consistent place that we can openly draw on to balance our diversity issues" (personal interview). Callier's persistent efforts to broaden Second City's horizons had begun to make a real difference.

Callier and Landry (and company) each chose a specific mode of surviving and thriving in Chicago's improv community. Landry and Oui Be Negroes established a locale that celebrates their difference—separate and segregated—though still linked to the official mainstream. Callier worked within the interstices of the Second City establishment, hoping to widen the cracks of opportunity and yet to resist the assimilative lure of the melting pot.

In 2000, both women chose to move their bases of operation to California. Landry relocated Oui Be Negroes headquarters to the less improv-saturated Bay area, though Chicago-based performers continued to participate in the troupe's touring shows. Callier became Second City's first African American producer with her promotion to head of the new Los Angeles theatre and training center. Her assignment included a mandate to create, pitch, and produce television projects for Second City. She and Angela Shelton continued to improvise dialogue for *Hey, Monie*, an animated series about two African American career women and best friends, produced by the woman-centered Oxygen cable network. Callier also agreed to stay involved as an advisor to the new black Second City in Chicago.

For Callier and Landry, their continued commitment to the improv genre, despite its obvious potential for abuse, stems from their vision not of its present reality in the world of mainstream improv-comedy, but of its eventual potential for finding and expressing a diversity of voices. Through their own determined efforts, both women found voice and visibility through Chicago improv. Like increasing numbers of improvisers, both would now participate in the dissemination of Chicago improv theory and technique to new places and new endeavors.

conclusion

As the millennium drew to an end, the improv world was again in flux. Nationwide awareness of improv had grown rapidly throughout the '90s, fostered by touring companies, regional teams, festivals, the internet, college and university troupes, television programs, and films. Increasing numbers of corporations and businesses began hiring improv consultants to help facilitate group work, creativity, and positive thinking. Eager students poured into Chicago in seasonal floods, but an increasing number of veterans were flowing out again, looking for ways to use their skills in less improv-saturated, more lucrative arenas. Chicago became a hub for the improv diaspora. Comedy-Sportz veteran Randy Smock explains, "If you are doing improv because you love to do improv, then Chicago is the place to be. If this is what you want your profession to be, you're probably going to have to leave" (personal interview).

Most new arrivals enrolled in classes at one or more of the city's "Big Three" improv theatres: Second City, ImprovOlympic, and the Annoyance Theatre. Each school of improv had something distinctive to offer. Students learned classic improvisation technique at Second City, the Harold and other long-form skills at ImprovOlympic, and creative confidence at the Annoyance.

But the boundaries separating important troupes or waves had begun to blur. Second City continued to cast key players from ImprovOlympic house teams, including most of the Family, many from Jane, and others. As early as 1995, elements of long form appeared on the Second City mainstage in *Piñata Full of Bees*.[1] The cast, mostly ImprovOlympic alumni, and director Tom Gianas set aside the standard blackout sketch. Instead, they allowed scenes to weave through one another with "callbacks"—recurring themes and characters reminiscent of a Harold—although the sketch format would return in later shows. Reflecting on the second and third waves' influence on Second City, producer Andrew Alexander says, "When Del and Annoyance opened, frankly it was the best thing that could ever have happened. . . . I'm looking now and saying, 'Where are the next ones going to come from?' because it only challenges us" (personal interview).

Mick Napier brought his Annoyance sensibilities and even a number of Annoyance actors into Second City, while mainstage improvisers were invited to join *The Armando Diaz Hootenanny and Theatrical Experience* at the Del Close Theatre on Monday nights. Players often belonged to several troupes at once, dividing their time among established companies and freelance endeavors. The atmosphere was less divisive at the management level, but more competitive among individuals as Chicago improv's population grew.

Women and people of color began to find greater opportunity in mainstream troupes, but audiences and players also continued to value identity-based troupes, such as Oui Be Negroes, Black Comedy Underground, Stir-Friday Night, ¡Salsation! and GayCo Productions, which flourished on tour, on their own, and in Donny's SkyBox. But issues of power and difference, race and gender, process and product still shaped the offstage and onstage experiences of every improviser, and the battle to find and assert a distinctive voice had to be fought by each new generation of players.

In the midst of this ferment, we may ask, Was there a *fourth* wave in the making? The philosophical model I have outlined throughout this book is only one way of looking at the billowing developments in Chicago improv, with its series of movements stepping forward to reclaim and reinvent the true spirit of the art form. Another perspective, however, might examine the tremendous increase in improv's reach and accessibility and the growing impact of technology on the dissemination of improv technique and philosophy far beyond Chicago. Not only are improv companies developing in many cities, but the internet has enabled improvisers everywhere to be in daily contact with one another. The fertile intersection of improv and technology has possibilities we cannot fully anticipate.

If a "wave" is defined as a fresh burst of improv idealism, the Playground co-op fits one possible description of a fourth wave. Second- and third-wave companies were often created by artists who felt excluded or manipulated by the policies and practices of established troupes. For the next generation of improvisers, however, even the anarchic Annoyance could seem to be a closed shop, with enigmatic politics and a guru (however unwilling) in the charismatic Mick Napier.

In 1997, a team of ImprovOlympians called Cinco de Bob found itself dismantled, its members redistributed among other teams. This was not uncommon, as producer Charna Halpern often discontinued groups deemed unsuccessful. But Cinco de Bob members were true believers in groupthink and team solidarity. They wanted to stay together, convinced they had the potential to grow. Nevertheless, Halpern refused to give them another chance.

Furious, the group began joking about the need for a competing theatre of "disgruntled players." The idea born of anger soon took on a positive energy (Francis interview). Cinco de Bob member Doug Diefenbach wrote and circulated an "Improv Underground" proposal. It was the design for an egalitarian improv utopia, based on the notion that "this groupmind idea can apply to living organizations" (Diefenbach interview). Diefenbach proposed a player-run co-op without an artistic director, identifying style, or commercial goal—no "backroom power elite" and "no gurus." A board comprising representatives from member teams would run the enterprise, but each group would retain artistic autonomy. They would "test the proposition that if an ensemble is committed to each other and to doing good work, they will find a way to improve and to succeed" (personal interview).

Diefenbach's idea struck a chord with a great number of improvisers who felt constrained by the "powers that be" (Diefenbach interview). Refugees from Second City's training program, ImprovOlympic, and other places met weekly to refine the plan. In April 1997, nine charter ensembles—including Cinco de Bob and the all-female troupe Red—paid forty-five dollars each to officially found the Playground. The following month, Mick Napier hosted a gala opening for the project.

The Playground grew quickly and ran quite smoothly. Diefenbach compares the group's management to an ideal long-form improv: "It's a wonderful orchestra of people who bring their strengths to the floor at the right time . . . it's an ever-changing mix of equals . . . we call it grassroots improv" (personal interview). At first, member teams and guest troupes performed on Saturdays at a local bar. Soon, the schedule expanded to include Friday nights and a regular rotation of shows.

Many improv veterans cheered the group on, donating time, money, and advice. Others predicted disaster and disillusionment. How many troupes could the Playground accommodate before competition set in? Even the move from one night to two created a hierarchy of preferred performance times. And equality was fine, but what about quality? Would the Playground become a dump site for troupes that weren't considered good enough for other theatres? Determined to maintain "a supportive environment where improvisers can grow as performers," the Playground's board devised a "professionalism committee" to oversee and assist member troupes that might be struggling (Playground guidelines). But the issue of quality control in a collective remains a thorny one.

Members worked hard to maintain their ideals, even as economic and logistical realities forced them to adjust their dreams. (A plan to pay performers was an early casualty, as production costs rose.) The Playground hosted scores of established troupes, including Oui Be Negroes, ¡Salsation! several popular ImprovOlympic teams, and a group of improvisers from Japan, while helping new or unaffiliated players form troupes though their Improv Incubator program. They also created RECESS, an outreach program providing free workshops for children and teens.

One Chicago critic marveled in terms that might once have described the Compass Players: "The idea of an improv co-op where people would perform just for the sheer joy of it was just too idealistic, too starry-eyed, too hippie-dippy Sixties to last, they thought. A year and a half later, [the Playground has] proved the naysayers wrong. . . . The loose, playful atmosphere of shows at The Playground virtually guarantees the kind of infectious exuberance everyone from Player's Workshop to Second City strives for, but few achieve" (Helbig, *New City*).

The following year, the co-op had increased to twelve teams with over eighty shareholder-players and a long list of guest teams eager to play along. The board launched a fund-raising campaign to secure and renovate a permanent playing space. With money and resources donated by friends, local businesses, established improvisers, and largely from the players themselves, the Playground Improv Theater opened its doors in March 1999.

Some of its members, inevitably, see the Playground as just another place to perform. But for Diefenbach and many of his colleagues, improv is a mission. In declaring themselves a nonprofit service organization, they wrote, "We believe that the value of improv goes beyond mere entertainment; rather, in a society filled with isolating and fragmenting influences, improv holds a societally valuable message: it demonstrates how teamwork, trust and support can make something wonderful out of absolutely nothing" (Playground archive).

Altruism aside, the Playground's true believers may not perceive the downside of groupmind. In 1999, Diefenbach stressed the value of recognizing that "we all have things in common." He explained, "Overlaying a feminist or race-conscious agenda tends to disrupt the work, because not everyone shares the same experiences at that level. Those are contentious issues and contentiousness kills. . . . [Players with that kind of agenda] are inward-looking and self-referential as you pursue the message, rather than outward-looking and 'commonality' driven by being connected to our shared reality" (personal correspondence). In conversation, however, Diefenbach acknowledged that "commonality" might too easily be read as heterosexual, white, male values and that a person of color, for example, would have "farther to homogenize" to meet his "common denominator" (personal interview).

Despite Diefenbach's tendency to homogenize, Oui Be Negroes' Shaun Landry recognized the co-op's meta-message of cooperation and collaboration through improv. She calls the Playground "one of the few places where improvisers are supportive, and unaffiliated groups feel welcome" (personal interview).

Veteran improviser Lillian Francis suggests that, "like most good grassroots movements," the fourth wave may be gathering force in American colleges and universities: "Practically everyone I know discovered improv at college and started by doing short-form comedy" (personal interview). When Mick Napier was a student at Indiana in the late '80s, he and the Dubbletaque gang had little more to go on than Jeff Sweet's *Something Wonderful Right Away*. Today's fledgling improvisers can attend (and organize) improv festivals, refer to improv pages on the internet, and even see modified versions of improv on television.

In 1998, Mission IMPROVable, an all-male troupe at the University of Massachusetts, produced the New England College Improv Jam. The guest list included a number of college groups and a team of invited professionals from ImprovOlympic. While long form was old news in Chicago, it was the first encounter with the Harold for most of the New England students. The Mission IMPROVable players were so inspired that they moved to Chicago as a group, to study and to work on being discovered. They were not alone. Just before the troupe was to go onstage at the Playground, Mission IMPROVable's Aaron Krebs explained the seasonal pattern of college improvisers' migration to Chicago: "[They arrive] every June, right after school, and then again in September—kids that worked all summer to save up to move out here like we did. The generation before us, last year, some people came from Florida State, from North Carolina and from New Jersey. . . . It's like a graduation. It's becoming a bigger and bigger thing in colleges and more and more people want to do it. It's just going to expand" (personal interview). Of course, individual players encounter different experiences when they arrive. The isolated strong women of the college circuit may find new allies when they hit town, while most men lose status when they move to Chicago's bigger pond. Mission IMPROVable hit the ground running, even persuading Halpern to let them stay together as an ImprovOlympic team.

Many players believe that improv's next wave consists of its rapid growth and recognition *outside* Chicago. While improv festivals draw some students to Chicago, they are also an effective means of disseminating ideas and even decentralizing improv activity throughout the country. In 1994, the Kansas

City festival (later called Spontaneous Combustion) was the first large, regional event to bring troupes together from all over North America for workshops, panels, and performances. More important, players could meet informally to share games, techniques, anecdotes, and opinions. By 1996, the Big Stinkin' Improv Festival was launched in Austin, Texas, expanding to an international festival in 1999 when it invited troupes from Canada, Australia, New Zealand, Holland, South Africa, Ireland, Scotland, and England to participate. The Texas festival was overtly commercial, aggressively recruiting representatives from the entertainment industry to scout for talent at their events.

In the latter half of the '90s, festivals were held in Portland, Minneapolis, Aspen, and New York with varying degrees of success. Skidmore College hosted the National College Comedy Festival annually, and smaller festivals on other college campuses demonstrated improv's growing popularity with students. In 1998, Frances Callier and Jonathan Pitts organized the first Chicago Improv Festival, a six-day extravaganza that showcased Chicago troupes, Chicago alumni, and other companies from New York, Minneapolis, and Los Angeles. Offerings included workshops with respected teachers and directors, including such improv luminaries as Keith Johnstone and Del Close. Callier hoped to make people understand that improv is not merely a technique or acting skill, but "an art form in and of itself" (qtd. in Kozlowski). Arts critic Jack Helbig saw the festival as a positive response to troubling times in Chicago's improv community: "There's an anxious lull, as many of the most talented performers leave town for higher profile possibilities on the east and west coasts. Which makes this a good time to gather the tribes—to see how far improv has come, what others have done with the form, and where it might go next" ("Critic's Choice").

In their second outing, Callier and Pitts expanded the festival, dedicating it to Del Close, who had died only weeks before. With sponsorship from cable station Comedy Central, the organizers were able to present the Groundlings, from Los Angeles, and Canadian Colin Mochrie of television's *Whose Line Is It Anyway?* The 1999 festival also featured a Gay and Lesbian Night and a Multicultural Night featuring Oui Be Negroes, ¡Salsation! and Stir-Friday Night. Whether this was ghettoization or special privilege may be in the eye of the beholder.

According to some players, the next wave of improv is its growing presence on the internet, on television, and in film. Throughout the '90s, the internet was an increasingly important part of improv subculture. Players exchanged information, traded games, advertised performances, made contacts, and solicited students through newsgroups like alt.comedy.improvisation. By decade's end, every self-respecting improv troupe had its own web site, and the quality of a site's design began to have an impact on a troupe's success (though, occasionally, sites were better than performances). Troupes post photos, reviews, and tour availability on their web pages and use the internet to send press releases directly to an editor's desk. National improv festivals owed their success and rapid growth to the internet, where organizers advertised, posted registration forms, and recruited troupes. Looking back at Oui Be Negroes' touring schedule and festival participation, Landry asserts, "Everything we've ever done has been as a result of the internet" (personal interview).

Internet resources for improvisers have proliferated, including the Improv Page, the New Improv Page, Improv Resource Center Chicago, the Living Playbook, and many more. Some sites are highly personal and idiosyncratic, while others list games, groups, or festival information. In 1998, a webzine called *YESand* began publishing news and feature articles on a monthly basis, also hosting a bulletin board/discussion list where players posted messages under the categories General, Plugs, Casting, Improv Theory, or Silliness. One discussion began by mourning the death of comedian Madeline Kahn, moved into a debate about gender roles in improv, and ended with plans for a Funny Women Improv Festival in Chicago (August 2000). The resulting event drew more than one hundred players from over twenty states, women who came seeking role models, support, and solidarity from other funny women. Performances, workshops, and panel discussions demonstrated that female improvisers throughout the United States were growing stronger, more skillful, and more confident, even as they continued to struggle with the gender and power issues discussed throughout this book. Following the festival, the *YESand* bulletin board posted kudos, congratulations, and thanks for "creating such a safe and supportive and funny environment" *(YESand)*.[2]

Improv performance has been broadcast over the internet through streaming video, and several versions of on-line improvisation, or interactive theatre, are gaining in popularity. The Annoyance Theatre plans a flash site for animation, original films, and "Living Mad Libs," an interactive game in which users can select features, including location, relationship, and activity, then watch their electronic improv unfold from a set of prerecorded sketches.

As it turns out, many improvisers are from the cognitariat—information workers whose day jobs involve sophisticated computer use. These self-described geeks may be drawn to improv for that very reason. The improv community offers human connection to professionals whose work may be isolating and provides a structured community for those who may be socially challenged. Many Chicago players are as involved in the on-line improv community as they are in the local scene.

Respected improv veterans and role models, Frances Callier and Susan Messing taught workshops and answered questions in a discussion panel at the first annual Funny Woman Festival in Chicago. Photo: Amy Seham

The Chicago improv community has a decades-long love-hate relationship with television. Second City's role as talent source for *Saturday Night Live* and *SCTV* brought it prestige, giving recognition to the art form. But dedicated players resented the idea that Chicago improv was merely a way station on the road to sketch comedy and sitcoms on the tube. Most agreed that *real* improvisation was incompatible with television. Television would never capture the spontaneity, audiences wouldn't feel the connection, and network executives would never take the chance. Mark Sutton believes that he could choose seven players from Chicago and present a fully improvised comedy that would be at least as successful as any recent episode of *Saturday Night Live*. He asserts, "They'll let you write crap; you can't improvise crap on TV, but, boy, they'll let you write it" (personal interview).

The late '90s, however, saw several new attempts at bringing improvisation to the screen. Comedian Drew Carey hosted the American version of Britain's *Whose Line Is It Anyway?* a half-hour pseudo-competition among four comic improvisers. *Whose Line* featured some of the most basic gimmick games popular at ComedySportz and other short-form companies. Comedians were challenged to present Musical Styles, Dubbing, Literary Styles, and other quick, accessible formats. Players focused on jokes and physical comedy rather than on sustained scene-building. Nevertheless, the performers seemed genuinely to be responding to real suggestions from authentic audience members—though it was also clear that the show was edited to feature the best (presumably) spontaneous moments. By contrast, a syndicated comedy show called *Kwick Witz* was an obvious fraud. An MC presented situations ostensibly to be improvised by performers who had clearly planned every joke beforehand. By their second season, *Kwick Witz* was constrained to add this disclaimer: "*Kwick Witz* performers have prepared their challenges in advance." David Alan Grier also began hosting a game show, *Random Acts of Comedy,* that used elements of improv.

In 1998, a special Chicago audition was organized for casting agents from *Whose Line.* More than a dozen of the best improvisers from Second City, ImprovOlympic, and the Annoyance were there, but not one was cast for the show. Halpern explained, "What they are really looking for are stand-up people who can do some quick one-liners, and then, buzz, the time is up. [The producers] are even saying, 'look, we know we're not purists here with improvisation, and we don't mean to be killing your art form, but this is what we really need.' So really top-notch improvisers are getting turned away" ("Laugh Tracked"). Nevertheless, many players credit *Whose Line* for increasing public awareness of improv as an entertainment form distinct from stand-up. Although women rarely appear on the show, African American performer Wayne Brady has become a role model for a growing number of black improvisers.[3]

While these shows are based on short-form improv, it remained for cable station Comedy Central to take a chance on the Harold. In 1991, a group of ImprovOlympic players and alumni created an event called *Virtual Reality* in which the Upright Citizens Brigade (UCB), a band of guerrillas "dedicated to undermining society through the proliferation of chaos," performed experiments (also called *pranks*) on its "clients"—the audience (UBC Newsletter). In reality, the show was a unique form of interactive sketch comedy based on the Harold structure. The players created scenes through improvisation, then devised a show in which characters and themes would overlap and finally come full circle as they might in a Harold. Retaining their UCB identities as a framework, the group devised several more shows, building a following in Chicago. A core UCB group, including Matt Besser, Amy Poehler, Ian Roberts, and Matt Walsh, then moved to New York to pursue possibilities for film and television.[4]

In the Big Apple, UCB opened their own improv performance and training center where they taught long-form structures and presented popular free performances of A.S.S.S.C.A.T., or the Automated Sprinkler System Siamese Connection Alternative Theater. Shows featured the Upright Citizens Brigade's own long-form structure, a thirty-minute improvisation based on a monologue performed by someone on their rotating list of guests (including a number of celebrities). In the spring of 1998, the UCB's seven-year mission to "obtain corporation sponsored television time within the mainstream cable network" was finally fulfilled with a regularly scheduled show on Comedy Central (UCB Newsletter). Dedicated to their improv roots, the group lists Del Close as "Mentor" in the show's credits and even hired Close to do the voice-over of their first season's opening.[5]

A group of Second City alumni, including Amy Sedaris, created *Strangers with Candy*, an "after-school special" parody briefly paired with Upright Citizens Brigade in Comedy Central's lineup.[6] Most improvisers, however, found their training suited them more for writing than for acting. Adam McKay moved from ImprovOlympic's the Family to the Second City mainstage, to *Saturday Night Live* as a writer, writing supervisor, then short film coordinator. Tina Fey followed a similar path, in 1999 becoming the first female head writer in *Saturday Night Live*'s twenty-five-year history. Poehler, Sedaris, and Fey are powerful role models for many rising women improvisers.

Other Chicago improvisers could be found on the writing staffs of *The Martin Short Show*, *Mad TV*, MTV's *The Blame Game* and *Mr. Show*, *The Drew Carey Show*, *The Conan O'Brien Show*, new animated series, and many others. In the same period, improvisational acting was highlighted in feature films, including the high-profile *Blair Witch Project*, *Waiting for Guffman*, and the critically acclaimed films of Mike Leigh.

As improv troupes proliferate in America and around the world, popular awareness of the form increases. The New Improv Page lists scores of troupes in thirty-six states and the District of Columbia and in thirty-one countries in Europe, Asia, Australia, and North and South America. Short form predominates, but long form is taught in California, New York, and elsewhere. Lillian Francis speculates, "I bet that the fifth wave is going to be [that] you will say 'improv' to someone and they know what it is. They will not say, 'Oh, you mean like stand-up.' Your average Joe will know what improv is" (personal interview). When the average Joe, Joanne, and John Kim down the street recognize improv as an art form open to all, we can better answer the question, "Whose improv is it anyway?"

When I began this book, I set out to better understand my own experiences with improv-comedy, to analyze why I found it so compelling, why it so often seemed to fail me, and what, if anything, I could propose that might help improv live up to its utopian promises. I discovered that the entire history of Chicago improv-comedy is the story of that very same quest. Each new wave of improvisers, disappointed in its predecessors' inability to achieve the dream, has asked the same questions: What is the essence of improv's appeal? What is the true mission and purpose of this art form? Why has it failed? How will we reinvent it? From the first-wave founders to the smallest third-wave team, artists have tried to make the ideal a reality: a new form of theatre that incorporates community, spontaneity, spiritual connectedness, self-expression, freedom, resistance, and laughter and is, at the same time, entertaining, accessible to all audiences, and open to every performer. Is it *really* too much to ask?

My study of first-wave improv helped clarify the hybrid nature of this genre. Improv's excitement comes from its internal contradictions. Improvisers are challenged to be at once unthinking and quick-witted; to be unselfconscious, yet aware of the audience, the scene, and the other players; to express individuality within a groupmind; to channel cosmic truths while parodying contemporary hypocrisies; to let go and at the same time to make do. The nature of the art is compromise, a fragile negotiation or fluctuation between the poles of process and product. The result can be very exciting, shimmering, and, as many have said, even magical. But this delicate balance is almost impossible to maintain. Players fall off the tightrope on either side.

As I have shown, there are pitfalls and traps at every turn, particularly for women and other marginalized people. There are rules that are not rules—or not the same rules for everyone. Like carnival, improv is free play for those who assert that freedom; but free play can turn into power games, especially when performers feel the pressure to produce. The first wave soon took steps to calcify, control, and ensure its commercial success and thereby lost the dangerous magic it never fully owned.

First wave's failure to fulfill its early rhetoric was attributed to commercialization—the loss of improv's ideals of community and spontaneity. Second-wave improvisers remade those promises with new structures and forms that expanded improv's reach. ImprovOlympic's rhetoric plunged deeper into ideas of spontaneity's link to spirituality and created opportunities for intense connection and subcultural belonging. Studying this company, I gained new insight about the fierceness of my old improv troupe's commitment to one another and the power of their belief that improv could not and should not be controlled. I saw also how unexamined spontaneity, for all its pleasurable sensation of flow and connection, can serve to feed sexism and racism at the deepest levels of myth and archetype.

ComedySportz underscored the competitive sports and business side of the game, stretching wide to franchise companies all over the country. Talking to the young girl at the Milwaukee arena (see page 109), I remembered my frustration with myself and with the other women at our theatre: Why did we sit on the bench instead of getting into the improv game? Why did we play by the rules while the men so often scored by breaking them? What showed so clearly at ComedySportz was something I had always known—that many women are (still) socialized to be self-conscious and tentative in their bodies, to avoid competition, and to mask their humor. While ComedySportz did not create these problems, it helped institutionalize them, along with the truism that women are just not funny. These larger societal issues must be addressed outside of the improv context, but can also be contested within it.

It remained for the third wave to reexamine spontaneity and community in terms of identity and the realization that truth, freedom, and the rules are not the same for everyone. Each third-wave troupe tried again to solve improv's problems and reconstruct its promise, working to find a new balance between conscious thought and spontaneous action. While improv is a valuable tool for overcoming inhibitions and self-consciousness, and while spontaneity produces pleasurable experiences of flow or even trance, most third-wave improvisers recognize that uprooting racism, sexism, and heterosexism is perforce a conscious process. We still have to think—to strategize—if we want to resist ingrained patterns and naturalized narratives.

I have imagined a replay of my harem scene with Patrick ("Wife! On your knees!") in the style of specific third-wave women who have devised *defenses and escapes* that help to level the playing field. In the mode of Susan Messing, of the Annoyance Theatre, who advocates total commitment to the role regardless of its potential humiliation (while using the scene partner's arrogance against himself), I might have thrown myself into an excessive and aggressively sexual incarnation of the concubine, showing *my* character to be the desiring subject. I once saw Messing in an improv show when she was endowed as a character with no arms or legs. Not one to be disempowered, she reached out her tongue and suggestively licked a fellow actor, inviting him to join her for great sex. No doubt she would have taken the "On your knees!" comment to be an invitation to begin her sexual work—and the shocked audience laughter would be hers.

As Mary Fahey of the Free Associates, I might have played a campier stereotype, commenting, through classic gestures, an ironic tone, and knowing glances at the audience, on the entire construct of the harem fantasy. Of course, had my encounter with Patrick happened at the Free Associates, he would likely have been quickly fired from the company. Moreover, the scene itself would have been far more circumscribed—I might have been a repressed homosexual concubine or a harem girl with a secret dream of owning a car wash. These structures in themselves would have guided me in the scene, minimizing Patrick's ability to manipulate me.

Had I been Stephnie Weir of Jane (a third-wave team at a second-wave theatre) there would have been no Patrick problem at all. More important, having played with Jane, Sirens, or Red, I could have returned to Snazz 'n' Guffaw with new confidence, greater range, and a stronger sense of my own voice.

Finally, my favorite scenario is the one where I get to be Shaun Landry of Oui Be Negroes. Patrick begins with "Wife! On your knees!" and I say, "YES*and*—fuck you!"

Of course, the issues are far more complex than these scenarios suggest. Improv can be exhilarating, fun, and creative, and I believe it can be a means to explore alternative realities and form temporary communities. Nevertheless, improv is quite a balancing act—it plays in the space between freedom and discipline, structure and openness, individual and group, process and product. Add too many rules and it's no longer improvisation and not much fun. But some goals or guidance seem to make it more likely that everyone will get to play and that the process will result in something interesting for an audience to watch. Players, teachers, and directors from every wave have begun experimenting with conscious tactics and strategies for creating a power balance without destroying improv's spirit or weighing it down with politically correct imperatives. On a surface level, manipulation of rules, structures, and casting and the reintroduction of a touch of Brechtian distancing have made a difference. But improv works on much deeper levels as well.

What energized me years ago, and what still fills improvisers with passion, is the joy of connection, the power of creation, and the ecstasy of flow. Improvisers in the third wave, and perhaps in a fourth wave to come, are particularly motivated to experience the kind of flow that improv offers—the concentrated absorption, *communitas*, the sense of oneness with others and with the action of the moment. For young people in a mediatized age, it is perhaps all the more important to manage the flow of images that bombards them from the outside through a kind of flow generated from within themselves. Improv offers the opportunity to strive for this kind of *letting go* and, in the meantime, allows players to make old images do new things.

The trickiest equation of all is that between awareness and flow, or consciousness and spontaneity. I think we must finally admit that simple spontaneity does not access cosmic *truth*, but something else—it accesses the sediments of experience and memory that form the sense of self. I believe these can be called forth, repeated, rearranged, juxtaposed with others, and used to create comedy—even to improvise resistant alternatives to the status quo. For people and groups whose lives have long been stereotyped or simply invisible, it can be important to say, "We can create through improv too." Improvised comedy drawn from the experiences of women, people of color, gays, and lesbians can work to demonstrate both our distinctiveness and our commonality. We are all worthy of being the subjects, rather than the objects, of the joke.

Clearly, nothing can emerge from improvisation that has not been learned, synthesized, and remembered by its players. Some teachers have assigned improv students *homework thinking* and journal writing in an effort to stir up and expand their improv vocabulary beyond the easiest clichés and pop-culture references. As the numbers of women and players of color slowly increase, players find they can learn from one another. But it is crucial to remember that increased participation and visibility is not the same as equal voice. Groupmind as true, unforced consensus may not be a realistic objective. But by listening to each other and respecting difference, players in diverse groups can begin to develop range and depth and genuine collaboration in their performances.

A number of male players in Chicago, serious about their art, actively seek the opportunity to improvise with women to experience a subtler, more relationship-oriented style of playing. Respected improv director Noah Gregoropoulos wistfully admits, "The women in Jane were all talented when they started, but they were significantly more poised, versatile and confident after doing time with Jane, [and] by far the best, most unforced, real, funny and compelling improvisation that I have seen [black improvisers] do was with a group of more than half African Americans" (Gregoropoulos et al.). Gregoropoulos and many improvisers, male and female, consistently strive to create the kind of good improv that allows every player the freedom to create. It can be an elusive goal.

Lyn Pierse of Australian Theatresports challenges coaches and teachers to uproot status imbalances at the training level: "Place girls and boys in non-stereotypical roles . . . discuss [stereotypes] with the class . . . offer them alternative ways to perceive themselves and each other" (304). Pierse has great hope that improvisation can not only demonstrate stereotypes and clichés, but also "give us the opportunity to challenge and break them" (304). Mark Gagné insists that improv instructors must teach students "how to think—not what to think—on their feet. How to work both intelligently and spontaneously" (personal interview). Gagné advocates teaching improvisers to confront stereotypes that emerge rather than depending on them.

Frances Callier fights racist, sexist, or homophobic choices by asking her players to distinguish between stereotypes and character: "Are you doing a humorous person who happens to be gay, or are you making fun of gay people?" She believes that the future of improv boils down to its fundamental teachings: "Mothers, how do you raise your sons? And if the mother is improvisation, we have to ask improvisation, How are we raising our sons and daughters? Are we raising our daughters to be strong? Are we raising our sons to be sensitive? Are we asking the men to give way to half of themselves? Are we asking the women to take what's rightfully theirs?" (personal interview).

As improv becomes increasingly popular through television (and throughout the world), it is crucial for beginners to learn more than the surface gimmicks and rules of the game. If they are serious about the art of improv, fledgling players must understand improv's history, its philosophical and theoretical roots. But even more important, it is incumbent upon experienced players to transmit improv's tradition of struggle and debate. As African American jazz musician Davey Williams has commented, "Free improvisation is not an action resulting from freedom, it is an action *directed towards freedom*" (qtd. in Corbett 221).

Players in the fourth, fifth, or sixth wave will come to recognize the difficulties of translating ideals into sustainable community and commercial comedy. But, like their predecessors, they will try, fail, and try again. This is improv's most valuable process.

Notes

Introduction

1. The British and Canadians are more likely to use the slang term *impro*, and they trace much of their technique to Keith Johnstone, whose work is discussed in the second-wave section.

2. In 1994, for example, Second City director-teacher Michael Gellman created "The Quest"—an improv structure for students based on the concepts outlined in Joseph Campbell's work on the heroic monomyth.

3. See feminist humor theorists Reginia Gagnier and Kayann Short on women's use of the humor of incongruity to question the status quo and the norms of femininity.

4. Improv practitioners depict the improv concept of "agree and heighten" in a variety of ways, including "Yes& . . ."; "Yes, and . . ."; or "Yes—And." I have chosen to emulate the YES*and* webzine and will adopt the convention "YES*and*—" throughout this text.

5. Second City touring company director Anne Libera established "the honey rule" to subvert the tendency of a male player's first line to immediately define his female scene partner as his honey—wife or girlfriend. "If a man walks out on stage and calls "Honey," says Libera, "I directed that only another man—or no one—was allowed to respond. After a series of gay scenes, the male players started to get the picture and come up with more creative alternatives" (personal interview).

Chapter 1

1. See "Interlude: The Third Wave" and chapter 6 for a further discussion of Second City's outreach efforts.

2. See *The Compass*, by Janet Coleman; and *Something Wonderful Right Away*, by Jeffrey Sweet.

3. In the '60s, avant-garde theatre groups, such as the Open Theatre and the Living Theatre, were, in turn, influenced by Spolin's games as well as by jazz improvisation. See Banes; and Schmitt.

4. See Coleman; and Sweet.

5. The early Compass Players included Elaine May, Andrew Duncan, Roger Bowen, Barbara Harris, Mike Nichols, Darden, Shelley Berman, Mark and Bobbi Gordon, and others. (Sweet xiv; and Coleman).

6. A performer in several touring companies, Asian American improviser Suzy Nakamura was never cast for the Chicago mainstage. She was, however, a founding member of Second City, Detroit, in 1993 (along with Angela Shelton and Jerry Minor). After her stint at Second City, Nakamura appeared on television's *West Wing* and *Daddio*.

7. Women directors at Second City have been few (particularly on the mainstage) but important. In Chicago, Canada, and satellite companies, they have included Sandra Balcovske (artistic director in Toronto for several years), Bernadette Birkett, Anne Libera, Jane Morris, Betty Thomas (the only woman to direct for Chicago's mainstage), Tracey Thorpe, and Barb Wallace.

8. Some gay improvisers claim Holland as a role model for his success and survival in the often homophobic world of Chicago improv. He was also one of the few players to befriend Joan Rivers at Second City.

9. Ironically, Myerson was fired from Second City for being too political. He went on to create his own improv troupe in San Francisco—the Committee.

10. Curry, whom Aaron Freeman calls "the Jackie Robinson of Second City," was a brilliant, uninhibited, and eccentric comedian. Second City archives reveal little about his short career with that company. Curry later directed Freeman's hit show, *Do the White Thing*. Curry died in 1985.

11. Senator Abe Ribicoff of New York first used the phrase "Gestapo tactics" when referring to Daley's treatment of the demonstrators.

12. A number of powerful women emerged at Second City in the 1980s and 1990s—Bonnie Hunt (1986–87), Amy Sedaris (1992), Rachel Dratch (1995), Tina Fey (1996), and several others. But these remained the exceptions rather than the rule, until the advent of gender-balanced casts in 1996.

13. See chapter 6 for a full discussion of Second City's Minority Outreach Program and the increased role of improvisers of color at Second City beginning in the '90s.

14. Another television program that made use of the improv-comedy aesthetic was *SCTV*, developed by the Toronto Second City in 1976.

Interlude 1

1. Cable programs taped at the Improv comedy club are largely responsible for many people's mistaken conclusion that "improv" means stand-up comedy.

2. Cable television also encouraged nontopical, apolitical comedy routines for purely economic reasons. A routine about suburbia, TV shows, airports, or dating miseries could be reused and recut into other comedy programming. Jokes about politics were quickly dated and unusable.

3. John Belushi's death in 1982 was a painful blow to Sahlins, Sloane, and the entire Second City community. His popular image continued to inspire young comic performers, many of whom flocked to Chicago and Second City.

4. Second City management resists the definition of e.t.c. as a second-tier company, pointing to the troupe's accomplishments and critical acclaim. Performers know, however, that the traditional progression through the Second City ranks moves from the training center, to the touring companies, to e.t.c., and, finally, to the mainstage.

5. In an agreement with Alexander, the Players Workshop was given legal permission to use the name "Players Workshop of the Second City" for their training program. Second City's new training center did not offer a beginning program until the mid-nineties. Nevertheless, there was some bitterness associated with Forsberg's displacement.

6. In 1993, Alexander also displaced longtime producer and "den mother" Joyce Sloane, Sahlins' virtual partner for many decades. Relieved of the day-to-day power and responsibilities of producer, Sloane was "kicked upstairs" to the mostly honorary post of producer emeritus. Her dethronement caused great consternation among many Second City players, alumni, and students.

7. Second-wave improvisers often view Second City as part of the mainstream.

8. "Subcultural capital" is based on cultural theorist Pierre Bourdieu's notion of "cultural capital." In *Distinction: A Social Critique of the Judgment of Taste*, Bourdieu defines cultural

capital as the value of education, upbringing, and the knowledge of cultural codes in determining social status.

Chapter 2

1. The standard arrangement gave ticket income to ImprovOlympic and a minimum beverage income to the hosting bar or restaurant. In 1995, ImprovOlympic opened its own theatre and abolished the two-drink minimum, although liquor sales remained an important income source.

2. Most ImprovOlympic shows begin with one or two short-form games to warm up the audience. Musical Styles was commonly used until 1997. It later became a signature structure for the house team Baby Wants Candy.

3. For clarity, I will adopt the convention of using capital letters to indicate the titles of games, for example, Musical Styles, Dubbing, Freeze-Tag.

4. The Harold is explained in detail later in this chapter.

5. Bourdieu defines "cultural competence" as the accumulation of skills and knowledge that allows a beholder to decode and thus appreciate a work of art (*Distinction* 2).

6. Shepherd used two words to name his enterprise, sometimes spelling Olympics with an *x*, while Halpern preferred one word, no *s*. For a brief period in the early '90s, the troupe was known as ImprovOlympia, because of one potential sponsor's concerns about a conflict with the U.S. Olympic Committee. But the troupe returned to ImprovOlympic in the mid-nineties.

7. Freeman also notes that their process included "smoking everything"—another link between drugs and improv as a means of achieving alternative realities.

8. Some Native Americans have soundly critiqued the New Age habit of borrowing their imagery and shamanic rituals of transformation, calling it "plastic shamanism" (Schneider 237). As Lisa Mayo, founding member of the Native American performance troupe Spiderwoman, put it, "What the white search for the shaman misses is the reality of the Native American here and now. They're not interested in that" (qtd. in Schneider 238).

9. Alan Myerson, founder of the Committee, also challenges Close's status as the sole inventor of the Harold, believing that most of the early long-form work in San Francisco was collaborative and/or independent invention.

10. ImprovOlympic's "manual of improvisation" lists two sample Pattern games that might derive from the suggestion "dog": "Game A: Collar; Police; K-9; Rin Tin Tin; Barking up the wrong tree; Firemen; 101 Dalmatians; Open 24 hours; I read it in the Sunday papers; Sentence; Death; Bergman; Bird dog; Bird Man of Alcatraz; Prison; Bondage; Collar. Game B: Loyalty; Man's best friend; Barking; Sit; You can have the kids. I'll take the dog; Stay; Caged; Divorce; Heel; Barking; Cat fight; His bark is worse than his bite; He's a stray." Each of these pattern games would inspire a completely different set of scenes based on the same suggestion. As Halpern writes, "Team A's use of the 'dog' theme revealed ideas about crime and punishment; Team B discovered levels of failed human relationships" (Halpern, Close, and Johnson 30–31).

11. While Close often proclaimed his low opinion of female improvisers in workshops and classes, a number of women found him to be a supportive mentor and inspiring teacher on a one-to-one basis.

12. Devoted to Close, Halpern managed everything from rehearsal schedules to laundry for the absent-minded genius.

13. Susan Messing later introduced a class at ImprovOlympic focusing on creating character through physicalization.

14. In 1997, one ImprovOlympic team refused to be disbanded. See the discussion of the Playground at conclusion of this book.

15. Schechner uses the notion of "liminality" in the anthropological sense of a threshold, margin, or transitional space in which conventional roles, rules, and hierarchies are suspended.

16. The "rule of three" is an accepted notion for many comedians who believe that it takes two repetitions of an action to set a pattern, causing the audience to laugh when a comic twist disrupts their expectations on the third repetition.

17. Turner's own adaptation of van Gennep is commonly termed "social drama" and takes the form of four phases: A *breach* of the normative social order precipitates a *crisis* in the community. Ritual and even performance activities may then be part of a *redressive mechanism*, which is followed either by *integration* or the community's recognition of a permanent *rupture.*

18. The theory is Turner's; the hypothetical modern examples are my interpretation of "spontaneous communitas."

19. One recent ImprovOlympic house team even chose to name itself the Tribe.

20. Close himself cited Csikszentmihalyi's idea of "flow" to describe the Harold.

21. In other words, some men cast themselves as the Marx Brothers, while the women must play either the unsmiling Margaret Dumont or the "pretty one" that Harpo chases around the room.

22. Fahey later joined the Free Associates (see chapter 5).

23. Members of Jane have praised the men on such teams as the Lost Yetis, Inside Vladimir, and Monster Island as excellent players who respected them as colleagues. Nonetheless, Jane gave the women something they couldn't get from any co-ed team.

24. Jane was coached by a number of veteran improvisers, including Mick Napier, artistic director of the Annoyance Theatre.

25. In a discussion of male versus female impersonation in camp performance, feminist theorist Kate Davy notes that "there is no institutionalized paradigm for reading male impersonation" ("Discourse of Camp" 233).

26. See the conclusion for a discussion of the Playground.

27. Farley's premature death in 1997 hit the improv community hard. He had been a particularly loyal alumnus of ImprovOlympic.

28. The cost of the musicians, food, drink, and other arrangements were subsidized in large part by actor Bill Murray, who had worked with and learned from Close at Second City.

29. ImprovOlympic veterans Miles Stroth and Noah Gregoropoulos took charge of the level 5 classes Close had once taught.

Chapter 3

1. Several improv-comedy theatres in Chicago are located on the strip of Clark Street known as Wrigleyville, within a few blocks of Wrigley stadium.

2. Rock has managed, coached, and directed teams in Madison and New York. His "Notes" are used in both places.

3. For Changing Emotions, the referee takes audience suggestions to create a list of emotions, including everything from anger to angst. Players improvise a scene based on another audience suggestion of a place or relationship. As the scene progresses, the referee calls out various emotions. The players must immediately shift the scene into each new emotional mode while justifying the change within the narrative. Musical Styles works in much the same way, except that the referee takes suggestions for styles of music instead of emotions. When the referee (or spectator)

shouts out a style mid-scene, the players must improvise a song in that style that furthers the plot of the improvised musical. (Improvisers also often play Film Styles and Literary Styles as well.) In Dr. Know-It-All, three or four players link arms to form a single "omniscient" being who is an expert on a subject suggested by the audience. The ref then takes spectators' questions, which the players must answer by taking turns speaking one word at a time, working collectively to form a single coherent answer. In Dubbing, two players present an improvised scene from an imaginary foreign film, while two other actors dub their voices from just off stage. The players on stage must move their lips when their voices are speaking and justify the words with action, while the speaking actors must justify the other players' actions through the dialogue.

4. For Story, players line up across the stage while the ref takes an audience suggestion for the story's title. The ref then conducts the story by pointing at individual players who must continue to speak until the ref suddenly points to a different player. Players are out when they stumble, stammer, repeat the last word of the preceding player, or draw a blank. In some versions, the eliminated player must then perform an elaborate death scene.

5. Chudnow's ComedyLeague of America has at one time or another included teams in the following cities: *Austin, Bakersfield,* **Boston,** *Buffalo,* *Chicago,* **Dallas, Denver,** *Eugene, Fort Lauderdale,* Fox Cities, *Green Bay,* Hartford, *Houston, Indianapolis,* **Kansas City,** Lake Tahoe, *Los Angeles, Madison, Milwaukee,* Minneapolis, New York, Orlando, Oshkosh, *Philadelphia, Phoenix, Portland, Provo, Quad Cities,* **Racine, Raleigh,** *Richmond,* Rock Island, *St. Louis, San Antonio, San Diego,* **San Jose,** *Santa Barbara,* **Washington, D.C.** Cities in bold are those that appeared on Chudnow's map in 1990, according to the *Milwaukee Sentinel.* Cities in italics were in operation as of 2000.

6. Patrick's replacement was Mark Gagné, who was later to found Chicago's Free Associates.

7. Stephanie DeWaegeneer has represented Houston and Chicago at a number of tournaments over the years and has seen a generational shift toward ever-younger players. She also admits that "diversity is an issue visible at tournaments" (personal interview).

8. The term "to naturalize" describes the way cultural representations can make human behavior and relations seem to be essential or innate rather than historically specific social constructions. See e.g., Roland Barthes's *Mythologies;* Linda Hutcheon's *The Politics of Postmodernism.*

9. In Theatresports, where judges are not drawn from the audience, spectators more often side with players against the judges.

10. The waffling foul was originally called the *wimping foul* (and still is in Canadian Theatresports). However, the limp-wristed gesture was too often interpreted, or deliberately performed, as a stereotypical gay or effeminate move. Chudnow changed the term to avoid those implications.

11. Some regional teams, presumably in line with their local audiences, are far more open about gay, feminist, and minority issues than those I have observed in Milwaukee, Madison, and Chicago.

12. Though direct references to queerness are frowned on in many ComedySportz venues, male players may play in drag or portray the suggestion "hairdresser," or any other stereotypically gay profession, as an effeminate caricature for laughs.

13. In several cities, the brown bag foul is often more liberally interpreted than it is by more conservative teams. The Chicago ComedySportz program states, "Obscenities, physical or verbal, that are *out of context* of the scene will not be tolerated."

14. In the 1990s and into the millennium, the increased prominence and prestige of women athletes in the Olympics, the Women's National Basketball Association, and elsewhere has been encouraging. It will take a very long time and unrelenting effort, however, for more positive

attitudes about female size, strength and assertiveness to reach the majority of high school girls seeking social acceptance.

15. Gaudet also points with pride to ComedySportz's official sponsorship of Gilda's Club, an organization that fights ovarian cancer in the name of beloved comedian Gilda Radner. Some of Chicago's fund-raising performances specifically featured female improvisers to honor Radner as a role model for funny women. Radner's 1989 death from ovarian cancer deeply saddened the entire improv community.

16. Chicago ComedySportz also occasionally experiments with its own brand of long-form improv with full-length improvised musicals and other projects.

Interlude 2

1. Most of the day-to-day work of reorganizing these systems fell to producer Sloane and associate producer Kelly Leonard, who was hired in 1992 to help shoulder these responsibilities. Leonard was promoted to full producer in 1995. Satellite companies also included Second City Edmonton (1979–82) and Second City London (1983–92).

2. French cultural theorist Jean-François Lyotard defines "postmodernism" as "incredulity toward metanarratives" (xxiv).

3. In his 1990 essay, "The Cultural Politics of Difference," Cornel West theorizes the present moment as a convergence of factors, including the weakened dominance of European standards of high culture versus popular culture, the establishment of America as a world power and cultural distribution center, and the decolonization of third world countries and cultural sensibilities.

4. Meadows performed briefly with the Annoyance Theatre and ImprovOlympic before being cast by Second City. In 1991 he was hired by *Saturday Night Live*, where he performed thankless bit parts into the millennium.

5. Del Close cast Meadows and Scott for his show *The Gods Must Be Lazy*. It was the first time any Second City troupe had included more than one African American (Patinkin 161).

6. Second City management does not acknowledge the existence of a "slot," minority or otherwise, in its casting policies, insisting that the company always hires the best individual for the job. Historically, in the experience of female and minority performers, however, opportunities were almost always limited to specific categories. It was far more likely for an actor to replace another actor of the same race and gender than for anyone else to be chosen. Casting innovations at Second City in the late 1990s have begun to dislodge these conventions.

7. The Native American women in the improvisational theatre group Spiderwoman, for example, saw the group's original diversity (including white, African American, and Native American women) as a "mask for white control." The group broke apart, and Spiderwoman now performs as a Native American women's troupe exploring Native American women's issues and experiences (Carlson 161).

8. The Compass Players also identified themselves as misfits. Third-wave improvisers, then, see themselves as misfits among misfits.

Chapter 4

1. Tristan Tzara was a leading artist in the Dada movement, publishing seven manifestos, between 1916 and 1920, that advocated chaos, discord, and chance over traditional artistic values of order, harmony, and meaning.

2. Performance artists such as the Kipper Kids and Karen Finley have used this "messy" aesthetic to make their own artistic statements.

3. As of 2000, the Annoyance did have plans to make several of their most popular shows available in script form.

4. Sung to a jaunty melody, the lyrics to the song's chorus are "Shit / Motherfucker / Fuck you, you cunt or a prick / Blooow job / Suck my dick." After hearing it twice, the audience is urged to sing along.

5. The Performance Group also used the Sharon Tate murders and Manson's trial in their environmental theatre piece, *Commune*, in 1970. While the tone of this show was very different from *Manson, the Musical*, the desire to challenge taboos and the mode of collective creation were similar.

6. See *Simulations*, by Jean Baudrillard: "When the real is no longer what it used to be, nostalgia assumes its full meaning. There is a proliferation of myths of origin and signs of reality; of second-hand truth, objectivity and authenticity. There is an escalation of the true, of the lived experience . . . a panic-stricken production of the real and referential, above and parallel to the panic of material production" (12–13).

7. The Bradys were a happy, blended family from two formerly single-parent homes—a fantasy of unity and stability that spoke powerfully to many children of that era. No problem was so great that it couldn't be solved in half an hour.

8. Later, Eve Plumb, better known as Jan Brady, agreed to guest star in several benefit performances.

9. Andy Richter, who took Mark Sutton's place as the MC of *The Real Live Game Show*, went on to write for David Letterman and eventually to appear as Conan O'Brien's sidekick on the *Late Night* television talk show.

10. Years later, Messing was finally cast for the Second City mainstage—details provided later in this chapter.

11. Blume gave permission for a one-time, very limited run of the show.

12. Napier also directed for Second City Northwest in 1991. Sutton and other members of the Annoyance have directed Second City touring companies, and Sutton directed a production of *Co-ed* for Second City in Toronto.

13. Second City owner, Andrew Alexander, and (then associate) producer, Kelly Leonard, supported this move to a gender-balanced cast. Alexander's Toronto troupe had long featured gender-balanced companies.

14. Messing co-created and performed in two Second City mainstage shows before she tired of that company's backstage politics and quit the troupe in 2000, returning to Annoyance and independent projects. She was replaced by Angela Shelton (see chapter 6).

15. See also my discussion of the lesbian character and song in *That Darned AntiChrist!*

Chapter 5

1. In Williams' *Streetcar Named Desire*, Blanche is the fading southern belle who comes to New Orleans to visit her younger sister, Stella. Stella is married to the working-class tough Stanley Kowalski, famously played by Marlon Brando.

2. An entire subgenre of improv performance is the interactive, environmental show in which the audience becomes part of the action. *Tony 'n' Tina's Wedding, Flanagan's Wake, Grandma Sylvia's Funeral,* and a variety of murder mystery shows use this technique.

3. From the song "I Am Woman," made popular by Helen Reddy: "I am Woman / Hear me roar . . ."

Chapter 6

1. African American jazz forms were also appropriated by white musicians, although many black jazz musicians deliberately adopted difficult improvisational styles that made it almost impossible to "steal" their musical licks (See e.g., Corbett, Ross).

2. Along with Callier, early workshops and Minority Outreach Program classes drew on the talents and experiences of touring company improvisers including John Hildreth, who would be cast in the e.t.c. troupe in 1994, and Suzy Nakamura, who joined the first Detroit troupe in 1993.

3. The title of this revue is drawn from a scene in the comic film *Animal House.*

4. Cooper's words resonate with those of W. E. B. DuBois, who wrote, "It is a peculiar sensation, this double-consciousness, this sense of always looking at one's self through the eyes of others. . . . One ever feels his twoness—an American, a Negro; two souls, two thoughts, two unreconciled strivings" (qtd. in Watkins 26).

5. Since 1992, touring companies have slowly been allowed, and then increasingly encouraged, to include original material in their revues.

6. In 1997, a highly publicized shooting at the Cabrini-Green housing projects was receiving national attention.

7. Both Stir-Friday Night and ¡Salsation! asked experienced white male directors (Rob Reese, Keith Privett) to mentor them in the early years, but also worked to develop directors from within their group.

8. Johnson was one of the producer/writers of *Soul Front* and was a member of the resident company in Detroit.

9. The title of the revue is a parody of "forty acres and a mule," the allotment given to freed slaves after the Civil War.

10. White improviser Jack McBrayer replaced Farahnakian midway through *Revelation* and continued in *History Repaints Itself.*

11. In 2000, Shelton replaced Susan Messing in *Second City 4.0.* Shelton thus became the second African American woman in forty years to play the Second City mainstage in Chicago.

Conclusion

1. An earlier long-form show, *Lois Kaz,* was presented on the e.t.c. stage in 1992.

2. Produced by Kathleen Puls and Susan Santaniello, and co-sponsored by the Playground, the Funny Woman Festival hosted individual comedians and improv troupes ranging from Boston's witty Improv Asylum and New York's sophisticated Flying Queens to the down-to-earth Wymprov from Eugene, Oregon. Unexpected Improv from Seattle, Washington, and Flaming Dykasaurus from Madison, Wisconsin, also joined Chicago's GayCo, Sirens, and Red on stage at the Viaduct Theatre. Susan Messing, Shaun Landry, Frances Callier, Debora Rabbai, Barbara Scott, Josephine and Linnea Forsberg, Charna Halpern, and many other leading women in improv led workshops and participated in panel discussions. Spirits were high, and organizers plan to make the festival an annual event. The producers hope to expand the celebration of funny women to include more diversity—improvisers of color and players from around the world.

3. Brady worked with the Los Angeles improv troupe Houseful of Honkeys, which played a

twin bill with Oui Be Negroes at the first Austin festival. The groups joked with each other about exchanging their token players—Wayne Brady for Hans Summers.

4. In Chicago, UCB included Horatio Sanz, Adam McKay, Ali Farahnakian, and others, but these players pursued other opportunities. Only the four actors mentioned above performed with the troupe in New York.

5. In the summer of 2000, Comedy Central announced the cancellation of UCB, outraging its devoted fans, who vowed to fight the decision.

6. *Strangers with Candy* also features Greg Hollimon, one of a few black improvisers who performed in a Second City touring company in late '80s and '90s.

Works Cited

Books and Journals

Atkins, Greg. *Improv! A Handbook for the Actor*. Portsmouth, NH: Heinemann, 1994.

Auslander, Philip. "Comedy about the Failure of Comedy: Stand-up Comedy and Postmodernism." In *Critical Theory and Performance*, ed. Janelle G. Reinelt and Joseph R. Roach. Ann Arbor: University of Michigan Press, 1992.

———. *Presence and Resistance: Postmodernism and Cultural Politics in Contemporary American Performance*. Ann Arbor: University of Michigan Press, 1992.

Babuscio, Jack. "Camp and the Gay Sensibility." In *Camp Grounds: Style and Homosexuality*, ed. David Bergman. Amherst: University of Massachusetts Press, 1993.

Bakhtin, Mikhail. *Rabelais and His World*. Trans. Helene Iswolsky. Bloomington: Indiana University Press, 1984.

Banes, Sally. *Greenwich Village 1963: Avant-Garde Performance and the Effervescent Body*. Durham: Duke University Press, 1993.

Barreca, Regina. *They Used to Call Me Snow White . . . But I Drifted: Women's Strategic Use of Humor*. New York: Penguin Books, 1991.

Barthes, Roland. *Mythologies*. Trans. Annette Lavers. 1957. Reprint, New York: Hill and Wang, 1972.

Bartky, Sandra Lee. "Foucault, Femininity, and the Modernization of Patriarchal Power." In *Feminism and Foucault: Reflections on Resistance*. Ed. Irene Diamond and Lee Quinby. Boston: Northeastern University Press, 1988.

Baudrillard, Jean. *Simulations*. Trans. Paul Foss, Paul Patton, and Philip Beitchman. New York: Semiotext(e), 1983.

Belgrade, Daniel. *The Culture of Spontaneity*. Chicago: University of Chicago Press, 1998.

Bergman, David. "Strategic Camp: The Art of Gay Rhetoric." In *Camp Grounds: Style and Homosexuality*, ed. David Bergman. Amherst: University of Massachusetts Press, 1993.

Blair, Rhonda. " 'Not . . . But'/'Not-not-Me': Musings on Cross-Gender Performance." In *Upstaging Big Daddy*, ed. Ellen Donkin and Susan Clement. Ann Arbor: University of Michigan Press, 1993.

Bourdieu. *Distinction: A Social Critique of the Judgment of Taste*. Trans. Richard Nice. Cambridge, MA: Harvard University Press, 1984.

———. *In Other Words: Essays towards a Reflexive Sociology*. Trans. Matthew Adamson. Stanford, CA: Stanford University Press, 1990.

Brecht, Bertholt. *Brecht on Theatre: The Development of an Aesthetic*. Ed. John Willett. 1957. Reprint, New York: Hill and Wang, 1974.

Brown, Rupert. *Group Processes: Dynamics within and between Groups*. Oxford: Blackwell Ltd., 1988.

Butler, Judith. "Performative Acts and Gender Constitution: An Essay in Phenomenology and Feminist Theory." In *Performing Feminisms: Feminist Critical Theory and Theatre*, ed. Sue-Ellen Case. Baltimore: Johns Hopkins University Press, 1990.

Carlson, Marvin. *Performance: A Critical Introduction.* New York: Routledge, 1996.

Coleman, Janet. *The Compass.* New York: Alfred A. Knopf, 1990.

Collins, Patricia Hill. *Black Feminist Thought: Knowledge, Consciousness, and the Politics of Empowerment.* Vol. 2. Perspectives on Gender Series. Boston: Unwin Hyman, 1990.

Corbett, John. "Ephemera Underscored: Writing around Free Improvisation." In *Jazz among the Discourses,* ed. Krin Gabbard. Durham: Duke University Press, 1995.

Crawford, Mary. "Just Kidding: Gender and Conversational Humor." In *New Perspectives on Women and Comedy,* ed. Regina Barreca. Vol. 5. Studies in Gender and Culture Series. New York: Gordon and Breach, 1992.

Csikszentmihalyi, Mihaly. *Flow: The Psychology of Optimal Experience.* New York: HarperCollins, 1990.

Davy, Kate. "Fe/male Impersonation: The Discourse of Camp." In *Critical Theory and Performance,* ed. Janelle G. Reinelt and Joseph R. Roach. Ann Arbor: University of Michigan Press, 1992.

———. "Outing Whiteness: A Feminist/Lesbian Project." *Theatre Journal* 47 (1995): 189–205.

de Certeau, Michel. *The Practice of Everyday Life.* Trans. Steven Rendall. Berkeley: University of California Press, 1984.

Diamond, Elin. "Brechtian Theory/Feminist Theory: Toward a Gestic Feminist Criticism." *Drama Review* 32, no. 1 (1988): 82–93.

Dolan, Jill S. *The Feminist Spectator as Critic.* Ann Arbor: UMI Research Press, 1988.

Douglas, Mary. "Jokes." In *Rethinking Popular Culture: Contemporary Perspectives in Cultural Studies,* ed. Chandra Mukerji and Michael Schudson. Berkeley: University of California Press, 1991.

DuChartre, Pierre Louis. *The Italian Comedy.* Trans. Randolph T. Weaver. 1929. Reprint, New York: Dover, 1966.

Dyson, Michael Eric. *Reflecting Black: African-American Cultural Criticism.* Minneapolis: University of Minnesota Press, 1993.

Faludi, Susan. *Backlash: The Undeclared War against American Women.* New York: Doubleday, 1991.

Fiske, John. *Power Plays, Power Works.* New York: Verso, 1993.

Foreman, Kathleen, and Clem Martini. *Something like a Drug: An Unauthorized Oral History of Theatresports.* Alberta: Red Deer College Press, 1995.

Frost, Anthony, and Ralph Yarrow. *Improvisation in Drama.* London: Macmillan Education, 1990.

Gagnier, Reginia. "Between Women: A Cross-Class Analysis of Status and Anarchic Humor." In *Last Laughs: Perspectives on Women and Comedy,* ed. Regina Barreca. Vol. 2. Studies in Gender and Culture Series. New York: Gordon and Breach, 1988.

Gitlin, Todd. *The Sixties: Years of Hope, Days of Rage.* New York: Bantam, 1987.

———. "Blips, Bites, and Savvy Talk." In *Culture in an Age of Money: The Legacy of the 1980s in America,* ed. Nicolaus Mills. Chicago: Ivan Dee/Elephant Paperbacks, 1990.

Goldberg, Andy. *Improv Comedy.* New York: Samuel French, 1991.

Gray, Frances. *Women and Laughter.* Charlottesville: University Press of Virginia, 1994.

Halberstam, David. *The Fifties.* New York: Villard Books, 1993.

Hall, Stuart. "What Is This 'Black' in Black Popular Culture?" In *Black Popular Culture, A Project by Michele Wallace,* ed. Gina Dent. Vol. 8. Discussions in Popular Culture Series. Seattle: Bay Press, 1992.

Halpern, Charna, Del Close, and Kim Howard Johnson. *Truth in Comedy.* Colorado Springs, CO: Meriwether Publishing, 1994.

Harris, Janet C., and Roberta J. Park, eds. *Play, Games, and Sports in Cultural Contexts*. Champaign, IL: Human Kinetic Publishers, 1983.

Hart, Lynda. Introduction to *Acting Out*, ed. Lynda Hart and Peggy Phelan. Ann Arbor: University of Michigan Press, 1993.

Hebdige, Dick. *Subculture: The Meaning of Style*. New York: Methuen, 1979.

Heelas, Paul. *The New Age Movement*. Cambridge, MA: Blackwell, 1996.

Hendra, Tony. *Going Too Far*. New York: Doubleday, 1987.

Hill, Doug, and Jeff Weingrad. *Saturday Night: A Backstage History of Saturday Night Live*. New York: Beach Tree Books/William Morrow, 1986.

Howe, Neil, and Bill Strauss. *13th Gen: Abort, Retry, Ignore, Fail?* New York: Vintage Books/Random House, 1993.

Huizinga, Johan. *Homo Ludens: A Study of the Play-Element in Culture*. Boston: Beacon Press, 1955.

Hutcheon, Linda. *A Poetics of Postmodernism*. New York: Routledge, 1988.

———. *The Politics of Postmodernism*. New Accents Series. New York: Routledge, 1989.

Innes, Christopher. *Avant Garde Theatre, 1892–1992*. New York: Routledge, 1993.

Janis, I. L. *Victims of Groupthink*. Boston: Houghton Mifflin, 1972.

Jarvie, Grant, and Joseph A. Maguire. *Sport and Leisure in Social Thought*. New York: Routledge, 1994.

Jenkins, Ron. *Subversive Laughter: The Liberating Power of Comedy*. New York: Free Press, 1994.

Johnstone, Keith. *Impro: Improvisation and the Theatre*. London: Methuen, 1981.

———. *Don't Be Prepared: Theatresports for Teachers*. Calgary: Loose Moose Theatre Co., 1994.

Jones, James M. "Racism: A Cultural Analysis of the Problem." In *Prejudice, Discrimination, and Racism*, ed. John F. Dovidio and Samuel L. Gaertner. New York: Academic Press, 1986.

Kompare, Derek. "Here's the Story of a Generation: *The Brady Bunch* and Generation X in the '90s." University of Wisconsin–Madison, 1996.

Lipsky, Richard. "Toward a Political Theory of American Sports Symbolism." In *Play, Games, and Sports in Cultural Contexts*, ed. Janet C. Harris and Roberta J. Park. Champaign, IL: Human Kinetic Publishers, 1983.

Lyotard, Jean-François. *The Postmodern Condition: A Report on Knowledge*. Trans. Geoff Bennington and Brian Massumi. Minneapolis: University of Minnesota Press, 1988.

Mailer, Norman. "The White Negro (Superficial Reflections on the Hipster)." *Dissent* 4, no. 3 (summer 1957): 276–93.

McCrohan, Donna. *The Second City*. New York: Putnam Publishing Group, 1987.

Mee, Charles. "The Celebratory Occasion." *Tulane Drama Review* 9, no. 2 (winter 1964).

Mercer, Kobena. " '1968': Periodizing Postmodern Politics and Identity." In *Cultural Studies*, ed. Lawrence Grossberg, Cary Nelson, and Paula A. Triechler. New York: Routledge, 1992.

Meredith, George. "An Essay on Comedy." In *Comedy*, ed. Wylie Sypher. Garden City: Doubleday, 1956.

Oglesby, Carole A. "Women and Sport." In *Sports, Games, and Play: Social and Psychological Viewpoints*, ed. Jeffrey H. Goldstein. Hillsdale, NJ: Lawrence Earlbaum Associates, 1989.

Omi, Michael. "In Living Color: Race and American Culture." In *Cultural Politics in Contemporary America*, ed. Ian Angus and Sut Jhally. New York: Routledge, 1989.

Patinkin, Sheldon. *The Second City: Backstage at the World's Greatest Comedy Theatre*. Naperville, IL: Sourcebooks Inc., 2000.

Pfeil, Fred. *Another Tale to Tell: Politics and Narrative in Postmodern Culture*. New York: Verso, 1990.

Pierse, Lyn. *Theatresports Down Under.* Sydney: Improcorp Australia Pty. Ltd., 1995.

Purdie, Susan. *Comedy: The Mastery of Discourse.* Toronto: University of Toronto Press, 1993.

Ross, Andrew. *No Respect: Intellectuals and Popular Culture.* New York: Routledge, 1989.

————. "New Age Technoculture." In *Cultural Studies,* ed. Lawrence Grossberg, Cary Nelson, and Paula A. Triechler. New York: Routledge, 1992.

Rowe, Kathleen. *The Unruly Woman : Gender and the Genres of Laughter.* Austin: University of Texas Press, 1995.

Schechner, Richard. *Between Theater and Anthropology.* Philadelphia: University of Pennsylvania Press, 1985.

————. "Drama Performance." In *Folklore, Cultural Performance, and Popular Entertainments,* ed. Richard Bauman. New York: Oxford University Press, 1992.

Schmitt, Natalie Crohn. *Actors and Onlookers.* Evanston, IL: Northwestern University Press, 1990.

Schneider, Rebecca. "See the Big Show: Spiderwoman Theater Doubling Back." In *Acting Out,* ed. Lynda Hart and Peggy Phelan. Ann Arbor: University of Michigan Press, 1993.

Short, Kayann. "Sylvia Talks Back." In *New Perspectives on Women and Comedy,* ed. Regina Barreca. Vol. 5. Studies in Gender and Culture Series. New York: Gordon and Breach, 1992.

Sills, Paul. "The Celebratory Occasion." Interview by Charles Mee Jr. *Tulane Drama Review* 9, no. 2 (winter 1964).

Speier, Susanna. "Stranded on Planet 'X.' " *The Drama Review* (TDR) 39, no. 2 (summer 1995): 10–12.

Spolin, Viola. *Improvisation for the Theatre.* 1963. Reprint, Evanston, IL: Northwestern University Press, 1983.

Stallybrass, P., and A. White. *The Politics and Poetics of Transgression.* New York: Cornell University Press, 1986.

Sweet, Jeffrey. *Something Wonderful Right Away.* 1978. Reprint, New York: Limelight Editions, 1987.

Tannen, Deborah. *You Just Don't Understand: Women and Men in Conversation.* New York: Ballantine, 1990.

Thornton, Sarah. *Club Cultures: Music, Media, and Subcultural Capital.* Hanover, NH: Wesleyan University Press/University Press of New England, 1996.

Turner, Victor. *Dramas, Fields, and Metaphors.* Ithaca, NY: Cornell University Press, 1974.

————. *From Ritual to Theatre.* New York: Performing Arts Journal Pubs., 1982.

————. "Liminal to Liminoid, in Play, Flow, and Ritual: An Essay in Comparative Symbology." In *Play, Games, and Sports in Cultural Contexts,* ed. Janet C. Harris and Roberta J. Park. Champaign, IL: Human Kinetic Publishers, 1983.

Ventura, Michael. *Shadow Dancing in the U.S.A.* Los Angeles: Jeremy P. Tarcher/St. Martin's Press, 1985.

Watkins, Mel. *On the Real Side: Laughing, Lying, and Signifying: The Underground Tradition of African-American Humor.* New York: Simon and Schuster/Touchstone, 1994.

West, Cornel. "The New Cultural Politics of Difference." In *The Cultural Studies Reader,* ed. Simon Durang. New York: Routledge, 1993.

Wilson, John. *Sport, Society, and the State: Playing by the Rules.* Detroit: Wayne State University Press, 1994.

Zadan, Craig. "Send in the Clowns." In *Drama on Stage,* ed. Randolph Goodman. New York: Holt, Rinehart and Winston, 1978.

Popular Press and Web Sites

Adler, Anthony. "In Your Face." *Chicago Magazine,* March 1992, 89–93, 108–11.

———. "The 'How' of Funny: Chicago's New Wave of Improvisation Aspires to More than a Punchline." *American Theatre,* December 1993, 14–19, 63.

———. "The Life of Brian." Unidentified clipping ca. 1993, 16. Annoyance archives, Chicago, IL.

———. "Love and Money." *Chicago Reader,* 12 November 1993, 9, 22–24.

Anshaw, Carol. "Days of Whine and Poses: Writers in Their Youth." *Village Voice Literary Supplement* (November 1992): 25–27.

Arbanel, Jonathan. "A Lasting Legacy." *Performink* 11, no. 31, 12 March 1999, 1, 6.

Bannon, Tim, et al. "Arts and Entertainment." *Chicago Tribune,* 7 March 1999, 4.

Barnidge, Mary Shen. Review of *One Drop Is All It Takes.* Oui Be Negroes at Turnaround Theatre. *Chicago Reader,* 14 March 1997.

Blinkhorn, Lois. "Zany Dick Chudnow." *Milwaukee Journal,* 8 March 1987, "Wisconsin Magazine" section.

Bommer, Lawrence. "Bitter Second City 'Rejects' Have Last Laugh with Satire." Review of *Second City Didn't Want Us.* Factory Theatre. *Chicago Tribune,* 6 November 1995.

———. Review of Oui Be Negroes in *Can We Dance with Yo Dates?* Sheffield's. *Chicago Reader,* 10 March 1995.

———. Review of *Citizen Gates.* Second City. *Chicago Reader,* 13 December 1996, sec. 2, 29.

Brustein, Robert. "Tonight We Try to Improvise." Review of *The Premise* and *To the Water Tower. New Republic* 148, no. 1911, May 1963, 28–29.

Caro, Mark. "This Bunch Can't Get Enough of the Bradys." *Chicago Tribune,* 2 November 1990, sec. 5, 1ff.

Christiansen, Richard. "Troupe's 85th Revue Finds the Spoofs Are up to Snuff." *Chicago Tribune,* 16 December 1999.

Ciesla, Doreen. "Creative Group Portrait: The Free Associates." *Strong Coffee,* January 1995, 4–5.

"Close Friends." *Chicago Reader,* 12 March 1999, sec. 1, 28.

Cole, Jeff. "ComedySportz Has Fun Expanding." *Milwaukee Sentinel,* 6 February 1990, 1ff.

Davis, Erik. "Rerun Resurrection." Clipping in Annoyance archives, Chicago, IL.

Enna, Renee. "Improvisation—with a Woman's Touch." *Diversions: News and Views of the Arts,* Pioneer Press, 15 April 1992, sec. D, 3ff.

Fleszewski, Jean. "Theatrical Olympics—More Than Stage Games." *SouthTWN/Economist,* 22 November 1981, Central edition.

Gregoropoulos, Noah, Hans Holsen, Jason Chin, and Jessica Halem. "Improv = Boys Club?" July 1998 and online posting (bulletin board conversation) on *Impravda,* 19 February 2000. <http://www.the-playground.com/chicagorat/impravda.htm#rob>.

Hayford, Justin. "Black Comedy Underground Makes the 'Boldest Choices.' " *Chicago Tribune,* 26 February 1999, 5.

Helbig, Jack. "Mick's Bunch." *New City,* 16 August 1990, 12.

———. "Critics Choice: *Cast on a Hot Tin Roof." Chicago Reader,* clipping ca. 1991. Free Associates archives.

———. Review of *Brainwarp: The Baby Eater* and *Dumbass Leaves the Carnival.* Annoyance Theatre. *Chicago Reader,* 22, no. 41, 16 July 1993.

———. "In Performance: the Playground's Improved Improv." *Chicago Reader,* 26, no. 40, 11 July 1997.

———. "Critic's Choice: Chicago Improv Festival." *Chicago Reader,* 27 March 1998.

————. Review of The Playground. *New City,* 10 September 1998.

Hemminger, Lisa. "Feature Made by Theatrical Troupe." *Screen,* 25 September 1995.

Hogarth, Marie-Anne. "Laughing Matters: Where Would Frances Callier Be without Improv?" *Chicago Reader,* 9 April 1999.

Holmstrom, David. "By Their Wits Alone: Comedy as Team Sport." *Christian Science Monitor,* 26 August 1997, 1, 14.

Horwitz, Simi. "Improv-ing on a Good Thing: The Growing Influence of Improvisation." *Back Stage,* 26 July–1 August 1996, 1ff.

Impravda. "Improv = Boy's Club?" Multiple postings, July 1998. <http://the-playground.com/chicagorat/impravda.htm#rob>.

Jevens, Darel. "Car Pool on Laugh Track: Improv Teams Try Different Route at Playground." *Chicago Sun Times,* 13 December 1997, late sports final edition.

Johnson, Allan. "Soulfront Gives a New Perspective to Second City." *Chicago Tribune,* 13 December 1996, North sports final edition, 12.

Jones, Chris. "e.t.c. Holds Its Own against Big House." *Chicago Tribune,* 21 December 1999.

Kim, Jae-Ha. " 'Coed Prison' Break." *Chicago Sun-Times,* 1 June 2000, Showcase/Arts and Leisure, 39.

Klein, Julia. "The New Stand-up Comics." *Ms.* (October 1984): 116ff.

Ko, Yumi. "Stir-Friday Night Woks!" *TASO Magazine,* April 1998.

Kozlowski, Rob. "It's About Time! The First City of Improv Finally Celebrates with a Festival." *Performink,* 13 March 1998.

Langer, Adam. Review of *Oui Be Negroes,* Cafe Voltaire. *Chicago Reader* 24, no. 7, 11 November 1994.

"Laugh Tracked." *New City,* 7 January 1999, 7.

Massa, Robert. "Much More Than a Hunch." *Village Voice,* 8 October 1991, 100.

Moe, Mechelle. "Annoyance Is Out, But Not Down for the Count." *Performink,* July 2000.

Neet, Melina. "We Be Negroes." *Pitch Weekly,* 10–16 August 1995, Metro Kansas City edition.

New Improv Page. "Improv Groups" and "Improv Festivals." 22 February 2000. <http://www.lowrent.net/improv/>.

Obejas, Achy. "Adios Annoyance." *Chicago Tribune,* 5 June 2000, sec. 2, 1, 3.

Olson, Jeana M. "Improvisational Comedy Reworked as Competitive Improvisation." *Daily Cardinal,* 23 January 1986, Performance section.

Pollack, Neal. "Women in Improv." *Chicago Reader,* 29 October 1993.

Ratay, Leslie. "The Sporting Laugh." *Milwaukee Magazine,* April 1987, 39.

Rath, Jay. "TheaterSportz: Zany Improvisational Theater Group Goes for Points and Big Laughs." *Capital Times,* 27 August 1985.

Russo, Francine. "Cagey." Review of *So I Killed a Few People. Village Voice,* 2–8 December 1998.

Sachs, Lloyd. "Second City at 30." *Chicago Sun-Times,* 17 December 1989, 1ff.

Saůers, Tim. "GayCo." *Gay Chicago Magazine,* 16 July 1998.

Scott, Wayne. " 'Your Butt' and 'Coed Prison Sluts'—Take Back the Night, Guys!" *Windy City Times,* clipping ca. 1991. Annoyance archives, Chicago, IL.

Shea, Griffin. "Theatre Profile: The Free Associates." *Performink,* 28 July 1994, 12.

Smith, Sid. "Beyond the fringe: Annoyance Theatre unabashedly lives up to its name." *Chicago Tribune* 7 April 1991.

————. "Funny Business." *Chicago Tribune,* 9 April 1995, sec. 13 (Arts), 24.

Smith, William. "Funny Business: Comics Taking Their Act to the Boardroom." *Chicago Sun-Times,* 4 September 1994, sec. B, 21ff.

Spitznagel, Eric. "Much Ado about Mick Napier." *Third Word,* 1, no. 4, January–February 1994, 32ff.

"Theatre Listings." *Chicago Reader,* 28 October 1994, sec. 2, 29.

"Theatres Take It to Limit and Beyond." *Chicago Sun-Times,* 28 August 1992, special advertising section, 16.

Upright Citizens Brigade. 15 December 1999. <http://www.uprightcitizens.org>.

Walls, Diane Levy. *"That Darned Antichrist!*—Review." *Nightlines,* 15 August 1990, 17.

Weisstein, Naomi. "Why We Aren't Laughing Anymore." *Ms.,* November 1973.

Wilcox, George. "TheaterSportz: Sports and Theater Collide in Comedy." *Daily Cardinal,* clipping ca.1985. ComedySportz archives, Madison, WI.

Williams, Kevin. "Second City has Unfunny Forecast in 'Soul Front.'" *Chicago Sun-Times,* 6 December 1996, 32.

Winn, Steven. "These Games Are Strictly for Laughs." *Sports Illustrated,* 26 November 1990.

Zeff, Dan. " 'Soulfront' Great Second City Show." *Daily Journal,* 18 December 1996.

YESand. "Women in Improv." Multiple postings on bulletin board, 1999 and 2000. <http://www.yesand.com/bulletinboard/>.

Other Materials

Chudnow, Richard. *ComedySportz Franchise Owner's Manual.* Milwaukee, WI, self-published, ca. 1988.

Rock, Mike. "Notes for Players." Self-published private player's collection, ca. 1993.

Second City Training Center Manual. Chicago, IL, self-published, ca. 1992.

Theatre archives: Documents, clippings, manuals, scripts, correspondence, inspirational material, newsletters, and publicity material from the Annoyance Theatre, ComedySportz (Madison, Milwaukee, Chicago), the Free Associates, Oui Be Negroes, the Playground, and Second City.

Classes and workshops: Second City (de Maat, Gellman, Libera); ImprovOlympic (Close, Halpern, Jane); the Annoyance Theatre (Napier, Messing); Madison ComedySportz, 1994–1999.

Performances: the Annoyance Theatre; ComedySportz (Madison, Milwaukee, Chicago); Second City; Second City e.t.c.; the Free Associates; Oui Be Negroes; Black Theatre Underground; the Factory Theatre; the Playground; ImprovOlympic, 1993–2000.

Interviews

See the acknowledgments page for a list of players, directors, teachers, and administrators who generously granted their time, thoughts, and support to this project.

Index

References to photographs appear in *italics*.

Jazz: appreciation, 18; beatnik, xviii; improvisation, xviii, 228, 236 n 1; subculture, 6
Jazz Freddy and Ed, 116, 158
Jermic, Butch, *205*
Jews, 11
JoAnne Worley Family Christmas Seance, 176
Johnson, Brandon, 206, *210*
Johnstone, Keith, xix, xxiii, xxvi, 36–37, 39, 44, 61, 79, 87, 219; "the creative child," 36; *Impro*, 36; masks, 36; status hat games, *96*; trance, 36. *See also* Theatresports
Jokes. *See* Humor
Jolovitz, Jenna, 201–02
Jones, James M., 189
Jonson, Ben, 9

Kafka, Franz, 18
Kansas City festival, 218–19
Kaye, Matt, 111
Kazurinski, Tim, 49
Keane, Chris, 88
Kentucky Fried Movie (film), 88
Kentucky Fried Theater, 88
Kerouac, Jack, 6
Kill Whitey, 209
Kingston Mines Company Store, 49
Klein, Julia, 15
Klein, Robert, 23
Knopf, Katya, 46–47
Knudson, David Paul "DP," 93–95
Kohlberg, Karen, 90
Kolb, Mina, 19–20, 21, 137
Kraft Foods, 111
Krebs, Aaron, 218
Krishnamurti, 50
Kulhan, Bob, *59*
Kwik Witz, 222

Ladies on the Couch, 158
Laible, Richard, 131
Lamb, Jenni, *172*
Landry, Shaun, 115, 190–98, *193*, 204, 209–10, *211*, 212–13, 216, 226
Larsen, Christian, "Creed for Optimists," 101
Latinos, 207–08. *See also* ¡Salsation!
Laugh-In, 176
Lazzi. See Bits

Leigh, Mike, 223
Leigh, Vivien, 169
Lennon, Jodi, 155
Leonard, Kelly, 29, 234 n 1
Lesbian theatre, 73
Lesbians. *See* Gays and lesbians
Leslie, Khristian, 210
Level Five students, 113
Level Six, 113
Libera, Anne, xxvii, 19, 156, 229 n 5
Libertini, Richard, 21
Liminality, 232 n 15
Lipsky, Richard, 99–100
Liss, Joe, *121*
Literary Styles game, 222
Liu, Jennifer, *207*
"Living Mad Libs," 220
Living Playbook, 220
Living Premise, 17
Living Theatre, 6
Long-form improv, xxvi, 10, 39, 48–49, 65, 78; *Harold* game, xxvi, 39, 41–42, 43, 49–55, 62, 63, 67, 69, 76, 114, 116, 119, 158
Long Play's Journey into One Act, 186
Loose Moose Theatre Company, 37, 87
Lost Yetis, 69, 70
Louis-Dreyfus, Julia, 34

Maat, Martin de, xxv, 114
MacNerland, David, 130, 131
Mad Magazine, 6
Mad TV, 223
Madcap, 161
Magic, 9
Mailer, Norman, "White Negro," 75
Mainstreaming, 117
Mamet, David, 182
Manson, the Musical, 142, 146
Manthey, Ken, 152–53
Marginalization: and improvisation, xxii–xxiii, xxiv, 120, 126, 188, 200; and loss of identity, xxv; of minorities, xviii, xxii, xxiv, 6, 120, 188–89; of women, xviii, xxii, xxiv, 66, 120
Marlowe, Philip, 181
Marple, Miss, 181
Martin, Bina, *70*
Martin Short Show, The, 223